The New Nightingales

Hospital Workers,
Unions,
New Women's Issues

Patricia Cayo Sexton

for
The Coalition of Labor Union Women

Introduction by Joyce Miller

ENQUIRY PRESS   1982
NEW YORK CITY

LC 81-068687

Library of Congress Cataloging in Publication Data

Sexton, Patricia Cayo.
  The new nightingales.

  Includes bibliographical references.
  1. Trade-unions—Hospitals—United States.
2. Hospitals—United States—Staff. 3. Hospitals—United
States—Personnel management. 4. Women in medicine—
United States. 5. Women in trade-unions—United States.
I. Coalition of Labor Union Women (U.S.) II. Title.
RA971.35.S48   331.88'1136211'0973   81-68687
ISBN 0-941494-00-4 (paper)   AACR2
ISBN 0-941494-01-2 (cloth)
Available from:

Enquiry Press
799 Broadway, Suite 325
New York City 10003 (212-982-2406)

The Coalition of Labor Union Women
15 Union Square, New York City 10003

PRINTED IN THE UNITED STATES OF AMERICA

for Alice Cayo Lindsey

The women are always called on for sacrifices,
the mothers for their families, the nurses for
the sick, the workers for the profit of employers. Now it is
their turn to enjoy the just rewards of their labor.
                                        John Sweeney

Lo! in that house of misery
A lady with a lamp I see
    Pass through the glimmering gloom,
    And flit from room to room.

And slow, as in a dream of bliss,
The speechless sufferer turns to kiss
    Her shadow, as it falls
    Upon the darkening walls.

Henry Wadsworth Longfellow,
*on Florence Nightingale, 1820–1910, British nursing administrator
in the Crimean war, widely regarded as secular saint of nursing.*

"I think," said Mr. Dooley, "that if th'
Christyan Scientists had some science
an' the' doctors more Christianity,
it wudden't make anny diff'rence
which ye called in—
if ye had a good nurse."

Finley Peter Dunne ("Mr. Dooley")

Contents

INTRODUCTION
Joyce Miller

Though some people outside the labor movement may be unaware of it, unions include millions of women among their members, and in many large unions, women members are approaching or have attained a majority of total membership. Overwhelmingly, these millions of women work because they have to work, to support themselves and/or their families. Their commitment to their jobs and to unionism grows as their job tenure lengthens. They are taking themselves very seriously and so is the labor movement.

This book is itself further evidence of the growth of interest in the role of working women in American life, and more specifically of its growth among members and leaders of the American labor movement. My own election to the Executive Council of the AFL-CIO also points perhaps less to my own merits and abilities than to the continuing growth in the stature and recognition of women in the work force and in the labor movement. Within labor, that growth is attributable in some large measure to the activities of the officers and members of the Coalition of Labor Union Women (CLUW) and to its fully committed advocacy of women's issues and women's rights.

The author of this work, Patricia Cayo Sexton, is a professor of sociology at New York University, but she is also a unionist, having been a member and local officer of the auto workers' union (the UAW), and a member of the bargaining committee of her American Federation of Teachers' local in years past. She, therefore, brings to this work both the knowledge and skill of the established scholar and the sensitive strength of the active unionist. Professor Sexton has also been a participating CLUW member, so in some ways she symbolizes the spread of CLUW's work into the academic world as well as into the factory.

The union that is most specifically the subject of this book, The Service Employee's International Union, has long organized in those places where women workers have been most harshly exploited. This union has dramatically improved the employment conditions of workers in health care who have become its members. Readers of this book will have presented to them in a highly readable and personalized form, descriptions of the way in which the union has benefited the lives of the women it serves. It will also point to the road that lies ahead and to the issues and problems of hospital workers that need more public attention and support.

In CLUW, it has always been out belief, as it is Professor Sexton's, that the first step most working women need to take is to join a union. A union can offer them the legal and contractual framework within which other issues, progressively over time, can be negotiated and settled. Without the protection of a union contract, women will remain vulnerable, fragmented, and essentially impotent in their efforts to deal with employers and secure the full benefits of their labor. Through the union, women will find what so many millions of them sorely lack, a close community of coworkers, a voice with which to formulate and state their views, democratically chosen leaders, and membership in a movement whose influence extends far beyond the shop floor.

CLUW has known that ultimately the best guarantee of decent working conditions, adequate salaries, and an end to discimination against women workers is a union contract. It has also known that the predominance of women in occupations that are poorly or almost completely unorganized is a prime reason for the poor conditions under which women work. Thus CLUW has always been strongly dedicated to the principle of organizing the unorganized. The insights contained in this book, and the ease with which so many women can identify with the experience of their sisters who are hospital workers, will make this book a useful tool in organizing. As we have seen historically, our influence gathers strength as unionism gathers members and support. At the bargaining table and in legislative halls, the strength of unionism is determined by the size and solidarity of its members.

Professor Sexton stresses the need to empower women, and she herself gives them the power to display their own grievances, desires and opinions in their own words. Her presentations make evident the intelligence and insights of these working women and the kinds of positive contributions they could make to improving productivity and lowering costs if they were recognized as having brains and an intimate knowledge of the work process.

Her analysis of the shortcomings of the traditional women's movement and its neglect of the 80 percent of the female population that is workingclass is excellent. She also buttresses the CLUW position that to be pro-female and to deal with women's oppression does not require one to be anti-male as the movement at times appears to be to some working women (and men). CLUW's view is that women and men working together through unions is one of the most important ways of achieving greater equality for women. In this book, the history of how Penn hospital was organized is a vivid reminder of the fact that male trade unionists can be valuable allies in the struggle of women for recognition.

What Professor Sexton says here, as an elaboration on CLUW's position, is that all steps toward unionism will depend on how well women members can articulate, and how well leadership can understand and translate into action, the work-related priorities of women and the issues that command their major concern. This book has taken on the unique task of examining and weighing those issues which are expressions of the sentiments of one large body of working women, hospital workers.

The most pervasive and profoundly felt issues of hospital workers, as the book points out, differ in many respects from those assigned highest priorities by professional and managerial women. Looking at working women in other kinds of jobs, we will certainly discover other "unexpected" issues to surface, issues that should be, but are not, on the women's national agenda. As the book clearly indicates, the millions of women who work for a living, and who may or may not be union members, work in a wide variety of jobs and under vastly differing work conditions, so they may be expected to have vastly different priorities. The concerns of women who work in restaurants, communications, auto, or apparel, for example, may differ markedly from those of hospital workers, even with respect to economic issues and fringe benefits.

CLUW has also sought, with considerable success, to put more women's issues on the *union* agenda—issues regarding the role of women in the union as well as the work problems of women members. We are firmly convinced that women need representatives at the highest policy levels within unions, as well as at all middle levels, if their voice is to be raised and heard throughout the movement. Certainly the new women's issues described in this book can be most clearly understood and transmitted by women representatives, and especially if they are dispersed in significant numbers throughout the union organization.

Professor Sexton has sensed that critical inter-relationship between women's issues, as they are expressed on the shop floor, and those representatives who carry and transmit the ideas to others and give them high standing on both the union agenda and the national women's agenda.

Since we in the labor movement deal on a daily basis with these issues, we are perhaps best able to inform the national agenda about them. To that end, we have consistently sought public forums in which the voice of women union members may be heard, and we are grateful to Professor Sexton for providing one forum, this volume.

PREFACE

The Coalition of Labor Union Women is a unique, dynamic women's group, founded in 1974 for the purpose of unifying "all union women in a viable organization to determine, first—our common problems and concerns and, second—to develop action programs within the framework of our unions to deal effectively with our objectives."

As ideas for this book percolated, I took them and a more formal proposal to Joyce Miller, the president of CLUW (and also the first woman member of the AFL-CIO Executive Council) who not only encouraged me to proceed but also obtained CLUW sponsorship for the project and later played a critical role in securing Ford Foundation funding for it. I am indebted to both Joyce Miller and Susan Berresford of the Ford Foundation for that aid.

Since about 80 percent of the more than 42 million women in the work force are workingclass (non-professional and non-managerial) women, and about seven million women are union members, CLUW's jurisdiction and its tasks are certainly vast enough to encompass a variety of research efforts, including this very experimental one from me.

The reputation of CLUW as a strong advocate of both working people *and* their unions opened many doors to our inquiries, but those doors were kept open by the perceptive and conscientious interviewing done by Lisa Polisar (the value of whose assistance goes beyond assessment), and by the substantial administrative work of Liz McPike (who also played a key role in conducting the second, and as yet unpublished, half of the research). I am certainly indebted to those who read the manuscript in its early, raw form and especially to Ruth Jordan, a kind mentor and positive critic, to Beverly Burris who added some final, balanced Texas seasoning and real substance to the whole, and of course to Rosemary Trump, a truly remarkable woman, and

1

Elinor Glenn who has played such a dramatically effective role in organizing hospital workers, and everyone else, over the years.

What this book says is not in any sense "authorized" by CLUW, so I am the sole source of whatever errors of fact or judgment it may contain. It needs saying, however, that a measure of CLUW's virtues as an open forum for the expression of ideas, even divergent ones, is the fact that, despite some differences in approach, it has given steady support to this effort and never tampered with anything said here.

When I began the project I had in mind a long-term venture that would eventually approach each union represented by CLUW (about 65 of them) and discuss with women members and leaders of those unions the theme of the projected series: the experience of women with work, unions and women's issues. A beginning was made on that grand project by selecting two unions, the Service Employees International Union (SEIU) and the Retail Clerks International Union (now the United Food and Commercial Workers' Union) for study. This is the first of the two projects completed.

The SEIU was chosen because of its size and significance (over a million members and the fifth largest union in the AFL-CIO) and because it has both a large female membership and a reputation of support for women's issues and women leadership. It is also known to be an active, hardworking, progressive union.

To say that the union was open and welcoming of our efforts does not fairly describe how supportive of our work the union's president, John Sweeney, and its officers and staff were, or how much time and help they gave us. We made it clear to them that nothing we learned in taped discussions with women members would be withheld, and that no punches would be pulled, yet we found that all our questions were answered fully and frankly, and nobody refused to talk to us or discuss the union's weaknesses as well as its strengths.

The project was made possible by the serious commitment of union president John Sweeney to the advancement of women's issues within the union—as demonstrated by the timely merger of the office workers' Local 925 (9 to 5) with SEIU—as well as by his specific commitment to hospital worker organization, as seen in the planned merger of hospital workers' District 1199 with SEIU.

The SEIU organizes a variety of service workers, including custodial workers, public workers, and hospital workers. We chose to study hospital workers because their jobs are so essential and their numbers so large.

Methods used in approaching this research included:

Interviews with leadership. We began the research by interviewing the top officers and staff of the international union's Washington, D.C.

headquarters, plus a number of women local union leaders from around the country.

Survey of women union leaders. Following those interviews we helped assemble a list of leading women officers and staff in the union nationally, and from the questionnaire on women's issues sent to them, we received 74 responses, a sizeable majority of the list.

Field studies. We then selected two local unions (associated with leading women in the union) and two hospitals (affiliated with those locals) for intensive field studies. The hospitals were chosen for their contrasts: a small non-profit semi-rural hospital in Pennsylvania, which was only recently organized, and a large county hospital in urban California with a longer history of unionization. The hospitals will be called "Penn Community" and "Cal County" hospitals to disguise, however transparently, their real identities.

Interviews with local leadership and hospital workers. A total of 21 union officers and staff were interviewed in the two locals, plus 32 hospital workers at Penn and 35 at Cal hospital.

Survey of hospital workers. From the responses to these interviews, a questionnaire on women's issues was prepared for distribution to women in the two hospitals.* Responses were received from 135 women at Penn and 262 women at Cal, or better than half of those polled, which included the entire female staff at Penn and one large sector of Cal hospital.

Interviews with management. Interviews with management were sought to confirm or contradict what workers and unionists said, but at Penn hospital, only a brief discussion with the personnel director was granted, and taping of the interview was not allowed. At Cal, a public hospital, we talked with managers at the highest levels.

The form this book takes is rather unusual, but not out of any pre-arranged design. The material seemed to take its own shape and it emerged as a kind of "family portrait" of women and their union, one that is highly personalized in its treatment of the actors and the organization, rather than abstract and general as most approaches to work experience and complex organizations are.

The form of the book underscores its main substance in that it gives women a voice, an opportunity to discuss matters that affect their work lives, and recognition for what they say. The voices of the workers and the unionists are sometimes separate and sometimes mingled, which is the way it is in real life too. My own voice is also in there, and louder than the sheer quantity of words indicates, since I also edited all the other voices.

---

*See Appendix A for the questionnaire form; the form used in the survey of women union leaders was almost identical.

While the book tries to let the women come through, the task has not been easy, for many wise people have urged me to interpret more and include more of myself in the account. I have resisted those urgings but not with total success; yet I have tried to listen carefully to what others say, without imposing my own voice on theirs.

Published data on living people and organizations are always to some extent historical rather than current. The people and organizations change even as they are being studied. Since this work began, the union has planned to merge with the Retail, Wholesale, and Department Store Union (RWDSU). About a third of RWDSU's membership is in District 1199, originally a union of pharmacists who took on the formidable task of organizing hospital workers. 1199's record of success with that task has been astonishing and its national reputation for innovative political and cultural efforts has grown. Since it is neither possible nor desirable to follow such organizational changes, this record must stand for what it is, a time piece that captures the main actors and events of its time. The currency of the data is not important. What is important is the book's effort to develop new ways of looking at *women's issues*. The people, the facts, the issues may change, but the *approach* remains essentially the same. The facts and details only illustrate general themes and perspectives.

The book does not examine the views of doctors, administrators, or the public with respect to hospital care or the experience of work. It is perhaps more than enough that it breaks the silence of workers and unionists on these subjects. Nor does the book focus on the registered nurse, the "professional" hospital worker, although her presence is often noted. Rather, the book is about "hospital workers," those non-professionals who assist in patient care and in typing, cleaning, cooking, and keeping the hospital going. References to literature on hospital workers are very slim since little is written about them. The RN, of course, is very different. As a "professional," she attends colleges where her instructors must do research, write, and publish in order to survive, so the RN is the principal subject of almost as much published material as her sister "professional," the teacher. That literature will not be reviewed here since it is basically marginal to the subject at hand; instead, a final bibliography will list some of the more related material.

This document begins with its main theme: the experience of work and redefinitions of women's issues, followed by a New Nightingale "sing-out" featuring three hospital workers (a nursing assistant, a lab technician, a registered nurse) who represent three levels of hospital skill. A section on conflicts introduces three kinds of contests within the hospital: the acute distress of the dietary department, the conflict between RNs and others, and a full-blown class conflict—that is, a strike at Penn hospital which resulted in its first labor agreement.

The next chapters move outside the hospital, into adjoining terrain: the union, its history, structure, mode of operation, female leadership, and the relation of hospital workers to the women's movement. This section does not pretend to describe, in any definitive way, the organization of the union or the role of women in it. What it offers is a brief guide to how the union works, who leads it, where women stand in relation to it, and perhaps how women, understanding its structure more fully, might use it more advantageously.

The second part on women's issues—the core of this volume—tries to analyze and illustrate issues as they are defined by hospital workers themselves, and it concludes with some views on how decisions are made in hospitals and how they might be made.

These discussions with hospital workers—the New Nightingales— grew out of personal impressions and sentiments. That is to say, I like the women, enjoy talking with them, and would like them to get the public attention they deserve. Unfortunately, the abundance of statistics and generalizations about "work and its discontents" gives us little real understanding of how women lead their daily work lives, experience their jobs, or perceive work-related issues. Personal documents are needed, individual and group portraits of workers, slices of real working life, statements by the women themselves—the handwoven fabric of their daily work lives. To this end, I have tried to make the mountainous statistics and theories about work life more intimate and familial by asking hospital workers: Who are you? What do you do? What issues trouble you? What do you want from your union or from the women's movement?

Not only can generalizations be misleading, inadequate, and lacking in any flesh and blood reality, they can also fail to take account of the astonishing variations among women and the work they do. Women have not one but many voices. On countless scores, however, their voices are united. Both the themes and the variations, the individual and the collective voices need to be heard. As a step toward recording this range, I have sought to make these accounts quantitative as well as personal, so that voices in each range could be heard. Thus, some numbers and percentages in this accounting are also included, but in a way that tries to illustrate some basic points rather than obscure them from readers who are not statisticians.

The book is about *these* hospital workers but, since responses from two very different hospitals turned out to be very similar, it is likely that certain shared experiences may be found among hospital workers generally. This likelihood is underscored by the fact that reports from national leaders about hospital conditions agreed in most cases with those of workers. As for other workingclass women (those who work in factories, offices, retail stores, etc.), the experience of work may coincide or conflict with those of hospital workers. Only inquiries such as this one can point up the similarities and differences.

This research could have taken the shape of a pamphlet or monograph rather than a full-length book, just as almost any book could, but the material turned out to be too complex and also, I feel, too valuable for that. These women rate a full-length treatment and they have gotten it. I regret that inevitably, but without intent, I have left out some key people from this account or given too much attention to some people and not enough to others. Since my purpose in this endeavor is to give full credit, I hope that those omitted will not feel too slighted. Good intent is not enough, but it is my only defense.

≈

THE COLOR-CODED CASTE SYSTEM,* IN THE WORDS OF ONE HOSPITAL WORKER

The hospital has a pecking order, a clear class, sex, and racial hierarchy, and much of it is color-coded. The color of your uniform tells your rank and in most cases it also tells your race and social class background. The doctors and administrators dominate the hospitals. They are male. The doctors wear white coats and the administrators business suits. Then there are the maintenance men who fix the machines and do the plastering and wiring—and wear blue collars. Then you have the male orderlies, the male chefs who have the highest paid jobs in the kitchens, the ambulance drivers, the guards—all of them with their special colors and uniforms.

Other than that, most jobs are staffed by women and the actual work is done overwhelmingly by women. The higher up you go in the hierarchy, the whiter the faces and uniforms get, and the more likely people are to be male and middle class.

You visit a hospital and you see the RNs—the registered nurses— who are usually white women. They *wear* white too. Sparkling white. White stockings, white uniforms. Some of them wear white hats. Even these RNs have distinctions based on who has a two-year degree, a four-year degree, a diploma from a hospital school.

Next in the pecking order, you see the LPNs—the licensed practical nurses. On the west coast, they call them LVNs, or licensed vocational nurses. They are mainly white women, although that is changing. In the cities, they're more likely to be Black or brown

*Color codes are not the same in all hospitals.

women. The LPN is sort of the technical nurse. She has training but not a college degree. She also wears white.

Then you see nurses' assistants (or aides or attendants) who have three to six months training and are overwhelmingly from the workingclass. They usually wear some color other than white—pink or green maybe. And they don't wear caps. The neighborhood surrounding the hospital determines the ethnic makeup of the assistants.

Also on the hospital floor where the patients are, you'll see a ward secretary, a clerical person. She doesn't type but she coordinates the floor and makes sure patients are where they belong and doctors have what they want. She's like a housemother keeping track of all the students on her floor.

On that same floor you might see, darting in and out of rooms, someone in yellow or maybe brighter pink who has a mop in her hand. In a city hospital, she's probably Black or Spanish or an older immigrant woman. She's a housekeeper and the lowest paid worker in the hospital, depending on where she works.

If you are there at lunchtime, you will see someone walking around with a tray of food. She's a dietary worker and she's probably wearing bright blue. She usually works in the kitchen and carries the trays up to the floors. In city hospitals, the dietaries are usually minorities, Black or brown.

You can't see all the little departments that keep a hospital going. The laboratory technicians. The people who work in a place like CSR (Central Sterile Room) and do all the sterilizing of instruments. The people who work in the laundry and wash and fold the linens. The people who travel around and draw blood. The various clericals who type the patients' records, keep files, do billings and accounting. The doctors' individual secretaries. The women who serve food in the coffee shop and work as saleswomen in the gift shop. Lots of people are tucked away in offices or kitchens or labs where you can't see them or notice them, *but they run the hospital.*

HERITAGE

1887 Job Description of a bedside nurse, from "Bright Corridors," a publication of Cleveland Lutheran Hospital

In addition to caring for your 50 patients, each bedside nurse will follow these regulations:

1. Daily sweep and mop floors of your ward, dust the patient's furniture and window sills.

2. Maintain an even temperature in your ward by bringing in a scuttle of coal for the day's business.

3. Light is important to observe the patient's condition. Therefore, each day fill kerosene lamps, clean chimneys, and trim wicks. Wash the window once a week.

4. The nurse's notes are important in aiding your physician's work. Make your pens carefully, you may whittle nibs to your individual taste.

5. Each nurse on day duty will report every day at 7 am and leave at 8 pm, except on the Sabbath on which day she will be off from 12 noon to 2 pm.

6. Graduate nurses in good standing with the director of nurses will be given an evening off each week for courting purposes, or two evenings a week if you go regularly to church.

7. Each nurse should lay aside from each pay day a goodly sum of her earnings for her benefits during her declining years, so that she will not become a burden. For example, if you earn $30 monthly you should set aside $15.

8. Any nurse who smokes, uses liquor in any form, gets her hair done at a beauty shop or frequents dance halls will give the director of nurses good reason to suspect her worth, intentions and integrity.

9. The nurse who performs her labors, serves her patients and doctors faithfully and without fault for a period of five years will be given an increase by the hospital administration of five cents a day.

One

FEMINIST ISSUES AND THE EXPERIENCE OF WORK

Self immolation is no longer considered the good life.
The American Journal of Nursing, editorial, August, 1926

This book is about one group of workingclass women—hospital workers—and their growing scepticism about the virtues of self immolation. It questions many feminist priorities and raises other issues that may be more relevant to workingclass women. It also explores the hospital worker's view of jobs, unions, and the women's movement, and searches for ways in which hospital workers, and others like them, can advance the many interests they share with feminists and unionists.

The women's movement has come upon hard times; its organizations are in some disarray and its progress is impeded on at least three fronts—abortion rights, affirmative action, ERA—and while women's studies flourish at colleges and universities, masses of workingclass women still regard feminists as dubious allies in a presumably common struggle.

History repeats itself in this respect. In the period surrounding the passage of the women's suffrage amendment in 1924, feminists suffered similar setbacks and for some similar reasons: cultural conservatism and backlash, a declining economy, shrinking opportunities, the dialectic rhythm of history. Then and now, the failure to sustain mass support for the movement, especially among workingclass women (who are eight in ten women) also figured in the movement's regression.

Feminists repeatedly acknowledge the major limitation of the women's movement—that it is largely white, middle-class, college-educated, professional, but in this case consciousness does not lead inevitably to action, and aside from several "mass" organizations, few large-scale feminist efforts have yet linked up with workingclass women or established networks among them.

In general, academic and literary feminists have written and spoken about what they know best, their own experience, assuming perhaps that it has universal applications. In fact, experiences differ, as does the language of discourse between feminists and others, the class idiom. Feminists who write have in fact created a special vocabulary and style which unite them as feminists (and provide an acceptably academic basis for women's studies) but which divide them further from workingclass women and widen the chasm into which feminist issues may be slipping.

Of course, the pressure on academic feminists to do research, write, and obtain funds for their work is likely to discourage efforts to reach out to workingclass women. Funds for such work are scarce even in good times, publishers are reluctant to publish (British publishers excepted), and the research itself presents discouraging problems. Far better for the subjects of research to be dead than alive. Living subjects change before they can be captured in print, so whatever is written about them today may not be exactly, or even nearly, correct tomorrow. Moreover, living issues are far more politically charged than dead ones, and living egos, both individual and organizational, can be so sensitive that almost anything said about them is seen as offensive. Since dead men (and women) tell no tales, the historian's job and methodology can be a good deal simpler than the sociologist's, in much the same way that the mortician's can be simpler than the surgeon's. Or, more accurately perhaps, historians have problems because their subjects *cannot* talk back while sociologists have problems because subjects talk back too much, change their minds, react and over-react to what is said about them. In any event, for those who must explore the present, cadavers are no substitutes for living subjects.

The academic feminists most involved with workingclass women have perhaps been the historians and documentary film makers who have explored the buried secrets of workingclass history, and those socialist-feminists who have recognized the key roles played by the workingclass in socialist theory and movements. Their concerns, however, might be even more valuable than they are if their emphasis were less exclusively on the past and on abstractions and theory, and more on the contemporary, the concrete, and the actual experience of living people.

Meredith Tax's history of the interaction between the women's and labor movements around the turn of the century, *The Rising of the*

Women, shows how middle-class feminists (and some male union leaders) delayed as well as assisted the causes of workingclass women, and it is in that sense exceptional to feminist literature, but it too is historical and also inclined to deny the validity of some family values cherished by workingclass women.[1]

Many feminist writers have been disaffected with living labor unions, as contrasted with some idealized unions of the past (the IWW and other dissident, and often deceased, unions) so their attention has also, for that reason, strayed from living women who must inevitably be seen within a context of living unions. In such cases, feminists may proclaim sympathy with labor, but sympathies seldom transcend the barrier of history or theory (unless labor is very weak or very strong— underdogs or giant killers) and in the end their critiques of labor can be more hostile than friendly.

Such views may be exemplified in an excellent book *about* feminism by a leading feminist author, Robin Morgan, who says the feminist movement should "not be based on gaining more privilege for those few women who already have some (white, upper- and middle class and professional women—many of you sisters reading this) at the expense of poor white, Third World and working-class women, but a movement which will fight for the needs of all women . . ."[2]

At no point, however, does the book deal further with workingclass or poor women, perhaps because feminism, whose history the book chronicles, does not deal very fully with the subject. At one point, the author notes that she was fired for union organizing by Grove Press which "had built a facade reputation as a left-liberal, avant-garde publisher,"[3] but the only further reference to unions or workingclass people involved a conversation with a *cab driver:*

"But the driver had seen my Womens' Liberation button. Oops. All the way home he proceeded to tell me how abortion was okay for them nigger and spic broads who breed so much, but no good for nice white girls like me. . . . Finally, at the end of the ride, he told me that if we women really pushed 'this liberation thing,' men like him were going to start killing us, literally. 'You talk about male violence—you ain't seen nothin' yet. These rapes and beatings are going to soar up, baby. You can't tell me I'm not a king in my own home and get away with it.' Besides, he informed me he was a union man."[4]

No doubt this is an accurate record of the author's experiences, but standing alone as it does, and as it may in the author's experience, it gives a distinctly *un*sympathetic view of the workingclass male, and by implication, the workingclass female, for the two are closely linked. Probably cab drivers' wives would challenge this stereotype of blue-collar bigotry as sharply as the author legitimately challenges the cabby's stereotypes of feminists.

Perhaps the chief point of contact between feminist academic-activists and hospital workers (and other workingclass women) has been the women's health movement. "In the late sixties and early seventies," write Marieskind and Ehrenreich, "two distinctly popular movements around health-care issues have emerged: a community movement centered in the Black, Chicano, and Puerto Rican ghettos of some major cities, and a women's health movement active in hundreds of towns and cities across the country."[5]

The movement dealt with issues unique to women—birth, gynecology, birth control, abortion—and it had two points of agreement among participants: that no one should be denied care because of inability to pay, and that consumers of health care should play a role in the management of health care institutions. By the mid seventies, the movement included some 1200 groups, thousands of participants, two national publications, and groups in Europe, Canada and elsewhere, but by the late seventies, the movement slowed and finally entered the doldrums along with other feminist and community-control activities.

WOMENS' ISSUES

Womens' issues are obviously not defined by popular referendum, but how they *are* defined, and *by whom* is apparently not known. However, at least two kinds of issues have been raised by two kinds of feminists. One group of professional and "radical" feminists (including writers, activists, academics on the political or countercultural left) have focused on the patriarchal family and the origins of sexism in private relationships. Another group of professional and "liberal" feminists (including policy makers, lawyers, organization staff) have attacked sexism in its institutional setting and addressed civil rights issues, legislation, discrimination in the workplace. In general, neither group has included many workingclass women in its ranks and neither group has defined or addressed the specific priorities of workingclass women.

Influential in the first group during the early seventies were the writings of radical feminists Kate Millett *(Sexual Politics)* and Shulamith Firestone *(The Dialectic of Sex)*, who attributed women's oppression (and the class system, hierarchies, and male rule) to the patriarchal family system which, as they saw it, was the basic unit of all historical societies.[6]

Firestone wrote, "Marx was onto something more profound than he knew when he observed that the family contained within itself in embryo all the antagonisms that later develop on a wide scale within the society and the state. For unless the revolution uproots the basic social organization, the biological family—the vinculum through which the psychology of power can always be smuggled—the tapeworm of exploitation will never be annihilated."[7]

While some feminists like Firestone called for an end of marriage and the family, others (including many lesbians) favored a virtual segregation of the sexes. In most cases, however, economic dependency was seen as the fundamental cause of womens' historic oppression, not physical and marital contact with men.

While these theories located many "tapeworms" of exploitation in traditional family roles (especially those of previous eras), they failed to locate much that typical workingclass women could identify with, and the call for an uprooting of the biological family and the self segregation of women did not win many votes among those to whom the message read "anti-family and anti-male." It was not that workingclass women were willing slaves to marriage and family, it was more that they related to them much as they related to work—that is, they had problems with both but their total assessment was more positive than negative. And for many, the highest priority was family life and, unless something clearly better came along, they would defend it.

They also saw (as educated women must have seen even more vividly) that male-female relations within the family are far more egalitarian than they were in grandmother's day and that women have more freedom and influence than ever before. They also saw that the reason for this (as feminists themselves pointed out) has been greater financial independence, and hence more choice, freedom, control over their lives.

While these writers influenced the early seventies, most self-identified feminists wished only to reform and improve family life and relations with males, not uproot or transform them. Some feminists pointed to the isolation, monotony, even triviality of housewifery and sought more stimulating alternatives in the marketplace. Many others focused on their own bodies and male violations of them—rape, wife battering, alcoholic and abusive husbands, lack of free choice on abortions, forced sterilization, male contraception, the treatment of women as property and sex objects, obstetrical and gynecological abuses by doctors, etc.

Raising these issues profited women of all classes, but the issues themselves seldom rallied workingclass women, whose major needs and priorities apparently lay elsewhere. Moreover, right wing groups used the confusion over feminist views of the family, female roles, and male abusiveness to win many converts among the confused. As feminist Barbara Easton puts it:

"Anita Bryant's attack on homosexuality as a threat to the family, or Marabel Morgan's Fascinating Womanhood movement which purports to teach women to hold onto their husbands through seduction, feed on fears of social isolation that have a basis in reality. The anti-abortion movement speaks to women's fears that motherhood is being devalued; this is a legitimate concern at a time when, for most women, there are no adequate alternatives to it. The solutions that right-wing movements pose to these problems are not only anti-feminist but inadequate. . . . These movements attract women not because they point to any viable solutions, but because they bring into the open problems associated with the breakdown of traditional family structure and roles. They provide arenas in which women can voice real concerns. It is time for feminism and the left to address these questions."[8]

The second group of feminists, turning to the law and public policy, raised issues of sexism in schools and on the job: equal pay for equal work; discrimination against women in hiring, training, promoting, terminating, etc.; affirmative action toward integrating women into "male jobs"; equity in social security and private pension plans; discrimination and sex stereotyping in schools. With respect to the intersection between job and family, the issues included: the treatment of pregnancy as a disability under workers' compensation, adoption of flexitime schedules, and the provision of child care facilities. Newer issues raised under the federal Civil Rights law included sexual harassment and comparable worth.

Except for comparable worth (still a developing issue) and in a different sense child care, this book argues that even these issues, *significant as they are,* do not tap directly into the major job-related problems of the majority of hospital workers—nor, in all probability, into those of most other workingclass women.

A strong undercurrent in the whole of the women's movement (most feminist groups included) has been an emphasis on careers and on achievement and equality in the highly competitive male professions and corporate world. Commonly assumed in the growing literature on careers (the academy, the arts, the managerial and corporate woman, the woman doctor-lawyer-merchant-chief) is that careers will not only elevate those few who can compete successfully with men for them, but they will also (1) provide "representatives" for women in high places; (2) change, improve, and humanize the institutions in which women function.

While all these opportunities unquestionably belong to women, careers as corporate managers and professionals are definitely not what most workingclass women seek, and even when they do, they find themselves at a distinct class disadvantage in the pursuit of them. As for "representation" and "humanization," the assumptions are as yet unproven. Women who are chosen for high office by their women constituents are likely to represent those women. Women who are chosen by their male superiors are more likely to represent *them*. Nor are women certain to humanize the institutions in which they function, and make them more hospitable to women workers, if they are trained and selected by those who have *de*humanized them.

UNIONISM

This book is also about labor unions, the work organizations that workingclass women most often join. In general the response of feminists to unions, much like their response to workingclass women, has tended to be distant and disinterested, and beyond that, ambivalent and suspicious. Again, responses are likely to be shaped by media stereotyping and by dualistic and purist approaches that see people and groups as either good or evil, rather than as possessing gradations of virtue, and that fail to distinguish among unions based on how *much* support each of them gives to *which* women's issues.

Negativism has other sources as well: the social class origins of most feminists, the search for alternatives to *all* established institutions, the critical stance of most unions toward Soviet communism (as well as the excesses of American capitalism), the difficulties involved—especially for outsiders—in organizing women, and a feminist focus on private life as the root cause of social oppression. Some feminists also see unions as the "sweethearts" of employers, an assessment that reverses the more popular image of unionists as tough, strike-happy radicals, and that hardly, in any event, suits the unfolding story of hospital unionism. Yet some feminists, even leaders of the women's health movement, women committed to social change, have been explicitly hostile to the role of unionism in hospital organization:

"The recent wave of hospital unionization has done much to reinforce the psychological industrialization of the lower-rank hospital workers. . . . In effect, the unions' message to the workers is, 'We can't do anything about the fact that you have a meaningless dead-end job, but we can get you paid more for doing it!'

". . . So by concentrating on economic demands, without in any way challenging the hospital hierarchy and its non-service priorities, the unions implicitly place the needs of the workers in conflict with the needs of the consumer—the ultimate alienation."[9]

Placing the economic needs of these minimum-wage workers in such an unfavorable light, disparaging wage demands because they conflict with consumer needs (the "ultimate alienation"), and understating the effects on the hierarchy of union gains, are only the tip of the iceberg. Commenting in a more general way on the responses of feminists to unionism, Carol Hatch says:

"The dominant trend in socialist-feminism in the United States has been to play down the importance of trade-union and workplace organization of women. Given that women's entry into the paid labor force in this century has been one of the central features of organizing production, it is peculiar that a strong left tendency—identifying as socialist and feminist—has been so unconcerned with the organization of women workers.[10]

"At least as common as ignoring the organizing of women in the workplace has been disparaging it. If it will not lead to the perfect struggle, it shows (dangerous) signs of tilting toward the (male-dominated, reformist-oriented, bureaucracy-dominated) right. . . . I suspect that fears of the labor movement's economism infecting organized women wage workers may be so strong because the essential niceness, as well as victim-like, nature of women is threatened by the idea of women descending to the pits of collective bargaining to win improvements in wage and working conditions.[11]

"Socialist-feminism as a tendency is still the main political identity of thousands of women, but with the dissolution of the organizations, the networks that have remained have tended to be the more established networks of left academic women."[12] Since a critical mass of these women, she says, study the private sphere—family, child development, women's history, gender studies—strong pressures remain to continue to focus on private issues.

"We were once the cutting edge of a mass movement, not just in the United States but internationally. We are now largely irrelevant to mass feminism, though we were extraordinarily important in its inception. How and why did we lose that role? . . . In any event, socialist-feminists have, I think, profoundly misunderstood the organizational potential of combining women's and workers' consciousness and the exponential rise that can take place on both levels. . . . If labor is to exist as a progressive force, it must recognize the potential of organizing women workers. And *we* must recognize that its continued dwindling as a countervailing force on both the economic and political levels would damage us immeasurably as feminists and socialists."[13]

Unions are in fact the only on-the-job advocates women have, and in their advocacy role they have measurably upgraded the security, independence, and job conditions of women workers—along with their economic status. While unions operate against formidable odds (corporate power) and possess no powers of instant gratification for members, they offer hospital workers the only means at their disposal for identifying and working toward the solution of job-related problems. Such an assessment will be validated, I believe, in the material that follows.

Throughout this book, hospital workers talk about their problems.

In response to what they say, critics might reasonably ask "Why do these problems exist?" and "Why don't unions solve them?" And unionists might reasonably respond that they have already solved (or reduced) many problems and that with more power they could solve more. They would say that this is the worst of times, not the best, for hospital unionism, given increased union-busting activities, hospital closings, public budget cuts, the rising tides of conservatism, and the innate problems involved in organizing low-wage, marginal workers. They would say they need all the help they can get from feminists and others in support of "mainstream" issues, those with an appeal broad enough to unite people of generally similar interests.

Support is especially needed because of the "overload" on unions—slim resources and an infinity of contending problems. Other movements (political, student, religious, civil-rights, anti-war, women's) have supported labor, but they have also raised obstacles to its progress. Perhaps a less sectarian, less purest approach to building coalitions with others would reduce these obstacles. Nothing is 100 percent pure, but impurities and wrong votes on issue *one* ought not to prevent like-minded people (or even the *un*like-minded) from working together on issue *two* or *three*. In particular, if the issues raised by hospital workers matter at all, support for them should be sought from whatever source and without regard to ideological deviations.

What this book says about feminism and unionism is that women's issues need to be looked at in a new light if progressive movements are to flourish. The issues raised by hospital workers are not new ones to their unions, far from it. Almost all are issues the union tries to deal with in bargaining. What is new, and not always perceived by unionists, is that most of these issues are women's issues, problems that have special meaning and priorities for women workers. Redefining them as women's issues may help direct leaders, inside and outside labor, to matters that concern workingclass women far more than some other women's issues do.

The women's movement has nourished and trained many women for union leadership, but its direct effect on hospital workers is more subtle where it is present at all. It has apparently affected them less through the issues it has raised than through its impact on consciousness and responses to authority. It has opened the eyes of at least some activists to the denial of their rights as women and as workers; it remains for unions to open the eyes of more feminists to the issues that affect their women members most critically.

The benefits of contact between feminists on one hand and unionists and workingclass women on the other, do not all flow one way. Workingclass women and unions contribute numbers, voting power, special internal knowledge about jobs and institutions, and an orientation toward basic work issues. Feminists offer new ideas, good internal *and* external views of many institutions, access to the media, support of social action, and a network of contacts in rather high places. The two do not share a common ideology at all points, but they do share strong commitments to equity on the job and they are, in that sense, two parts of one movement.

WOMEN'S ISSUES, JOB SATISFACTION, AND THE ALTRUISTIC MOTIVE

It is puzzling that people who perform what educated people regard as "disagreeable" jobs so often say they like them. Most hospital workers we talked with complained about their jobs, but most of them also insisted that they liked or even loved their work. Here, the distinction between the "job" and the "work" may matter, for what these women are usually saying is that they like what they do (the content of their work) but heartily dislike many of the conditions under which they do it.

To find out more about their positive responses, in the study of two hospitals we asked what women *liked most about their jobs*. The two leading factors chosen were: "useful work; helping sick people", and "the people I work with." A close third was a factor unrelated to the work itself, but very much related to the family ties of women: "the job is near home."

An overwhelming 74 percent of those surveyed said they *disagree* with the statement: "I would be happier if I didn't have to work at all." Such responses are so hypothetical that they may not mean much but they do indicate that women have strong positive feelings about their work.

"Caring" is a major theme in the positive responses to work— helping the sick, doing useful work, taking pride in work. It is apparently what makes hospital work gratifying and interesting, despite the long list of complaints raised about the job. For these women, work is likely to be useful, meaningful and seldom routine, boring, or alienating, as some experts on job alienation assume it to be.

But such positive responses can turn sour when women feel they cannot give good care, when they have no time for it, or when staff, supplies, equipment, supervision are inadequate. Perhaps the underlying complaint women have with hospital management is that it does not care enough about the patients, for it is such caring that makes work rewarding. Most women believed that the hospital's mercenary interests take priority over concerns about patients, and 93 percent *agreed* that the "hospital cares more about money than about patients."

Supporting our findings about positive responses to work, another survey found that only 22 percent of 17,000 hospital nurses were either moderately or very dissatisfied with their jobs (and only 8 percent of industrial and school nurses).[14] Thus, a sizeable proportion of hospital RNs were dissatisfied, but most were satisfied with their jobs. The survey also found that the feeling of accomplishment at the end of the work day, coupled with opportunity to help other people, was for these RNs the factors most highly correlated with job satisfaction.

It is ironic that patients sometimes regard hospital workers as uncaring or hostile when in fact most of them (with some genuinely grim and apathetic exceptions) complain more about the poor quality of patient care in the hospital than about the poor care given workers.

Hospital workers often cannot *give* good care, but mainly because staff shortages and poor conditions make it impossible. While hospital workers are not "goodie-goodies" typically, they perhaps care more than other people about the quality of the work they do; and it is because they care (about work, patients, and now about themselves also) that they turn toward unionism and other collective action for support.

This book catalogs some hospital worker complaints, but it should be kept in view throughout that, contrary to some prevailing views, these women are generally more satisfied than dissatisfied with their work. In the following passages, hospital workers talk about caring and altruistic satisfactions.

I feel good when I help somebody. That's mainly why I like my work. And that's why I'm a union steward. I'm not only helping the patients, I'm also helping the people that help them. I was taught by Catholic nuns in a Catholic school. They were totally anti-union, so I was too. But I worked in a place where I couldn't give good care. I was tired all the time, frustrated all the time. When an LVN and I were given eight critical care patients to work with, I got fed up and called the union. I blew my lid: "Now what the hell is this fucking union going to do for me?" I was mad. I said, "I want somebody down here now." That's how I got started in the union. I began to realize that to give good care, nurses would have to fight for it themselves, and use whatever agents they had to get it.

Nurses were brought into the intensive care unit from everywhere because of our complaints, and we got a one to two ratio of nurses to patients. Suddenly, patients were being taken care of. Monitors appeared all over the place. Everything the patients needed was coming in. In other words, the union responded to the nurses' needs and helped alleviate a lot of problems. But the nurses are afraid of the union and it's hard to get them to take action. I like to see the nurses effect change for patients through collective effort. It stems from being a nurse, that's why I like it.

It's very stressful working in a hospital, but it can be exhilarating. At the end of the day you feel you've really done something for someone. You see a dying patient come in and later you see him walk out. You feel you've saved a life. If he doesn't make it, you feel very bad, but you know you did all you could. I like to encourage patients and try to help them accept their illness. My patients come in and can't do anything for themselves, but they walk out feeding and dressing themselves, everything.

When people are ill they think no one cares. I'll never forget one patient in the arthritic ward. She was crying, and I asked her "What's the problem?" She said, "I just feel like I want to scream." I pushed her out on the patio and said, "Now scream." She screamed at the top of her lungs, two or three times, then she was okay. She said, "I really appreciate that."

I never had a chance to do anything for my own family. As soon as I was out of high school I lost my mother. Now I take people under my wing as if they were mine. I get a thrill from that. I do it outside as well as inside the hospital. I go visit the little elderly people, and some of them call me "mama", If they ask me to do anything for them, I go out of my way to do it. I like caring for old people, but the way they're treated in convalescent homes got me. I had to fight it, that's why I went union. My heart wanted to expose these homes for the way they treat people.

I like bedside with patients. Sometimes they say things that really cheer you up. You also meet other employees, all different types, and it helps to make your day. Sometimes the patients can't communicate with the doctor, they're afraid, so they talk with me about their problems. Lots of times I know more about the patient's history than the doctor does even though I'm just an aide. Very often the patients just want somebody to talk to, and sometimes just a few words will encourage them. But we're not there to talk to them, we don't have time for it. We have to do so much half-assed stuff with patients. It bothers us, makes us feel guilty, that we can't care for patients properly, but we just can't do any more. We don't have enough people.

The nurse today wants to do a good job. She walks out of nursing school and into the wards saying, "I'm here to help the sick and needy," but she soon learns there's no way she can do that, and do it right, because the hospital cares about one thing only, money. She gets frustrated and quits. Nine times in ten, the next hospital is as bad as the last one.

Hospital workers have a real sense of altruism about their work, a real dedication. The Catholics used that against us all the time in organizing campaigns. "Dear fellow employees: We here at St. Mary's don't want outside influences in our hospital. After all, we're dedicated to our work, we're giving part of our lives to this work," and so on. Even the janitors and maids have a sense of dedication. They want to give good care but they're frustrated by administrators who are so cost conscious.

I had a brother who was a priest, and I talked to him about the social teaching of the Catholic church, a very wonderful teaching, that people have the right to join unions. He agrees with me that their implementation of that teaching can be absolutely awful.

Hospital workers are not called New Nightingales because they have abandoned the traditional altruism of nursing. On the contrary, they have extended it, learned to care in newer and better ways, and recognized that saving others does not require one's own suicide. Unionism for them is merely an extension of that caring.

In justice to the real Florence Nightingale and the real heritage of nursing, however, it should be pointed out that the Nightingale mystique is based on myth more than historic fact. As a feminist review of the woman and her work verifies, the real Nightingale was anything but submissive or witlessly self-sacrificing in her personal life, though she did indeed oppose the suffrage and feminist movement of her day.[15] Not only did she refuse to submit to expectations that she pursue a lady-like, sheltered Victorian life-of-leisure, she became a determined mover and shaker in the man's world of medical care. And she was not reticent about claiming credit for what she did. Perhaps the New Nightingales are the legitimate heirs, after all, of the real Nightingale's achievements.

Two

A NEW NIGHTINGALE SING-OUT
THE SENSE OF SELF AND OTHERS

In the following, three New Nightingales talk about what they do on their jobs, how they perceive their work, and how they relate to collective action through their union. They also talk about how their new sense of self-and-others affects their job of caring for the sick. In their comments, the altruistic motive (caring for others in the old Nightingale tradition) is mixed with a newer and more complex sense that caring also about oneself, one's family, one's coworkers is a necessary extension of the altruistic motive and that improving conditions for workers can also improve them for patients. Thus, the altruistic motive is supplemented, not replaced, by the collectivist motive.

These women are not "ideal types," only individuals, yet their jobs and experiences extend through patient care from "unskilled" to "professional" work. One is a registered nurse, one a technician, and one a nursing assistant (or aide). Sandy Butterfield, the RN, works with radium therapy in a cancer clinic at Cal hospital, and though she is not assigned to regular ward work, as most RNs are, she shares many of the responses, both positive and negative, of RNs to their professions.

≈

THE WOMEN—IN THEIR OWN WORDS

SANDY BUTTERFIELD, REGISTERED NURSE

I got into oncology through my own illness. I had a tumor and it took six months to find out for sure it wasn't malignant. In that six months I went absolutely crazy. I thought my father and everybody were trying to kill me. I was nuttier than anybody I've ever seen. After I came out of that, and got through an ulcer, I became a nurse and ended up in oncology. I felt I had something to offer people because I'd been through it.

As an oncology nurse, a cancer nurse, I interview patients when they arrive, find out about their strengths and weaknesses, and what problems they may have during therapy. I follow patients through therapy and I do death and dying support and nutrition support. Right now I am educating the staff about nutrition supplements, hoping they will prescribe them to patients. The nurses prepare the radium needles so the doctor can implant them. We load the radium ourselves, and then go into surgery, scrub, and circulate.

The department is unique and almost a closed entity. The staff physician stays here for four years of residency. It's not like a medical clinic where residents rotate in and out every month. The same ones are here all the time. Our patient count is down to almost 50 percent of what it normally is. The new doctors have to be re-educated about what radiation therapy can offer. In the past it was used only with people who were on their way out the door, but it cured many people and some new doctors don't know that. There's a competition between the different cancer treatments. Medical oncology, for instance, doesn't say, "Maybe radiation can offer something my chemo-therapy can't." They won't send patients to us.

The staff in oncology is under a lot of stress because the patients are dying. They should leave the ward about every six months to get relief from the stress. When I was head nurse on the gynecology cancer ward, I tried to rotate people out for a period of time. All you see here are failures, people who are going to die. That's one reason I went down to ambulatory care, because I could see successes there; for every patient that died, eight more lived. It's very hard to give up somebody you get attached to, and then physically clean up their body. If people on the cancer floors could go to the clinics for awhile, and see some cures, it would keep people in oncology longer. Our turnover and burnout rates are very high.

They will take anybody to work the cancer floor, but most new grabs, unless they *choose* oncology, aren't seasoned enough to face it. We see bodies totally demolished by disease and experience the terrible psychological strain of working only with the dying, so nurses don't stay more than six months. We need staff that really wants to work here, and we need more breaks. We're supposed to get 15 minutes in the morning and afternoon, but more times than not, we don't get them. The cafeteria is miles away, so we have to sit in the break room, even to eat, and usually we're called out while we're in there.

I get very anxious about the radium. I don't want to handle it. They say it's safe now, but in 20 years will they say it's safe? I wear a radiation badge that it takes them six months to read. In that time you could get cancer and die. In most places, the radium is handled by technicians or physicians, not by nurses. I resent doing it, I don't need leukemia.

A lot of nurses waste their training. They teach us to *think* in nursing school, and they teach us that we have our own realm and skills, but on the job we find we have no realm at all. Unless we have a specialty we're stuck. We do what the doctor orders and we do not think. It is absolutely boring here because I'm given such mundane tasks to do. I've been a cancer nurse for seven years, and most of the work I do could be delegated to ancillary personnel. I like teaching and I like counseling, and I like working with the children and helping them have a less traumatic experience in therapy.

An aide should make up the trays for surgery, not an RN with four years of college and seven years of cancer experience. There is nothing to putting instruments out on trays. An RN should not be responsible for tearing down charts on patients who have expired, it doesn't take any brains to put a bunch of papers together, staple them and put them in an envelope. Why do you need an RN to show the patient where the room is? The RNs do it because the old style nursing said, "This is what nursing is." The old nurses define themselves that way, and they are proud of it.

Primary care is great for patients. They get better much faster when the same people work with them throughout their illness. If I as a nurse get to know you, I'm going to know your pain needs, your food needs, your bathing needs, and I can sit and just shoot the shit with you so you don't get so lonely. But you need more staff in order to give primary care.

The patients are lonely and afraid. On the 11 to 7 shift, the family is gone, the television is gone, the person next to them is asleep, it's dark, and they are frightened. A lot of times they wake up scared to death. That's when they need people the most. A patient like that should have primary care on *that* shift. Sometimes the primary care should be on the 3 to 11 shift, when the family comes in. Maybe the family is adding stress to the patient's life, and the nurse should be there to handle it.

The County hospital has problems because it gets the poorest patients and the roughest cases. Its equipment is worse than in private hospitals, and the system itself is an absolute mess. We have a crew of supervisors who have been in the system for thirty years and are waiting out their retirement. They have been "countified" and are not willing to change anything. They say, "It's been like that for thirty years and that's how it's going to be." When people come in with other experience and education, they get washed out by the system. I'd say this is the worst job I've had, and I've worked the V.A. hospital which is supposed to be the pits. Still, I'm staying in oncology, if not in this hospital, then another one. If I didn't need the money, I'd still work. In one sense, I'm lucky. I work a steady shift Monday through Friday. The only trouble is having to cover the late clinic one week out of four because some rule says an RN has to be there. But other staff is there to care for people, so all we do is sit and wait.

If an RN treats other people on the staff like they're idiots, they'll get their backs up, but if she shows them she'll go to their level, get her hands dirty, they'll back her up all the way. It's how she treats other people, and how she works with them. Most doctors don't know how to deal with women or with subordinates. They want everyone to jump because they are the doctors. Well, I'm a doctor's daughter and I don't jump for them.

SALLY PEARMAN, TECHNICIAN

Sally Pearman is a "tech"—specifically, a radiological technologist or x-ray technician at Penn hospital, and her skill level is somewhere between that of a nursing assistant and an RN. Most x-ray techs in her hospital are women. Men go into it, she says, because they need it to get into nuclear medicine and ultra sound, higher paying specialties.

≈

The human body is fascinating. I'm always learning about it and I never get bored. I like working with people and helping people. There's a religious aspect to it, and that's not corn, it's a true feeling. Love of medicine made me decide to become a tech, and I picked x-ray so I could get rich quick—ha! There were three options for me: The Peace Corp, physical therapy (which required a college education) or x-ray. The Peace Corp was out. Eleven cents an hour isn't my bag. Physical therapy training I couldn't afford, but x-ray was on-the-job training. The fact that my sister is an x-ray tech helped draw me in.

It was intriguing to think I'd be working with people, seeing the x-ray of a head or a large bowel. I might grumble a lot but deep down inside the fascination and the sense of a higher power is always there. The human body is awesome, miraculous.

The cases we have! A child might come in and there's a suspicion of child abuse. We find out the child's history and with our x-rays we can prove if it's child abuse or not. Or someone's been in a hideous accident and been put together with screws and bolts and pipes, and they're *walking*. Or someone has a heart attack and they've been shocked twice to bring them back to life. They come down and talk to us and laugh. We see people get better as we help them along, see them healing. It takes a lot of compassion and sensitivity.

A hospital should be a functioning machine like the human body, where everything works for one purpose, but in this hospital nobody understands how other departments work. A patient may need a kidney test but hasn't been cleaned out for it. We call the floor he came from and tell them the patient needs cleaning. Ten minutes later they call back and say, "Why didn't Mr. Smith have his kidney x-rayed?" We had just told them why. The problem is lack of communication and cooperation.

I see so many things that are detrimental to patient care and employee welfare. I am pushing to get equipment that would help transport patients. The hospital keeps saying, "It's not in the budget. You don't need it." Meanwhile you get patients with broken legs and broken backs, and you're moving them around like crazy on draw sheets. With this new apparatus you move them only once, very carefully, and that's it. Supervision won't listen to what we say. They think about their budget rather than their patients.

Patients have certain rights now. They can question their doctor, change doctors, see reports of exams done on them. They can look at their charts and say, "What are you doing to me and why are you doing it?" instead of accepting whatever the doctor does. There are a lot of incompetents in the medical field, and the only way this can be changed is by public pressure.

People think it's appalling that a union should be in a hospital; they associate unions with industry and coal miners. When I first started out I was anti-union too, but I saw the problems evolving and now I feel you need a union everywhere, if it's a good union, and ours is good because of the people who run it. I tell my employer, "I'm a good technician and I deserve more than you're giving me, but you won't listen so I have to get a third party in here, with legal status, to make you listen."

The patients need care, but so do I; I need clothes, a car to get around in, nourishing food. I'm worth something too, and I have my own life to live. The union gives me a say, a way to speak out about things I feel are wrong. Now we can improve patient care and benefit employees at the same time. It's taken us about six years to get a union in here, and it's still a constant battle. Lack of communication, cooperation, respect are the basic things.

In x-ray the doctor in charge was a very good man so people felt they didn't need the union, but I went to union meetings and found out about problems outside of x-ray. They were horrible, appalling— the scheduling, the staffing, the rotating shifts, the work load—and "if you don't like it, there's the door."

You get very close to people when you work with them day in and day out. The employees here do quality work, they're compassionate with patients, they take pride in their work, and they do not deserve to be hassled and put down all the time. The supervisor writes them up because they take five extra minutes on their break or call in sick. Someone's son might phone because he needs five dollars for his Little League, and the hospital refuses the call. These things are petty but they happen and they shouldn't. People come to me and weep on my shoulder. Some of them come with their personal problems. I don't like to see them get pushed around by the personnel director, who is a downright mean man, so I try to help them.

If you keep telling workers they're not worth anything, and you don't pay them anything, their work is going to be inferior. People deserve a pat on the back, some praise, and some real rewards. You can't create good morale and a desire to work without that. Happy people can take better care of patients. Anybody can deal with physical problems, kidney infection, appendicitis, ingrown toenail, whatever. But hospital care often falls short psychologically, and that's a big part of curing patients.

In the next contract, we will be dealing with scheduling. We go seven day stretches with absolutely no compensation for overtime. It's a long hassle, the seven day week. It causes a lot of tension, a lot of mental and physical strain. You work seven days, and the next few days you spend in bed resting or gulping aspirin for headaches. So we'd like compensated scheduling and more weekends off. Before the union came in, many people only got one weekend off every six or seven weeks.

Some department heads use the schedule to punish us. "I don't like you, so I'll create problems for you, put you on seven day stretches, or rotate your shift two or three times a week." The grievance procedure on this is not explicit in our contract. This is only our first contract. As we go on, the language will become clearer.

Supervision is really nailing people for sick time. They've called people who have had major surgery and told them they had to come back to work right away or be suspended. Doctors' excuses for your illness mean nothing. I'd like them to tell some of these doctors that what they say means nothing to the hospital.

They had an antique portable x-ray machine and they would not buy a new one. One day I plugged it in and it shocked the heck out of me. Patients could be injured that way, and using a defective electrical apparatus around flammable anaesthetics could blow the hospital up. The equipment has to shock someone, or blow someone up, before they will get rid of it.

Nurses are on the top of the heap and technicians are fall-out. It's always been a professional battle, a battle for respect. Nurses are "professional" and above everyone else. I think anybody that gets paid for their work is professional. The technicians are getting more recognition now because we're getting more education.

Our department head is a model of what a supervisor should be like. She's easy to talk to, intelligent, and she doesn't play popularity games. She'll be very honest with you and tell you exactly what she thinks. She's also very fair, she can see if someone is being a little lax and the other technicians are taking on an extra load. If equipment doesn't work well, she'll get it taken care of. If we ask her to help us, she will do anything. Her door is always open. She really cares for her people and she sticks by them, which is a quality very few supervisors have. We go to her with problems, but if the problem involves finances, her hands are tied. The higher-ups control the funds.

I'm a member of the National Organization of Women, and it's important for me to be involved with the struggle for women's rights. I like the car door opened for me, but I don't like people to treat me as an inferior just because I'm a woman, that's garbage. I'm a novice at the women's movement. I've gotten involved through the union. I am not domesticated, and I can't see house cleaning or changing diapers as a life's work, even though I love children. I've got to grow mentally, physically, whatever, through experiences and knowing people and achieving my goals.

Women are underdogs, so it's a challenge to me, an intriguing one. I went to a women's meeting recently. One woman was on welfare, one had a masters in psychology, another worked as a chemist, and one was a housewife. That's what I like, meeting people, learning about them.

I have a good job and no problems because I'm a woman. I'm respected in my field because I've earned it. But the fact is other women have problems, and I am a woman. Somewhere along the line it would affect me, so I want to know about the problems and the solutions. If I can leave this corner of the world a little better place, then I have done something.

When I first tried to organize a union, I went into the coffee shop on my day off and talked to people. There was almost a court hearing over that. I was subpoenaed and the director of personnel took me to court. He told me I was breaking the law by talking to people in the coffee shop. He called me into his office and read me up and down, and left and right. The case got thrown out because he didn't have a leg to stand on, but he scared the heck out of me, calling me into his office and accusing me of being a criminal.

Our local knew how to organize people. They knew how to talk to them and deal with their problems. They cared. They had a sincere interest in workers as people. That's where the hospital fell short. They didn't care about you as a person, only as someone to get the work done and bring in revenue. "Just work, don't ask questions."

I have gained a lot of friends through my union activities. People trust me. They know they can come and talk to me and air whatever's in their guts, and even get angry with me. It's a fantastic union and there isn't anything in the world I wouldn't do for Rose Trump.* If I were to pattern my life after someone it would be her because I have complete admiration and respect for her. She brought the union up from practically nothing and developed a great organization. She's very respected by the people who work for her, under her and with her. It sounds like Abraham Lincoln, heh?

VIRGINIA WILTROUT, NURSING ASSISTANT

Virginia Wiltrout is a nursing assistant at newly unionized Penn Hospital. The work related issues she discusses might, in shorthand form, be called the "eleven S's": security, staffing (and speedup), scheduling, stress, safety, sick-time, sexism (and segregation), step-up (promotion and upgrading), supervision, schooling, and speaking out. These do not at all exhaust the list of problems confronted by her or other hospital workers, but they do include most of the important ones. Among the anguished complaints of assistants and others low in the hospital pecking order is that they are not treated with the respect and dignity they think is due them. These verbatim comments from a woman of obvious intellect, courage, and concern point up the validity of the complaint.

≈

My husband didn't want me to work. We had what I call "friendly arguments." He felt that a woman's place was in the home. But it got to where we wanted things we couldn't get. I'm a heck of a good budgeter. I had to be. Whatever money he brought in was A-1 with me, but I saw we could do much better if I worked. When my sister got killed in a car wreck, I said, "I am going to work in a hospital." So I did. My emotional state at that time, losing her, was bad. That's what told my husband, "Let her go." He's very understanding when the emotions are concerned.

He doesn't mind me working, except when I come home so tired and angry. Last month he told me to quit work about two dozen times. My phone rings off the hook constantly in the evening. But he

*president of local 585 SEIU

understands the union part because he has the same thing. It's either him or me on the phone about the union.

We tried to improve our conditions at the hospital but we had no job security. The personnel director's favorite saying was, "There's the door. If you don't like it, leave." But the door swings both ways, and that's why the union got in. Management would not talk to us or try to work our problems out. They just said, "No. That's the way it is." So we had to go for job security and for some way of saying: "Wait a minute. This *isn't* the way it is. These are your workers. They take care of your patients. You have to give them what they need to work and live decently." Only when the union came in did we get a say.

Wages are *not* the number one issue. If they were, the union never would have gotten in here. It's working conditions. Anyone will tell you that. Staffing is the number one problem. Scheduling is the number two problem. Wages used to be miserable—and benefits? There weren't any. The union can make a big difference there, but what we wanted was a voice and a contract to back it up, so that when we argued about conditions, they couldn't fire us.

I like being around patients. What I don't like is that we don't have enough time with them. They want to talk. They ask all sorts of questions to keep you at their bedside. But you have to rush past them. It aggravates the patient, people rushing around like that. It should be an easy-going atmosphere for them. They have aggravation enough just being there.

The patients ask: "Why don't they get you girls more help?" And we kid them: "Boy, we've got you fooled. We pretend to work hard and you fall for it." They laugh but they know we work too hard. I try not to let them think they're a burden to us. At home I do my work and I can sit down, it's not overwhelming. At the hospital, we're like robots, working machines. I find myself running when I'm at that hospital. Then somebody says: "Hey, slow down." I catch myself and slow down to a walk. We get so little rest. There's supposed to be a ten minute break in the morning, ten in the afternoon and a half hour for lunch. Very seldom can we take the afternoon break.

People work seven days under constant pressure, so when they get home they pass out on the couch. They're too tired to go anywhere and they call in sick to recuperate. Not one supervisory person works a seven-day stretch. You can't function right or think straight when you work seven days in a row. Your nerves are frayed and you take it out on patients and coworkers, or on your family when you go home.

We'd like every other weekend off, to be with our families. They could give it to us, and they could give us a five-day week, but they won't. The contract says, "at least every third weekend," and they won't give us more.

The job itself, I love. The work I do, I love. The pressure I'm under, I'm very dissatisfied about.

You're constantly running, and then they say, "Well, did you straighten the utility room up?" or "Did you put more soap out?" You're thinking, "Blankity, blank." All these bad words come in your head and you figure, "Boy, I'd like to give you a wet floor mop in the face."

On nights, there isn't much supervision. Everybody knows their job and they do it. On days it's different. The supervisors are all there and they like to bark orders. "We need this *right now*. Take these instruments down *right now*. Get that patient out of bed." Blah, blah, blah. You try to take it all with a grain of salt, but it gets to you.

The head nurse puts an awful lot of pressure on us. It's unnecessary. When she's not there, all the work gets done, and people aren't as uptight about it. She never goes out on the floor. She might walk around and say, "I'm the head nurse," but that's all. Most head nurses don't know what they're doing. If they had to work the floor one day a month they might learn something. They don't have any concept of what the actual work is like and how much time it entails.

My head nurse gets agitated if you complain about anything, so you learn not to bother her with problems. She wouldn't allow us to work as a group, but a lot of patients can't be handled by just one or two people. Four or five are needed. When she's not there, we go in as a group and do it. The work flows smoothly and things get done. There's no harassment, and you can *find* people to help you. When she's there people disappear. Everybody tries to stay clear of her.

The hospital harasses people about sick time. The personnel director says, "I won't accept anybody's doctor's excuse." If he feels you shouldn't be off, *even if you have a doctor's excuse,* he won't pay you. I'm the union steward and I keep telling him, "We have a contract here and we're entitled to sick days." Girls come in even when they're sick, simply because he harasses them if they don't. A girl came in today coughing and choking. I said, "My God, you should be home." She said, "No, they'll write me up." If you miss even two or three days, they write you up for abusing sick time. I'm waiting for them to write me up. I'd tell them where to shove it. Management doesn't understand. Why bring sick workers into a hospital? They only spread their germs.

A hospital isn't a safe place. I injured my back once, many people do. A patient fell out of bed, grabbed me and threw my back out. I was off for about six weeks. Now they have a surga-lift to move patients, a miraculous thing, but it's been broke for six months now.

The administration values the RNs more than us, even though we pick up vibes from patients that the RNs never get. I can tell the RN more about patients than she can tell me because I am with those patients more. I roll them over, rub their backs, put them on the bedpan. I know when something's wrong.

I was told when I was hired, "the patient comes first," but I've found this is not so, and it's very disturbing. The hospital is more concerned with piddly things. It boils down to the dollar sign. We get lectures on budgets and not using so many supplies, and blah, blah, but none on patient care. They don't ask, "Did this patient get his back rubbed? Did you turn this patient every so often?" I say, "Forget about that utility room, that it wasn't straightened up twice today. The utility room will be there tomorrow. Maybe the patient won't be."

Only a few people in administration know what they're doing. They need to overhaul their system from the top on down. They're keeping people from doing their job right and enjoying their work. If you like your work, you do a much better job.

I'm not interested in becoming an LPN or RN. No way. I've seen too much of it. I've talked to several people that were going on for RN but backed out. They said it required too much paperwork and it would take them further away from the patients. They don't want this. I plan on staying here until I get done or until they throw me out.

The orderlies and aides have to be paid the same wage now, that's sex equality. One orderly on our floor thinks he deserves more than the aides. I don't object to that. Maybe I should be more for women's lib but the orderly assists with autopsies, sets up traction, does male catheterizations. Of course, the aides do things the orderly doesn't do, so it might even out. Some girls would do the orderly's job, even though it's a man's job. I would. I said, "If you want me to assist with an autopsy, I would gladly." That would be very interesting, but I'm not going to push the issue because other women would feel they'd have to do it too.

Women get treated pretty decently by men here and we don't hear much about sexual harassment. I don't feel discriminated against as a woman, only as a union member.

The personnel director should want things to run smoothly but he's really an agitator. He puts the union down constantly. "It's *your* union. This is what *your* union did." These head nurses and administrators never admit to themselves, "I've benefited from this union too." They did benefit. They got hospitalization benefits, for one thing. They don't belong to the union, but they get the benefits. "Union" is still a bad word to them.

The supervisors have their pets. Three or four on our floor get their benefits, but it's "kiss my ass" and "yes, m'am." That provokes me. I'm treated pretty equal with the rest. When I'm not, I know why, because the head nurse hates the union. She tries her best to get at me, but I don't let her know it bothers me. And that bothers her. If I'd whine about it, she'd be tickled to death. She flipped out when I asked for a week over the Christmas holidays, but there's no reason not to give it to me. The patient load is way down at Christmas and there's less work to do. They don't want to because all the supervisors and clericals want off then. But now they have to go by seniority on vacation time, and they can't refuse me.

Certain things I'll fight for tooth and nail, whether we can win them or not. Like scheduling. We should have a schedule a month in advance, but we get maybe three weeks notice. You need to know ahead of time in order to plan your life. If we got a monthly schedule posted, it'd relieve some of the tension. As it is, we're treated like a pack of kids. The head nurse leaves the week's schedule laying in an envelope. It's marked "Do not open," as if to say "these bad kids are going to sneak a look." We walk past and wonder, "What's in there? What has she got me down for?" When it's posted, we all run to the board to see our schedule. It's pitiful. If they'd only let that go, that little grain of sand in our shoes, that rubs us so bad. But they really don't care for their workers.

Some people feel they're being harassed. I say, speak out, tell them about it." But they don't. They go along like puppies. A few supervisors like to dish out orders, but I get along with them too because I open my mouth. They can't get away with anything around me. It's hard to get people involved, and there's a few that say, "The union isn't doing anything for me." Blah, blah. They expect you to work miracles. They forget what benefits we have gained.

Women are more resistant to joining unions than the men. Usually the women aren't head of the house, and they're more or less under the man's wing, like myself really. Most women feel this way: "Why rock the boat? We've got a job, but it's only a supplement to our husband's income. With a man it's his livelihood. He's the head of the house and he *has* to have security." Now the women are learning they *have* to work just like the man and they're entitled to decent treatment too.

I don't know why I became a steward. I didn't want to be that involved. But people said, "Who else is going to do it? We don't want a hothead in there as a steward." The people work hard and don't need somebody pounding on the table and shaking everyone up. They need someone to go down and talk to them calmly and bring back their exact words.

I handle everything, even arbitration. It's a lot of work and a lot of hassle. Every day three or four people come to me with a problem, and they call me constantly at home. I'd love to let somebody else do it. But it's quicksand. I'm getting in deeper and deeper. I'm getting more and more gratification out of going down to Brenner's office and saying, "This is the way it has to be." People tell me, "You're not the type of person to make demands," but I'm getting to the point where I am. I'm getting more and more forceful. I'm getting aggravated. They're not living up to their end of the bargain. I don't know if I can walk away from it now. I get really thrilled by the development of our union, and being part of it.

We had a fabulous steward's training program at a local college. Before that, I thought this union was just a handful of people, but it's so big. It's everywhere and draws information from everywhere. You don't feel so alone when you know that. You don't feel like, "Oh, this is such a little hospital. We'll never get anything accomplished." The union isn't little at all. It isn't just a few people pushing you ahead. It's a whole group behind you saying, "Go get it. You worked for it and you deserve it." It gives you a very secure feeling. When the union first came into the hospital, it was like you and I and the neighbor down the street organizing a car pool. But the more I stepped in, the more I saw how big it really is.

We went to Washington, D.C. and heard people talk who came from California, Canada, everywhere. They had the same problems we had, but they'd had a union longer and had solved some of the problems. So it gave us hopes of things getting better. I loved it. After the meetings, Rose Trump took us for a ride around Washington. Oh, God, you could tell I'm a hick by the way I went on. I suppose they laughed at me afterwards. She took us to the Lincoln Memorial. I can't describe the feeling that came over me when I walked up and looked at it. You stand in such awe of a figure like that. With the kind of bosses we have, you need someone to look up to.

Three

THE CULINARY BATTLEFIELD

It's true all over. The kitchens are hell-holes

Hospital dietary departments are as notorious for their working conditions as for the food they serve. Perhaps for this reason, discontent in both Cal and Penn hospitals was highest among kitchen workers, with the runner-ups in this category being laundry workers, and for similar reasons. Both the kitchen and the laundry were described as "hell holes," and the workers in them as the most exploited and consequently the best organized of hospital groups.

In both hospitals, women reported that the kitchens were hot, humid, crowded, hazardous, pressurized, poorly managed, often chaotic. In such a setting, the deadlines of meal service had to be met regularly, and a continuous, copious supply of food ordered, stored, served.

In its organization, the kitchen resembles the assembly line more than other hospital departments do. Workers deal mainly with inanimate objects (food and kitchen tools), and they usually perform simple, repetitive tasks at high speed, often under the close surveillance of people who lack both supervisory and culinary expertise. Because dietary workers deal mainly with objects, they receive few of the compensatory satisfactions available to those who care for the sick.

Working with inanimate objects is only half the problem. The other half, dietary workers claim, is being *treated* like inanimate objects. When workers protest such treatment, the hospital may simply hire more supervisors to control them, thus adding to the surplus of "unproductive supervisors" and to the discontent of workers, which at Penn hospital contributed to its final unionization. Since then, the distress in the hospital's kitchen has been reduced, but serious problems, affecting patients and the public as well as workers, still remain. If hospital food is unpalatable or nutritionally deficient, patients suffer most in the end, but the general public also suffers because it pays much of the food bill.

Kitchen conditions may reflect a larger health care problem: the medical profession's general neglect of diet and nutrition in treating the sick. While doctors routinely prescribe pills and chemical treatments, those chemicals entering the body as food are usually matters of indifference to the profession, despite the extensive and growing body of research showing that nutrition (and exercise) are linked to numerous ailments, including such mass killers as heart disease and cancer.

Medicine's indifference to diet and nutrition is perhaps associated with both profits and prejudices. Prescribing pills is far more profitable than preventing illness, or curing it, through nutritional approaches. A patient, after all, does not need a doctor's prescription to purchase and consume a nutritionally appropriate diet. Prejudice and sexual bias may also play a role, since the kitchen has been a universal symbol of female enterprise and confinement, much as the implements of war have been symbols of male enterprise. Since food, diet, nutrition are the basic products of that historic female enterprise, they may be seen as essentially marginal to hospital operations, along with the dietary workers associated with them.

Dietary workers complain much more about *job conditions* than about the work itself, despite the routine nature of the work. The disabling symptom they complain most about is "tension," the sense of being pushed, mistreated, frustrated. Much of this tension is attributed to the malice and incompetence of supervisors, the "devils" in the kitchen's "hell hole."

Complaints about supervisors include: incompetence, laziness, uncaring attitudes, favoritism and unfairness, bossiness, misconduct, corruption, malice. Resentment often focuses on the special privileges claimed by supervisors: they may do what is forbidden to others—eat kitchen food, take long lunch breaks, rest while others work, come late to work.

Supervisors are charged with incompetence at many levels—in dietary, administrative, and personnel skills; that is, in knowing about food preparation, organizing the kitchen, and directing the work of others. Their behavior, it is said, often passes from indifference into misconduct, and then sometimes into corruption and misappropriations of (or kickbacks from) the vast sums of money spent on kitchen supplies.

The ultimate responsibility for the kitchen's distress, of course, lies with those higher up in the hospital hierarchy, with those in charge of assigning priorities, allocating funds, and getting things done. Adequate funding could overcome many of the kitchen's problems: low wages, staff shortages, safety, facilities that are antiquated and inadequately cooled, supervisors who are untrained and uncaring.

The following are quoted passages from interviews with dietary workers about their jobs. At their request for anonymity, real names have not been used.

≈

THE WOMEN—IN THEIR OWN WORDS

JOANNE LAUGHLIN, PENN HOSPITAL

When the patient count's really high and the menu's really bad, you don't get done, and you don't get your breaks. You're sweating and you're running yourself to death. You tell the supervisors about it, but they don't give you help no matter what.

The menus aren't organized at all. Everything that's real hard to prepare comes up at one time. Then maybe the next day everything is real light and easy to do. Chef salads, coleslaw, things like that are hard to prepare. You have to clean your cabbage and cut it up, clean your carrots, cut them up, make the dressing. It takes a lot of time. They never ask us if the menu has too many complicated things to prepare in one day. They had this same menu when I first started here four and a half years ago. They're supposed to give us new menus, but I haven't seen them.

Our supervisors are the main problem. They're not qualified. They don't know what they're doing. Once our dietician was fired and we didn't have one for a long time. But we knew what had to be done, and everybody worked together and did it. We didn't need to be told. The kitchen never worked better. Now it's back where it was. They never order half the things on the menu, and they are getting into ordering cheap surplus foods. It's disgusting.

They ran out of lemon pudding because the company isn't making it any more. But they leave it on the menu. They tell me to use lemon pie filling instead. On my own, sometimes I mix it with milk and vanilla pudding, and it's not so bad. You can't dish out lemon pie filling in place of pudding, it's awful.

They did the same with chocolate pudding. One boss said, "They don't make Hershey chocolate no more." We just laughed. We're not that stupid.

Another incident. They used to buy blueberry muffins. Suddenly they say, "blueberry muffins are too expensive to buy, so Shirley will have to bake them." Once Shirley ran out of blueberries. When I asked the dietician for some, she said, "Shirley doesn't make them, we buy them ready-made." She was the one who told Shirley to bake them, and Shirley had been doing it for six months.

We have five bosses over less than 30 people. They do nothing but sit around, read their papers, crochet. We're not allowed to eat, but they are. They can take anything they want from the refrigerators. If we're caught, we get written up for it. If it's going to be a rule, apply it to everyone.

They used to have favorites, but not so much since the union came in. They're still very nasty, and they walk around like they're better than us. The dietician is very high class. If she says "good morning" to you, you're lucky. She only says it to a few people. If they'd get rid of a lot of the bosses, people could get more work done. Even if we're short handed, they'll sit back and won't lift a hand to help. They come late to work almost every day, and they act like you're a slave or a servant. The five of them will get in their office and laugh and giggle and read their papers. When you go to them with a problem, they just shrug their shoulders. We used to worry about our patients and what they're getting. But when your bosses don't care, why should we?

When the new dietician came in, she started this budget thing right away. Whatever you'd say to her, she'd say, "I'm looking over my budget." The patients are paying for good food, but they're getting garbage. I figure she's getting some kind of kick-back for keeping her budget down.

The hospital hates the dietary department. We were the strongest for the union because we were treated the worst. They lost so many good workers in there. It's sickening. They should want to keep their good workers. But they don't care. You get so you can't stand it in there. You're treated like an animal, but you're just as human as they are.

The heat is terrible. They say nothing can be done about it. There must be *something*. Some days it's 100 degrees in there. We walk in and five minutes later we're soaking wet. They say air conditioning costs too much. The two vents in there are not even near the ovens.

If the sink breaks, they say the broken part isn't made any more. It's that old. We had a leak about a month ago. They tightened it a little. They couldn't buy a new part. It still drips. They stick buckets under it until inspection comes. Then everything's straightened out.

I also got stuck with bagging bread for lunch. You stick a piece of bread in a little bag, fold it shut, put it on a tray. You do five loaves of bread for every meal except breakfast. You put silverware in the little bags too.

After I took my stuff to the floors, I had to set up the trays for supper. You take a tray, then a placemat, then a napkin. Then you take the patients' names and put whatever they're allowed to have on the trays. You had to have a computer upstairs to do all this stuff.

The stuff came out so hot from one machine that you'd burn your fingers. Sometimes the cook wasn't so good. She couldn't put potatoes on at the same time as the meat. You'd have to help her do that. My arms never stopped moving. I couldn't stop for a drink of water.

Once a week I had to put away an order. That was a ball. After supper I'd get the snacks out—cookies, milk, pop, juices. I had to mix orange juice. It was frozen concentrate and it was a big pain because you had to wait for it to thaw out. At 8 o'clock I'd start on my rounds. I went to every floor, every room and asked people what they wanted. They didn't remember from one night to the next what was on the cart, so you had to repeat it in every room: how many kinds of juices, milk, cookies.

People on calculator diets, who could only eat certain things, were allowed four ounces of skim milk and five crackers. That was fun—*five* crackers. There's two in a package, so you'd have to take them apart to get that fifth one. Then you put the crackers in a little bag, just like the bread.

By the time the day was over, I was always at least a half hour overtime, but they'd never pay me for it. It drove me crazy, so I got out of the kitchen. I also had no love life. I worked steady afternoons. When I got done at about 10:30 at night, there was nothing to do. On my days off, I just sat around and rested, from running all week.

Inspection is once a year. We always know when they're coming, so what good is it? For a week ahead, all we do is scrub and clean. The inspectors should surprise us, so they can see how things really are. Nothing's supposed to be put on the floors in the coolers and freezers, but they're always piled high from floor to ceiling. They have walk-in coolers, but you can hardly get in, and when you do, something may fall on your head. Clara had stitches in her head because some stuff fell on her. They weren't concerned about her head. They only cared about what fell on her and if it got wrecked. It's very hazardous.

There's 12 people that work good, steady shifts. The others rotate, maybe two days one shift, two days another, one day the third. The contract says if you've been on a job two years, you should have a steady shift.

I've been trying to get in Volkswagen, or some place that pays more money. I work hard. I'm not one that sits and takes 20 minute breaks. I like my job, but the bosses make me hate it more every day. The conditions are terrible.

I was raised on a farm, and I like to move around. My mother always said, "You wouldn't like factory work." The jobs I had sitting at a typewriter, I couldn't stand. I wouldn't want a job like maintenance, with all men. If there were more women, maybe. I could do the maintenance work. That's no problem. I was going to bid on ward clerk but I couldn't get steady days. That's why some people stay in dietary, they have a steady shift.

DOROTHEA McDONALD, PENN HOSPITAL

You're under pressure in the kitchen. You're being watched all the time to make sure you're working constantly. They pick certain people to watch and others can do what they want. I get watched all the time because I'm the steward. When the girls have a problem they talk to me on my working time. But they are not allowed to do that.

One girl's uncle passed away and she wanted to go to his funeral. She had to explain to the personnel director how the man could possibly be her uncle when he was so much older than her. He asked her a flock of questions. But he didn't believe her, so she couldn't get time off.

The supervisors know absolutely nothing about diets. If you have a question, you look it up in a diet manual because the answer the dietician gives you is way out of the ball park.

Our dishwasher throws hot water at you, really hot. People get burned. They report it to the supervisor: "Well, get the guy to come in and look at it." You call him but he never comes.

The grids under our steamer are very dangerous. If you walk on them, you could fall and break a leg. They said they were getting them welded. It's six months later, and they're still not fixed.

The sick rooms aren't posted the way they should be. Two weeks ago, one girl took a tray into a hepatitis room, and the dishes were sent back and washed with the others. The room wasn't posted for contagion, so how was she to know?

Men are treated better than women in dietary. Out of 35-36 people, there are two temporary men and one full timer. The full timer is looked on as better than the women. He relieves the cooks, so it's a higher classification and more pay. Some girls had been there longer, but he got the job because he'd cooked in a bar. But the women are experienced too. They all cook every day at home. He doesn't.

ALICE NELSON, PENN HOSPITAL

You'd get a new supervisor in dietary and think he was OK, but pretty soon he'd stab you in the back. I left because I had a battle with my bosses. They gave a good job to a girl with no seniority at all. I had three years there, and I wanted the job. It made me so mad I was boiling. I went to the personnel officer, and he called down the head dietician. She made out like I was a big liar, that I'd said I didn't want off my shift. They had said the job wasn't up for bid because nobody would do it steady. But this girl had it steady. After I complained, they put her on other jobs once in awhile, so it wouldn't be so steady.

They worry about remodeling the hospital, but not the kitchen. That's why people leave dietary work, the horrible conditions in the kitchen. That and the bosses. Thirty workers can tell the personnel man the same story. But if one boss says, "It wasn't that way," they say, "Okay, we believe *you*, not these 30 other people."

Our bosses came to work drinking—drunk. If we reported them, their supervisors would come to the kitchen two hours later. They didn't want to catch them drinking. When one boss took her crochet lessons and sat for three days and crocheted while we ran our legs off, we finally reported her: "Is this what you're paying her to do?" Her supervisor came up hours later, and she wasn't crocheting at that moment. Once she read newspapers all day.

Dietary is put down by everyone. But what is a hospital without food, without feeding the patients? A good diet can help the patients get well. But their attitude is, "You have no education so you're dummies." The nurses don't want any part of us. They treat us like dirt so we scream and fight back.

DOLORES RODRIGUEZ, CAL HOSPITAL

I like to work but not when I get pressure from the supervisor. She is like a sergeant. She's always watching, just watching. Maybe she doesn't want to talk to us, the Mexican people. When she talks, you don't know if she is talking to *you* or to another lady. She likes to boss, not just me, but another three ladies over there, Mexican. It is only the Mexican ladies that she bothers. We are only three, four Mexicans in the kitchen.

MARSHA HILL, CAL HOSPITAL

What's good about the job? Ha, ha. I see nothing good about it. We need more help. There's more men cooks than women cooks, and the cooks get paid more than we do.

I applied for intermediate worker, which pays more. People got that job who haven't been here as long as I have. I didn't hear anything after I applied, and I haven't asked because I don't know *who* to ask, or if anyone would want to answer me. I come in at 10 am. I'd like to come in earlier because I have a little girl at home. I always work weekends. I've never had one off. On the tray line in the kitchen, they work two weeks early and two weeks late. They keep changing shifts. It's awful. I'd get mixed up and maybe one week I'd come late, and it would be early.

I slipped and fell a few times. There's always water and food on the floor. It gets hot in the kitchen, and there's no air conditioning. It gets 100 degrees and I can't breathe.

I like to work *together* and get along with people. I don't like friction. There's so much tension in the kitchen that I just can't work. If I was rich I wouldn't work. No way I'd be working, no. I'd like more training and another job. That would be nice. I'd like to see the union get more people to help out in the kitchen. The trouble is the hospital doesn't respect our work. A nurse gets more respect. They look down on us.

The place has gone down hill. The new system they put in doesn't work. They didn't even tell us they would start it. We didn't have any meetings, any idea of what was going to be done. They just gave us job descriptions and told us to do it. A lot of people aren't cooperating. We could do our jobs much better if they'd talk to us first, ask us what we think, or explain things to us. But the supervisors just do things their own way.

A UNION REP IN PENNSYLVANIA

It's hot in there and tension is high because they have to work in such a hurry. A lot of work and a lot of tension. But the administration thinks it's not important enough to worry about.

Dietary's a special problem because it has so many jobs within it. If you don't have a good supervisor the little problems and these little jobs can get out of hand. At Penn they don't have good supervisors. They're not used to making out schedules. Dietary departments have a lot of both part time and full time people, so schedules get messed up.

You have a lot of younger people in dietary too, and this creates a problem. They have to be worked with, more than an older person. They get upset over their schedules because they have young children and a lot of things to do. Dietary's always had the biggest problems, and it's always been strong for the union. They never can voice their opinion in there. Supervisors think they don't have an opinion. They should be allowed to talk these things out, but it has to be the supervisor's way and no other way. If we can straighten out the scheduling, a lot of problems will be taken care of; that causes more stress than anything else.

A UNION REP IN CALIFORNIA

Turnover is high because of poor administration. The supervisors are not sensitive to the employees' needs, so the union has to take problems to a higher level. We've been winning a lot of those grievances.

People leave because of salaries. Some of our lowest paid workers are in laundry and dietary. But I don't see that much turnover in the laundry. They're treated slightly better than in dietary. The turnover is very high across the board, but the majority of the problems are in dietary. It has to do with the supervision mainly.

Occasionally we get a good supervisor, but usually we're dealing with incompetent people. It's a problem in other departments too. A lot of nurses come up from the ranks. They were terrific nurses working on the wards with the patients but they're completely incompetent as administrators. They don't know personnel policy, they don't know how to deal with employees. This is true in all our hospitals.

Dietary has a sweat shop atmosphere, and nothing is being done to alleviate it. The women are being shoved aside and neglected. There's no improvement as far as the machinery and equipment they work with, that could make the job a little easier. The hospital just doesn't listen to the women when they complain. The union, under the contract, can't touch most of these problems.

ANOTHER UNION REP IN CALIFORNIA

At Cal hospital, the dietary department is without a doubt the biggest mess in the hospital. One reason is that it's always run by a dietician. They are trained in nutrition, not supervision. So you find terrible or capricious treatment of workers, and a lot of hostility in return. Strange things happen in those big kitchens. Once 24 cases of turkeys suddenly disappeared from a kitchen.

These dieticians are asked to be nutritionists, administrators of huge budgets, purchasing agents for the kitchens, and personnel managers. They are trained for none of these jobs except nutrition, which is usually lousy in the hospital. The food's lousy. A lot of patients won't eat it, and the nutrition is lousy.

Dieticians are also very anti-union. They don't know how to work with unions and they refuse to accept them. They're arrogant, inefficient, and often corrupt. I think it comes from lack of training and experience. But it's true all over. The kitchens are hell holes. They have impossible schedules to meet and they do an overall job that satisfies nobody. They're vicious in their personal relationships. If you're a dishwasher, that's where you stay. You can't become a cook. They won't train the workers. There's no upward mobility in the kitchen unless the union insists on it. The laundry is also a hell hole. The laundry workers are the most exploited group, the most badly treated, and the best organized group as a result of their bad treatment.

The dietary department and the laundry department are downgraded. Look at their salaries and you can see that. If you think you're valued by the hospital, just look at your wage. If it's low, you're not.

Four

CONTESTANTS: RNs AND OTHERS

You have to wonder why only about half the registered nurses want to work in hospitals. What is it about that institution that makes it so impossible for people to work on it? The reasons are a lot broader than scheduling and staffing. Those are just symptoms of deeper problems.

The central conflict in the hospital is the classic one between management (and doctors) on one side and labor on the other—the governors and the governed. This contest is also a *de facto* sexist conflict since the governors are largely male and the governed female.

A secondary struggle also occurs in the hospital because a buffer class—the RNs—stands between the main contestants. While RNs have had notorious difficulties with those above them, their main conflict is with ancillary staff. This conflict is not sexist on the face of it, both groups being largely female, but sexism nevertheless shapes the conflict since the contestants are put into positions of conflict in the first place by their male managers. At any rate, this secondary conflict tends to obscure the main one: the conflict between management and labor over wages, staffing, scheduling, etc., so that complaints with more distant policy-makers (as in the case of dietary workers) are deflected to supervisors who are closer at hand.

The RN is a "professional," a college woman; her pay is often twice that of the practical nurse's, and her authority over other workers in patient care is usually considerable. Complaints against her, from below, charge that she is paid too much for what she does, that she is bossy and too uppity to help out much with routine tasks.

The RN also has complaints. If she is an old Nightingale, she complains about employees' insubordination and selfishness. If she is a New Nightingale, she complains about the low status of her profession, the high-handed behavior of doctors and administrators, and the fact that she is over-trained and under-paid for what she does on her job.

Central to the RN's problems has been nursing's inability to carve out more professional tasks for nurses. Training has been extended and moved out of hospitals and into academies, where it has become more theoretical, less practical and presumably more professional and prestigious; and some routine skills of the RN have been given to others, but few claims to new ground have been staked out. The result for the RN: more years of schooling, an actual shrinkage in her scope of practice (on the lower end), and rising frustration at being over-schooled for her job.

Underlying these problems has been the RN's lingering vision of the dedicated missionary who serves without pay or gratitude and submits to the demands of those in authority without question or struggle. These visions stand in the way not only of the RN's progress but of those below her in the hospital pecking order, for *their* jobs are defined in relation to *hers*, their scope of practice is limited because hers is, and their frustrations are usually mirror images of hers. The nurse's apparent preference for working with doctors, as one study shows, rather than either fellow nurses or aides, also suggests that her view of doctor-nurse relations may put her in conflict with the long-term interests she shares not only with other RNs but also ancillary staff.[1]

≈

THE WOMEN—IN THEIR OWN WORDS

Nurses feel they have been whipped by medical directors and chief physicians, who are male and who have put them in a little box and not allowed them to do anything. It's the old measure of power: how much space do you give a person? Look at the physician's and top management's space, then look at the nurse's little box. Now nurses are saying, "Why can't we get a director of nursing in here that's willing to take those men on?" So nurses are feeling their power. They're realizing they can give that power back to the directors of nursing.

The RN's problems? They've got as many bosses as there are doctors on the floor. They're highly trained professionals and they're treated like errand girls. They're expected to clean bedpans and carry food trays. They have to fill in on all levels and all shifts, and they're expected to do the work of an orderly, an LVN, an aide. Doctors scream at them and call them to task for anything. No one controls what a doctor can do to a nurse.

The conditions are bad, the hours are long. They're expected to work every other weekend, or sometimes every single weekend. True, they get time and a half, but it's horrible to work so many days in a row. Their schedules and conditions are no better than the aide's or LVN's.

They're supposedly in charge of the floor, and God forbid something should happen to a patient. It always comes down to the nurse. If the wrong prescription is written by a doctor, the nurse is expected to realize that the patient shouldn't get it. Nurses have been suspended for not doing that.

They're expected to work in violation of their license. The licensing requires a certain ratio of nurses to patients in the Intensive Care Unit, for instance. If those nurses are not there, the nurse in charge can lose her license, simply because her coworker didn't show up. Before the union three nurses complained they were in violation of their licensing and all of them got three weeks for complaining. That's what we're dealing with. If you're a conscientious nurse, get out. People die in the corridors.

In some hospitals the doctors are partners in the business. At Kaiser Permanenty, one of the biggest hospital complexes in southern California, the doctors supposedly work out of altruism. They get a salary, but at some point they become partners and share in the hospital's profits. The nurses never share profits.

Economically and professionally the nurses are in trouble. It's very difficult to watch people die needlessly because of a doctor's order, or because you're under-staffed and over-worked and can't do anything.

The biggest issue for RNs is work load, staffing. It's a vicious circle. If there aren't enough nurses, the work load is heavy. If the work load is heavy, you can't find enough nurses.

Nowadays women can get some traditionally male jobs. They climb telephone poles, and they get off weekends and make a lot of money. That's where it's at. Nursing is a shitty job. Women go into it because it's a female occupation. They feel safe in it. We have a lot of Filipino nurses and some Japanese, Chinese, and East Indian nurses. To them, nursing and teaching are upper middle class professions.

The stress on nurses leads to the high burn-out rate. They'll jump from one job to another, trying to find one that's less stressful, more compatible with their home life. They're also looking for higher paid positions, with recognition. They'd love to teach patients, instruct them on how to take care of themselves. The staff nurse's job is dead-end. It's like a clerical job. And nobody pats you on the back for a job well done. There's probably no position where people are trained so well and make so few decisions as in nursing. When you come out of nurse's training it's a big shock to find that what the books say is not necessarily so. It gets worse the longer you're in nursing. Short cutting, finding faster ways to do things, becomes a way of life. You do it to survive, but you don't like it.

The other big problem is your direct supervisor. Sometimes you're lucky and get a good one. But with many of them, you wonder, "What the hell are they doing in nursing?" They stay in those ivory towers. Some have never worked on floors with really sick patients. If they have, they never see or empathize with the problems of nurses.

The good supervisors, who want to do something, usually can't. Even the very good directors of nursing can't get anywhere with the hospital administration or with the board. It always boils down to, "What is it going to cost?"

A lot of RNs have to tell the doctors what medication and treatments to use. And they have to do it without offending the doctor. They have to make them believe it was their idea. It's an RN doing a doctor's work for a fraction of his pay and doing it in a very demeaning way. It's poor little helpless female and the strong male who gives her all the answers: the Nancy Nurse image.

The relationship of RNs to doctors is a big issue in the hospital. One day the doctor will learn that the nurse is not a maid. In the last ten years it's gotten much better. Nurses are using their power and the nursing crisis is helping them. Doctors respect them more.

Some nurses, even without a union, are going down in groups to their management and saying, "We've had it. Either you give it to us or we're gone." They get what they want. A group of nurses in Santa Monica Hospital (non-union) did that. It was amazing. They negotiated a contract on the spot with management. No experience whatsoever with contracts either. The nurses came to a meeting, about 400 of them, and negotiated from the floor of the meeting. That's a realization of power. The only problem is (I had to laugh) if they had a negotiator's experience, they could have gotten a whole lot more. That was the limit of their power to change things.

A UNION REP DESCRIBES THE CONTEST AT CAL HOSPITAL:

There's a horrible pecking order in the hospitals. Young RNs are rude to the people they work with. I hear the word "teamwork" so often, but I don't see much teamwork. The LVNs feel the RNs look down on them. The nursing attendants feel the LVNs look down on them. Everybody looks down on everybody else.

Relations between RNs and other people were bad, but now they're worse. With the competition for RNs, their benefits are skyrocketing. But it's not happening to LVNs, attendants, clerks. So the nurses are resented.

I was an attendant at one time. A lot of RNs above me I respected, and a lot I didn't. When they got a benefit more than I did, it hurt. Better not get a unit where RNs, LVNs and attendants are all in the same local. Too many problems. By law, the RNs are supposed to be separated out.

They work on a team basis now. Let's say there are 30 patients to a team. They might have one RN (required by law) and maybe two LVNs, and four attendants. But the attendants may function just as well as the RN and the LVN because they've been there longer. In California, the attendants and LVNs stay around and are very dependable. The RN can go out and do better, so she is more transient and less dependable. So the hospitals use the LVNs and attendants to train the RNs, which is very frustrating to them. The LVN knows the practical application *and* the theory. The RN comes in with just the theory, and has to be taught the practices by the LVN.

The RN wants to be a supervisor or coordinator. She doesn't like bedside care but she has to do it at Cal. With changes in the state law here, the LVNs can do almost everything the RN does. But to get accreditation, a hospital has to have: number one, doctors, and number two, RNs. That's the state mandate. The law does not require LVNs or attendants.

The RN is in demand and can write her own ticket. She's being catered to and, as a result, the unit is full of pay inequities. The ancillary staff doesn't complain about the RN being a supervisor. Their complaint is that they have to teach her, and then turn around and be supervised and evaluated *by* her. To top that, the RN is paid much more.

A WORKER DESCRIBES THE CONTEST AT PENN HOSPITAL

If a patient wants something for pain, she'll complain to us, the aides. We tell the RN and keep going back to her, but she won't do anything. The patient wonders why you don't help her. If a patient asks for a bed pan, the RN says, "I'll get someone else." Patients don't understand why *she* can't do it.

We have an RN who gives out medication. She's just there to babysit us. We've run that place without an RN, so we don't need her there. She feels we're supposed to do all the dirty work and she's supposed to just sit. The RNs pass the medicine for 20 patients. They used to do it for the whole floor, 40 patients. Now it's cut in half, but it still takes them all day. They're supposed to do the dressings and help us with baths and beds, but usually they don't. The ones that don't help us, get mad at the ones that do. The patient suffers.

One RN had a patient, a male with urinary tension who had to be catheterized. "Oh, I don't know how to do that. You do it," she told the LPN. But the LPN wouldn't do it. The supervisor was called, but the LPN still wouldn't do it.

The younger nurses say, "I'm an RN and I will wipe no B.M. I will only give orders." When I run into those kind, we have it out. I've never seen any type of nursing that a nurse is too good to do.

Sometimes we all meet and say what we think about RNs not helping us. We usually end up in a big fight, and it makes things worse. The clinical supervisor is really good. If we threaten to complain to her, the RNs get on the ball fast. The LPNs want recognition for the duties they perform, which are basically what RNs do. It isn't the title that concerns them, and they don't want to become RNs. It's the money they want. The RNs are paid far more.

If by chance RNs get on patient care, they're like raving maniacs. They demand to have an aide work with them constantly, and they expect everyone to come and help them. Not *all* the RNs, but the majority. Our hospital may be the only one where the RN does no patient care at all. Some RNs say that if they had to work on the floor, they'd quit. When you get that far removed from patients, you forget what a nurse's main reason for being is.

Five

NOTES FROM A STRIKE

Remember the dignity of your womanhood. Do not appeal, do not beg, do not grovel. Take courage, join hands, stand beside us, fight with us.
                                    Emmeline Pankhurst, feminist, 1888

When a strike was called at Penn hospital over the terms of the first contract, only RNs, clericals, doctors and administrators continued to work. Few of the strikers had ever engaged in any kind of direct action before, so it was a new and daring experiment for them. Most had the backing, not only of the union but of their husbands, fathers and sons who, in this Pennsylvania mining-steel community, gave solid support to the strike.

Despite such backing, most women admitted to being frightened by this unprecedented public challenge to authority, but some mastered their fear, came forward, and led the strike. Most of the women strikers had serious grievances of their own, but some walked the picket line out of concern for coworkers. Recollections about the strike, its causes and aftermath, include the following:

COMMENTS BY ROSEMARY TRUMP, LOCAL PRESIDENT:

At Penn hospital the union won two units by majority votes. The hospital continued to fight us with their anti-union consultant firm. They made up wild accusations and tried to undo the election results. But we mobilized the community, our own members and labor reps in the area, to put pressure on the hospital.

Finally we staged a demonstration to force bargaining. The local police and hospital officials over-reacted and the police chief threatened to get dogs and fire hoses to chase us off. We had a very heated exchange, and I said, "Will you guarantee me this in writing? I always wanted to be on national news. I'll make sure that NBC and ABC are here to see this. You with your big badge and big billy club, batting down our women and their babies."

I called the state police because I could see this guy was paid off by the hospital to give us a bad time. Fortunately we got a community relations person from the state police to intervene. So we were able to force them into bargaining. *They* created the union for us, the employer did.

Very good leadership came forward. The employer finally made an offer but our members considered it inadequate. So we had our first strike and we got our first contract. We made big gains in that contract and we've worked hard with the stewards to iron out the problems you have in the first year of marriage.*

We struck for 12 days and we picketed around the clock. The hospital admitted no additional patients during the strike, only emergency cases, and they released patients as they got better. They had the top floor completely closed and part of the third floor. So a big building was sitting there without money coming in. It puts pressure on the administration to get back to the table and negotiate.

COMMENTS BY STRIKERS

During the strike the hospital told us they were admitting all new patients, just to make us feel guilty about not being there to take care of them. It was an out-and-out lie. They also said the picketers were responsible for deaths in the hospital during the strike. They even got families to blame the picketers for their relatives passing away. Of course, the patients were all being taken care of by the RNs, the doctors, and the others. For once, the nurses weren't just parked at their desks.

Clerks did the housekeeping, the dietary and the aides' work. They passed trays, changed beds, cleaned floors. At first it was fun for them, something different. They'd come home laughing and joking about what happened. Then it got on their nerves. Nobody wanted to

*See appendix for a description of contract gains. According to federal tax returns, before the strike, one doctor in the hospital, (a pathologist) was paid $192,592 for the year, another (a radiologist) $151,076, another (an anesthesiologist) $108,249, and two other doctors were paid more than $50,000. The executive director of the hospital was paid $37,692. At the same time fully employed (40 hours, 52 weeks) dietary aides earned $6,552; nursing assistants $7,046; LPNs $7,926; nuclear technicians $11,065. RNs averaged about $14,000. The hospital itself listed a net worth of $5.7 million.

be there. They still had their own work to do and it was backing up on them. They worked lots of overtime and were very happy when the strike ended. Not enough clericals signed union cards to even think of getting them into the union. Several clericals wanted desperately to get the others in, but they realized it was hopeless.

It was more or less the dietary department that started the union campaign. I guess maintenance too, a little bit of every department. One lady I work with was very unhappy about her job and got the union started, but then the hospital gave her everything she wanted so she backed down.

All of the aides were for the union. We had nothing. Supervisors could fire you for anything. No questions asked, no recourse. The LPNs were really being degraded. "You're just an LPN, so you can't do *this* and *that*." The hospital had hired a lot of new graduate LPNs, and that helped get the union in. They had never been treated like that, anywhere, and they were very upset. They were doing a good job and being told they were dummies. When somebody new came on the floor, the head nurses would show their authority and tell them off in front of everybody. It's no fun to be degraded in public.

* *

I was working in the kitchen when I joined the union. Then I went to housekeeping, but I couldn't forget about my friends in the kitchen who had it so bad. I tried to sign up people in housekeeping. Half of them wouldn't talk to me because they were so set against the union. That's funny; they were against it until the contract was signed. Then they loved what they got out of the strike. A few are still bitter. Most of them were just scared to death. At first they would run and hide when they saw us coming. A lot of them still say, "Oh, I don't want to talk to you. I'll get fired." When we started to picket, more and more of the housekeeping ladies came out. One thing was nice. None of our people crossed the picket line. We had only one that stayed in the hospital. For 12 days she didn't come out. They got some retirees to cross the picket line, but none of our girls, not even the ones that were so against it, crossed our line.

A few were told by their husbands and sons, "The union's in, and you're better off with it." The women would come out to the line and say, "My husband told me to come out, so I'm going to help you." It was really nice. I was tickled that they stood up and came with us. And they were tickled when they saw that the union got them their bonus, better pay and a pension.

They're older women in housekeeping, and they're scared about their jobs. A lot of them lost their husbands, or their husbands divorced them, so they feel insecure. It's the only job they ever had, and they are so thankful the hospital gave it to them. That's why they didn't want to fight for a union.

I'd like to see the RNs included in the union. It would make a world of difference to us. They are satisfied too easily by the hospital. If the RNs were union, the hospital would think twice about causing us trouble. When something's not going their way, the RNs are all for the union. But when it is, they don't want to bother. The last time the RNs voted, the union lost by two votes. The part time nurses voted against it. They weren't going to get as much from the contract. Now a lot of them wished they had voted "yes." Next time the vote will carry. When we were organizing, the RNs weren't allowed to associate with us or even take breaks or eat lunch with us. They were told not to. A lot of them did it anyway.

The hospital pushed us into a union. It was a matter of fairness. We were discriminated against, harassed and pressured. We wanted to be able to talk. It was like being in jail. We weren't allowed to discuss certain matters with certain people. The wage scale was locked in a drawer. We had to get permission to see it. They had no seniority list. They just went by who they liked. If they liked you better than me, you got the job. They had no open bidding on jobs. Strictly a buddy system. We wanted the security of knowing they couldn't fire us because they didn't like us. Before the contract, only three Blacks worked in the hospital. They were always given the nasty jobs. They used to complain, "Niggers down South don't work this hard." You can't run a floor on bigotry. Everything has to be divided equally, which is what we wanted.

Organizing was a gradual thing. Momentum kept building up, and it was like being drawn into a vacuum. They laid the path, starting out small, a leaflet here and there, and you're drawn in. I'm not one to be suckered into anything unless I really want it. They laid this union business out and I knew "that's what we want." It was strange. I get along fine with the administration, but I saw what was happening to the others, and I didn't like it, so I got drawn in.

*   *

My father got me involved with the union. He used to work in the mines, but he got sick and spent a lot of time at the hospital as a patient. He said, "What you need is a union. You people are worked to death." So when local 585 came in, I decided to work along with them. I helped organize. I talked to people. I went to union meetings. I stuck my neck out. I sat in on negotiations. You can't believe how bad your employer is until you sit in there and listen to what people say.

During the strike, the "volunteers" would almost run us down trying to cross our line. They were the worst. Some crawled up over the hill and snuck in. It was ridiculous. One truck went in and out of the hospital just to agitate us. If we said anything to them, they called the police. People in the community volunteered for strike breaking. The ministers even went in to do the cooking. A few doctors were behind us and would tell us to keep up the good work. They even said they'd transfer some patients to other hospitals.

I don't think there should be strikes. But if that's what it takes, I'm all for them. I was on the picket line day and night. People say, "You had a good vacation when the strike was on." Well, it wasn't a vacation. The girls you work with cross your line. You resent it. They know how hard you work, and yet they're in there (primarily RNs) making money, doing your job, and keeping you out on the street. Some day it will blow over and we'll be able to forget the hard feelings.

Myself, I wasn't scared for my job during the strike. If you don't help yourself, who's going to help you? You have to take a step forward somehow. People respect you much more when you stand up for yourself. They'll stand back and say, "Oh, well, maybe we can't do this to her. She'll fight back. She won't lay down."

Job security was a huge problem before we got our contract. People were afraid of losing their jobs. When we started to organize, supervisors would say, "Don't talk to that union organizer or you'll lose your job." That's why we lost the first two union votes.

The union guaranteed us that if we showed the others not to be afraid to vote union, we'd never get fired. So I picketed, got my picture taken like everybody else, and never got fired or punished. I didn't have a family to support, so I didn't need to worry.

We had problems signing women up if their husbands weren't union. If they were salaried, forget it. They'd be against the union. Only about ten percent had husbands who didn't belong to a union, so that worked for us.

My husband's been a union man since he started at the steel mill. He says, "A union's as strong as its members. If the members aren't strong, you might as well throw the union out the door." He wouldn't go to work without a union. I was out on the picket line, and got my picture taken. I was worried about that picture. My husband said, "Don't worry. I've had my picture taken on picket lines and I'm still working after 32 years."

At first my husband was against my being active. He is self employed, a dairy farmer, so he's non-union. He figured it would be a hassle, and I'd lose my job. He said, "Why don't you leave the union to somebody else?" I said, "If everybody felt that way, nobody would do anything." I wanted to get in and help. He understands more now and he accepts it.

The union organizer was a terrific talker. He could tell us what we wanted and needed, but he didn't stand on a pedestal and say, "You've got to do this or that." A lot of people get turned off if union officials come on too strong.

You have to talk *to* people, not above them or down to them. Then you can grow. You have to have women organizers too. Definitely. It isn't a man's world, it's a people's world. We had two organizers, a man and a woman, so we got both points of view.

Our union attorney is a fabulous man. I can say 1800 words, and he can say the same in three. Some management people come at you full blast and angry, like a herd of charging elephants. He steps out of the way, says a few words, and they're just like little pussy cats. He laid it on the line, even to members, and told them the raw truth about how long the strike might last.

*   *

You get a lot out of it. You beat them. It's a terrific feeling to win and know there's nothing else they can do.

I loved being on the strike committee and negotiating the contract. Everyone should sit in on negotiations. You understand the contract much better when you help write it. I kept thinking, "Oh, I'm stupid and I don't know how to answer what the hospital says." But you learn more than you think you can. When you give them a good answer, you say, "Did that come out of me?" You surprise yourself. You do it and you wonder how.

The twelve of us on the negotiating team all came from different departments, so you learn a lot about other departments in negotiations. We sat across from management. I got so mad at them sometimes I could have wrung their necks. It wasn't like we were asking a lot. Instead of saying, "We'll try to work it out," they'd say, "No way. No way."

You meet people during a strike that you've never seen in the hospital, and you get to be friends. I enjoyed it even though it took me away from home an awful lot. We held meetings sometimes twice a week. Sessions might last until two in the morning. And then we had to drag ourselves to work the next day.

I became a steward after the strike, and I've learned how to handle grievances. Now I can talk to people that have problems and answer their questions. I couldn't have done that before. If you're a steward, the minute you sit down in the cafeteria everybody converges on you. It's a chance to air their complaints. Stewards should have an office and certain hours to talk to people. I like being a steward because I want people to get a fair shake, but it does take a lot of time. Stewards should really be paid. I could be doing my chores or taking care of my child in my time off.

At least the hospital listens to us a little now. Before the union, we wanted a suggestion box. No names, no nothing, just suggestions. I never knew they had one until last week. They had put it in a year ago. It was hidden behind the cashier's office. They didn't tell anybody it was there. They do things like that.

Before the union came in, whenever you got reprimanded or written up, it went into your personnel record. You couldn't check that record to see what it said. Now you can, and you have grievance procedures to protect you.

The strike got us a lot of what we wanted. Nobody could have gotten more than we did in a first contract—a dental plan, paid pension, a bonus, a wage increase. We got every third weekend off. We asked for every *other* weekend, but we knew we wouldn't get it. We got protection against being fired or disciplined without cause. I'm not satisfied with everything, but it's a good stepping stone. Each time we negotiate, the contract will get better. Some day there'll be a big management turnover, and the people with a big mental block about unions will go. Then we'll work together. The union's everywhere. They have to accept it.

After the strike, what upset me most was that management gave the RNs everything we got, plus an extra personal day. They gave *them* things they said they couldn't afford to give *us*. They also gave them a bigger raise than we got. They did all that for spite.

There's nothing in the contract about staffing. That's a problem. The hospital says it's none of our business. I don't know if the union can change that.

Another problem is that the hospital won't settle grievances at the first step. They take everything to arbitration. They want people to get fed up with the union, so they drag their feet all the time.

The first year for a union is like baby walking. Start them out slow. Pretty soon they'll stand up and run. We may not run but we'll stand up and face the hospital. I had no reservations about the union. If you have no security, the job isn't worth anything. Besides, everyone has a right to be represented and to be heard. It takes a while to get used to having that. Even now some people are a little afraid to speak out. They haven't felt the union's strength yet.

We've laid a foundation, something to build on. What we need is more cooperation and a willingness to be fair and talk things over. Why shouldn't unions be in hospitals? We're working people, and we work as hard as people in factories, so why not? If we do a good job at the hospital and people benefit from the union, they won't be able to beat it down or hide it. The information spreads like wild fire. "This union is a good union. It's working for the people." The next hospital can point to Penn and say, "Well, look, that union is working very well." That will be enough for me.

If it becomes an albatross around our necks, I'd say, "Get rid of it." I want people to be satisfied. If it comes to the point where the union isn't benefiting us, then I'd work against it. But I feel this will never happen, because of my experience with it.

Six

SPOKESWOMEN

The union has been a very valuable consciousness-raising tool. Women can appreciate themselves more.

The women's movement and the labor movement help each other. The sisterhood that results is remarkable . . . on women's issues, we're all sisters.

THE WOMEN—IN THEIR OWN WORDS

ABOUT ROSEMARY TRUMP,* BY A MEMBER OF HER LOCAL

This local is exceptional because of Rose. From the minute they put her in as trustee of the local, it was clear, "This isn't some little piece of fluff, this is somebody that knows what the hell she's talking about." She's got more energy. She talks faster. She walks faster. And she does things. When she says she's going to do something, she doesn't back down from it.

That's why she was re-elected president of the local without opposition. Nobody wants to tangle with her. I wouldn't want to go up against her. She's that aggressive. Some men dislike her because of it,

*Rosemary Trump is President of Local 585, SEIU, Pittsburgh. She is also the first (and only) woman to become a vice president of the International union.

but they also respect her because of it. She's shown she can do everything they can do and usually better.

Rose is someone to really look up to. I admire her. As far as women's lib is concerned, she went a giant step, where others have been tiptoeing along. Her image comes across as one that knows what she's doing, where she's going, and how to get there. Such confidence has to rub off on everybody around her. You feel really in awe of her and her knowledge and her ability to do things. You know that when she answers you, that's the answer you need, and she's not going to change her mind a week later. She puts that image across to men too, but she's not an overbearing woman. She's a fantastic person.

BY ROSEMARY TRUMP

If it weren't for the women's movement, I wouldn't be a vice president of this union. Betty Friedan basically articulated most of my feelings and helped me understand myself.

Most women are taught by their mothers that their lives should revolve around making their husbands happy and raising nice beautiful children, and that if they had to go to work, it was too bad. "Try not to let it interfere too much with your primary role in life, your family."

I've always been very rebellious. I guess it's genes. I'd like to say that my parents taught me differently, but frankly they tried to put me in the same dolls' house. I love my mother very much, and I have immense respect for her. But I'm not sure that in her own mind she doesn't really think, "Gee, it's too bad Rosemary couldn't have been a nurse and worked eight hours, and then gone home to take care of her family."

Most little girls like baby dolls, right? I never played with dolls. Once in a while my sister would say, "Oh, let's play house." I didn't want to. I'd rather play cowboys and Indians. My sister was older and our next door neighbor was older. They always got to play the good guys and I had to play the bad guy. I never liked playing the bad guy. Maybe now I have a chance to play the good guy for a change.

I never perceived myself in a traditional female role. I was always the leader in school, in class, and always the nonconformist—and an outsider because I didn't conform. I liked playing boys' games—football, basketball, baseball, and tag. Girls play hopscotch and jump rope. But I can't jump rope too good even today. I was lousy at hopscotch. It was boring to me. Girls were expected to stay indoors more during recess and lunch, whereas I liked the outdoors. That's where the boys played. I tended to associate with the male gender, which created tensions because the boys really didn't like playing with the girls.

I was even a rebel in high school. I refused to take a chemistry course from this terrible teacher. So they threatened to withhold my diploma. Finally they gave it to me and I went on to major in government at American University in Washington, D.C.

I'm 35 years of age now. I was born in Smithfield, Pennsylvania, a small rural community near the West Virginia border. My mother is a school secretary. She used to own her own restaurant, which I grew up in, washing dishes at age 10, waiting tables. After I graduated from college, I came home for a year and took over the business, while she took typing and shorthand courses to get this job at the school district. My father had a small grocery and gas station. Previous to that, he drove a truck and delivered bread, and was a member of the teamsters' union.

I didn't go to college with the notion that I'd end up a social worker. When I applied to college, I really had in mind becoming a foreign service officer, a diplomat. When I came home to close my mother's business, I did it because I knew that if I didn't, my mother would soon be dead. I just stayed on.

After that first year at home, I got married. My husband was an industrial designer at that time. We spent the next three years in Boston, and I got my first job as a social worker in the welfare department. Welfare mothers were being organized, and I became active in that. My supervisor had encouraged me to write memos downtown about improving our services to clientele, but I'd get stock replies like, "Thank you for writing," etc. So she suggested I get involved with the union. It was like a lightbulb going off: I said: "Yeah, that's right. I never thought of it." I marched down the hallway, contacted a steward, and said, "I'm going to join the union. And not only that, I want to be a steward."

I helped organize that building and then other buildings in the city when SEIU put some money into organizing. I became one of the first full-time organizers for Local 509.

My husband decided to get his masters degree in industrial design at Carnegie-Mellon, so we moved back to Pennsylvania. A new collective bargaining law for public employees had just been signed in the state, so I contacted the International union, and John Geagan, who had just come on board as the general organizer, about the possibility of organizing social workers here. He persuaded David Sullivan to hire me. David had not hired any female organizers before that, so I was one of the first two females hired.

After three years of steady organizing, I was very drained, to put it mildly. On election night after our first big victory, I felt like someone had taken a thousand pound rock off my head. But we kept on going; and we now have a union of over 6,000 members in the Pennsylvania social services union.

Then Local 585 needed someone to provide it direction. I was the only person they could conscript into doing it. So they made me the trustee of the local. I was faced with bargaining some 30 agreements as well as organizing in school districts.

I thought this local didn't want me because it was male dominated and run by the school janitors. But the chaos in the local forced the International to take action, and I decided it would be a challenge to administer the local. I was only 27 then, and I was put in charge of a potentially large union. So a lot of credit goes to the International union for having confidence in me. We're fortunate in having a very liberal leadership that doesn't fight women tooth and nail.

The last ten years of my life have been consumed with the union and little else. For a period I had no time to do anything else, and that created personal tension with my family. But that's behind me now and fortunately I have a great support staff, and I can actually sleep at nights.

A law firm in Pittsburgh specializes in keeping the union out. Our union makes them wealthy because of the fees they get from employers for trying to keep us out of city hospitals. Within three blocks of here, there are about 20,000 unorganized health care workers. No major downtown hospital in Pittsburgh is organized. And no *public* hospitals in the area provide medical-surgical services. The public hospitals provide geriatric care only. Hard to believe.

Hospital workers in San Francisco probably have the best wages, hours and conditions, or at least they're on a par with New York City. Registered nurses in *this* area make about as much as the *aides* in San Francisco make. The difference is, the hospital industry is organized in San Francisco but not here. It's just day and night. We are more typical of hospitals in the country. We've organized only three hospitals in the last five years. It's been a major struggle.

It was all-out warfare getting a union at one hospital. Four brothers owned the hospital. They felt very threatened by us. They were afraid their empire might have to be shared and they pulled every dirty trick in the book. They fired people, suspended them, transferred them, coerced them, threatened them with the loss of benefits if they joined the union. They committed so many unfair labor practices that we were able to get a bargaining order there. And that's almost impossible to get. I'm sure they hoped they could destroy the union after the first agreement, but it didn't work. We were able to develop a good steward system, work on solving problems, bargain the second contract and work on a job classification system. That brought the union together, and last year we were strong enough to go out on strike when the employer made an inadequate offer.

We try to have an ongoing training program for stewards, but we have limited resources, so we really can't focus enough on explaining the union to new employees. Unfortunately five years from now, many of the people who took part in the struggle will be gone, and the new people won't appreciate what has happened.

I'd like to believe I can make every member happy 100 percent of the time, but it doesn't happen that way. Sometimes you have to stand up and say "no" when a member is wrong. So it is necessary to change staff assignments sometimes, when personalities don't click. That is the advantage of having a large staff. You can do it.

Most of our members have an uncle or a grandfather that either belonged to a mine or a steel union. Those are industrial unions. SEIU is not. We are based on a craft concept. The power is based in the local rather than the International, and every contract is a "chapter" of the local. We have separate contracts and separate chapters for each occupational group, each craft. Our members often think their chapter is really the local union. Again, it's the experience of the area. AFSCME* is also heavily concentrated in this area. They also have an industrial structure, where every institution they represent is a local union. That makes it even more confusing to members.

We encourage our chapters to develop a steward system. The chapter is where the action is, as opposed to the local union. But the local has a monthly meeting. We advertise it and any member with a problem who wants to raise hell can come and do it. We welcome it. We want them to air their problems. The reality is that not many attend. I can say, "Gee, that's bad," but on the other hand, it's very good too. When members come, it's because they have problems. I tell members all the time, "The squeaky wheel gets the grease. If you don't squeak, I don't know that you have a problem."

Our staff reps don't often get involved in day-to-day grievances. The chapter leaders can help themselves. That's the way it should be. Those leaders are around 40 hours a week. Our staff isn't. The service rep is primarily used in a consultant role. If a problem can't be resolved and the case has to go to arbitration, staff is brought in. Or they're brought in during bargaining. We don't have the resources to go out looking for problems if they don't exist. We have to respond as things come up, and it's impossible to know where the fire's going to blaze

* American Federation of State, County, and Municipal Employees.

next. Now that our staff is experienced, I use my time more for administration and organizing. I try to grab the reps when they're in the office and say, "What's going on out there?"

In an anti-union atmosphere, it's hard to organize anybody—men *or* women. In the absence of an anti-union campaign, I'm not sure that women are more difficult to organize than men. The difference is that society has given approval to men having unions, but not to women. The women are more susceptible to pressure.

In an organizing campaign we frequently have female issues— scheduling, child care, shift work, health and safety, heavy lifting (particularly in geriatric facilities), personal leave, the use of sick leave for small children, pregnancy leave, part time work. We try to deal with those concerns in organizing.

Once the shop is organized, we couldn't have any more solid union person than a woman. Frequently they are more solid than the men. Once they find the confidence and the leadership they trust, women tend to be very sincere, diligent, and dedicated. Maybe it's a sorority type of atmosphere. A kinship develops among them around a central core. You couldn't want anybody more dependable on a picket line than a woman. They'll be there.

The union has given women an opportunity to become assertive in a structured way, that is, helping their coworkers. Perhaps men have been able to enjoy that in football or by going to the local clubs Friday night. Women are expected to stay home while their husbands are down at the bar or the Elks. The union gives women a chance to play leadership roles. It's a new experience.

Some of our women leaders say their husbands pressure them to be less involved in the union. But during a strike many women have extremely supportive husbands. They wouldn't make it through otherwise. One of our best women says the union gave her a feeling of self confidence and independence, and helped her deal with the suffocating relationship she had developed with her husband. It saved her marriage. The union has been a very valuable consciousness-raising tool. Women can appreciate themselves more.

ELINOR GLENN*

I'm the daughter of a suffragette and a building tradesman. My mother says the problem with the suffragettes is they went out of business when the vote was won.

*Elinor Glenn, retired, was the General Manager of Local 434, California, and a member of the International Executive Board of SEIU.

I grew up in New York and studied theater at New York University but the depression hit and the world was coming down around me, so my interests changed to economics. I volunteered as a labor organizer on the waterfront. That was my beginning. I married a young unemployed writer, so I worked. One of us had to. I was the worker and he was a creator. When we came out to Los Angeles, it was the same. He wrote, I worked. I have since remarried. My husband is a former union organizer and a strong supporter of women's rights, and my son is a young labor attorney who fights for women's rights.

During the depression I was a WPA remedial reading teacher, an actress, and a vice president of my union. When war came I worked for the government and organized federal workers as a volunteer. I was fired three times for organizing and reinstated each time by the CIO Central Council. In 1946 I was elected president of my local of the United Public Workers.

I told my business manager of the union, "Okay, I want to be an organizer."

He said, "Forget it."

I said, "Why not?"

He said, "You're a woman."

I said, "So?"

He said, "You have to go out at night."

I said, "Well, I go out at night. I'm not a member of a religious order."

"The workers won't have confidence that you can handle grievances," he said.

"You mean, they have enough confidence to elect me president of this union, but won't have confidence in me as an organizer?"

I proposed that I be put on a three month probationary period. They agreed and I became a staff organizer.

At first the workers at the hospital said, "Where's Sam?" (the General Manager of the union.)

I'd say, "Well, he's going to be here next week."

At the end of three months I said, "I'm bringing Sam to the next meeting."

They said, "Who's Sam?"

I later became general manager of the union. When the executive board considered me for the job, the same conversation I'd heard 20 years earlier was repeated.

"How will people feel about a woman manager?"

They thought for a few seconds and said, "Well, this woman they will be terrified of."

I took the job, and it works. Of course, it works! I was the first woman, by the way, (along with a colleague, Gloria Marigny), to be elected to the International Executive Board of our union. Now there are six.

A woman is a hell of an organizer. She's sympathetic, and she establishes a person-to-person relationship. And she's not abused by employers like men are in an organizing situation. When I was pregnant, I worked through my seventh month. The pregnancy didn't handicap me, it helped.

On the picket line, the women are absolutely committed. They'll fight like hell during a strike, like they're fighting for their children. They're as easy to organize as men, except in certain ethnic groups. The Hispanic woman will ask her husband for permission to join. It's a family matter. The husbands are uneasy. For instance, once we had a young Chicana in negotiations. It's 3:00 am and she's weeping. She says her husband will be mad about her being away so late. I called her husband and spoke with him. He was very hostile. I guess he thought she was out with somebody. I suggested he come over, and he did. He saw what was going on, left quietly, and she had no further problem. This is a new role for Hispanic women, but when you get them active in the union, they're terrific.

We're becoming sensitive to the special problems of minority women. Black women have worked away from the home since slavery. It is no big thrill to them when middle-class white women raise the slogan, "We're going to free you to get out and work." Black women say, "Look, free me so I can stay home, or have a choice of working or staying home."

When the Hispanic woman has a grievance, she usually comes to the union office with a male relative. As the male gains confidence in the union, we try to address the wife and encourage her to express her own ideas. It helps if a woman union rep handles the grievance. Both the woman and man feel more secure. A Black woman with a grievance pursues the remedy independently.

Even child care has a different cultural meaning to the Black woman than to the Hispanic or Asian woman. If somebody in the Hispanic family is sick—anybody, a child, a grandmother, an aunt—the Hispanic woman stays home and takes care of that relative. So the hospital hires the Hispanic woman one day and fires her the next. We're trying to resolve that.

We've learned to deal with racial conflict and reduce it. One of our stewards, for instance, heard there was going to be a rumble between Blacks and Hispanics in the hospital. Our women leaders went on the loudspeaker outside where people were gathering and cooled the tensions. The union mediates a lot of racial conflicts that way.

Our union just completed a most exciting project. It's a story for the future of health care because it affects both upgrading for our members and the shortage of nurses. Hospitals have even been recruiting nurses in foreign countries. Some hospitals pay a bounty of a thousand dollars to anyone bringing a nurse to them. But these young recruits are very transient. They stay awhile and leave. They have no ties to the community or to the patients.

For 15 years my union and I fought for apprenticeship training programs like the building trades have. I'm happy to say we finally got a law in California that provides funds for such programs. So we are now training 100 LVNs to become RNs. The apprentices work 32 hours, go to school for eight hours, and get paid for 40 hours. They've brought the community college *into* the hospitals, so that the hospital is now the campus. The program can make a dramatic change in health care. It can reduce the hospital class system, offer upgrading to disenfranchised people, and provide a committed RN staff. Hospitals resist upgrading our people because the training is very expensive. This program provides the funds for it.

In California during the depressions some unions tried to organize public employees. In the sixties, following President Kennedy's executive order on collective bargaining for federal employees, there was a rebirth of organization.

We organized hospitals because the exploitation was so severe there. Nobody sat down and said, "Let's go out and organize them." Our phones were ringing. People were ready.

We moved into nine county hospitals. I'd go into the cafeteria, sit at a table with the women, and talk about issues of importance to them. With the men workers, I'd go into their dressing room. We'd put up a sheet separating them from me, we'd talk about the union, and I'd sign them up right there. The guards would come and escort me out. Later I got those guards to join the union.

It was an asset being a woman organizer. We could go places other people couldn't. I'd get a white coat, so I'd look like a doctor or a nurse, and I'd walk all over that hospital. There'd be five of us. With five we could reach 500. We'd get one person from each floor and make them stewards. Then we'd work out a campaign. We'd learn what issues bothered people. In those days it was mainly bread. They were hungry. They'd get a few dollars and they'd have to kick back to their supervisors. They were at the bottom of the pecking order and they had no dignity. The union penetrated that system by organizing the entire hospital, top to bottom, except for the physicians.

It was truly rank-and-file organizing. I myself came from the ranks and fought my way up to organizer. We started with seven members at county and now we have 7,000. I always found it very easy to organize in the public sector. Once the barrier of legitimacy was removed by Kennedy, it became even easier. I love organizing, and I'm still doing it.

*   *

The strike by our local of the county hospital in 1966 was an historic strike.

Before the strike, union committees (led primarily by women) met simultaneously with the nine county hospital heads. Thousands of our people began gathering in the halls of the county hospitals. Nothing was going on. They were just trying to find out if the committees were getting any concessions from management.

The hospital heads finally agreed to contact the Board of Supervisors, which was meeting downtown, and support the union demand for a decent wage increase. The response they got from the Board was rage: "The employees won't get *any*thing, not even the 43 cents a day we offered before."

When they heard that, masses of workers grabbed their pocketbooks, walked out of the hospital, and marched four miles in the blazing sun to the Board's office. The social workers and the clerks joined the other workers.

The Board called the Fire Marshall because so many people came. The Marshall told them not to sit in the aisles. The social workers had arrived first, so the hospital workers sat on the social workers' laps. It was a marvelous experience. The biggest outpouring of workers in the county's history. Nothing went on that day at the work site. It was almost like a general strike. The hospital workers reached agreement and went back after three or four days. The social workers stayed out for three weeks and finally won their demands. When the Board gave a bonus to the scabs, the social workers went on strike again and got it reversed. We won a substantial wage increase. The following year we had a contract, or what they called a "memorandum of understanding."

That was the first agreement covering public workers in California. It was the right time and the right place. And it opened doors up and down the state of California for organizing the public sector. It changed the labor picture from paternalism to mature collective negotiations. A few years after the strike, an orderly collective bargaining system for public employees was set up. Women played leading roles in those events.

In the seventies we got involved with tax questions. We analyzed budgets of billions of dollars, and we helped the community identify wastes so that money could be used to hire more workers and improve patient care.

We built community coalitions long before it was fashionable to do so. In the mid seventies our local assembled 1500 people (from 300 different organizations) to go to the state capital and demand tax reform. We called ourselves the Committee for Tax Justice. I got that name from the idea of social justice. We saw that *other* taxpayers' groups just wanted to penalize the disabled, the poor, and women. We saw no justice in that. Ours was the first Committee for Tax Justice. It began in California and spread to the International union and the whole country. We lost on Proposition 13 in California. But on Proposition 9, people realized it was waste, not services, they wanted to cut out.

Our union played an important role in eliminating waste. We pointed out that County hospital was losing over $400 million in revenue from state and federal governments by not hiring enough clerical workers to process medicaid applications. The Board doubted it but finally substantiated our claim. As a result they hired 400 additional workers, primarily women.

*   *

Our local has quite a reputation in the community. We have coalitions with all kinds of ethnic and political groups, across the spectrum from right to left. We don't give them a loyalty check, but we do maintain our own identity. We set up coalitions on rent control. We set up the first women's committees in California, and injected women's issues into the life of the union. We have actively represented patient interests. In East Los Angeles, we supported parent groups that were set up to save the clinics. Our members would not have lost jobs if the clinics had been closed, they would have been transferred, but we *cared* about the children in the clinics.

With the attack on public workers, supporting the community to protect health services is even more necessary. When we go into hospitals to organize, we're known as a union that works with the community. It helps us in organizing.

The county system has been hit very hard by Proposition 13. Workers have not lost jobs but they are being overworked. Hiring has been frozen. Emergency wards have been closed, and many hospitals have been closed. They haven't been replaced by alternative health systems. The result is that the poor and sick are denied opportunities for health care.

The whole medicare and medicaid program is in desperate straits. Surgeons get less, for instance, for operating on a poor person than on an elderly person. They get less for operating on an elderly person than on a private patient.

In other places, consulting firms are trying to break up the union, but we don't face that here. They recognize the union but they still try to screw the workers. We're there to see they don't do it. We educate the workers on how to fight. We're not counselors. We're fighters, teachers, negotiators, organizers.

A woman social worker and a male custodian from the deep South organized this union. She was white and he was Black. Those two people. That's the character of the union. The social workers and custodians were once the most advanced union group. They subsidized the organization of other hospital workers.

In our local, four of the five top officers are women. Seven out of ten staff members are women. The General Manager of the local (who succeeded me) is also a woman, Ophelia McFadden. She is one of only two Black women who head large unions in California.

Organizing women is one of the four goals of CLUW. It's the one that interests me the most. We're not getting to the women.

The first time CLUW met they asked how many officers of national unions were present. Very few hands went up. I was one of them. We ask the same question now and it's thrilling to see all the hands that go up. It's very exciting work. We support each other in union fights. We walk each others' picket lines. It's that kind of network. We've made an impact. We're no longer an object of humor.

The women's movement and the labor movement help each other. The sisterhood that results is remarkable. Women are transcending the jurisdictions between unions. Two unions may be fighting like hell in some election, but on women's issues, we're all sisters.

The fight on women's issues has had a very salutary effect on the men. Their consciousness has been raised and the rules of the game have been changed. The feminist movement was once directed toward fairly middle class women, many of whom didn't work. The interests of working women are more job related—pay equity, retirement, careers, child care. Before the advent of CLUW, working women didn't have a home in the feminist movement.

Seven

ORGANIZERS AND LOBBYISTS

Women like to be organized by women. It encourages them to say, "If Nancy can do it, I can too."

I can remember when clericals thought they were just working for pin money. That's changed. It wasn't so much the women's movement as the economy—they came to depend on those wages. And the more you see your job as essential, the readier you are for organization.

THE WOMEN—IN THEIR OWN WORDS

NANCY MILLS, ORGANIZER

It's been a torturous road. Boy, I don't know where to begin. I went to Antioch College, primarily because I didn't want an education. I wanted to work. But my father wanted me to get an education and that was the best compromise. As part of my education at Antioch I had several different jobs. They sort of reflected my interest at the time in creating social change. I started out doing mental health work with emotionally disturbed children. Then I was a social worker. Then I worked with Saul Alinsky for awhile, then with the government on juvenile delinquency.

When I got my degree I worked for a Nader organization on agri-business, of all things. Spent time jet-setting around the country investigating agri-business's effect on small farmers and farm workers. I did that for a couple of years. Then I reached a terrible crisis. I looked around and I thought, "Oh, my God, I do *not* want to spend the rest of my days testifying before Senate committees on agri-business." I had

*Nancy Mills is an organizer for Local 880, SEIU, Boston, Massachusetts.

no idea what could make real changes in this country, so I took time out.

Some friends were organizing LPNs and the workers engaged in a "high noon" action. On their lunch hours they gathered in the lobby of the hospital to demand union recognition. The hospital's response was to arrest the entire bunch for trespassing, and then fire about 50 of them. The NLRB—Labor Relations Board—didn't cover them then, so it became a big community issue.

My friends asked me to join a support committee, and I did. Then they asked me to help organize another hospital, and I did. I had no intention of sticking with it, but I worked in that hospital for three years as a ward secretary. I loved it. You get a real sense of collectivity working in a hospital, spending eight hours a day with the same people, working around life and death. It's intense and exciting. We won that election and I later took this job as an organizer. I've loved every minute of it.

The local is new. The people who started it had been active in welfare rights organizing in Boston. They weren't out of a labor or hospital background. At some point they decided that the best way to change poverty was to organize the working poor—hospital workers. They got funds from the International to do that.

Their heads were bashed in the first few years, trying to organize some of the Boston giants. In some cases they couldn't even get 20 percent of the vote. So they put their tails between their legs and ran to smaller hospitals in the suburbs. They had some real victories there. The industry is incredibly strong in Boston. It's a health care *empire*. Harvard Medical! How much stronger, wealthier, more powerful can you get? They use it very well against us. They have no money to pay workers a decent wage, but they hire the most skilled and ruthless union busters in the business and pay them a fortune.

Massachusetts has more health care workers, per capita, than any state in the union. They're also the least organized and lowest paid. Management is strong partly because workers have been weak. The race problem is one reason they've been weak. The tension in Boston around race and integration has been incredible. Unions didn't understand that very well, and the workers themselves didn't understand it. So a lot of mistakes were made. For a long time, the resistance of white workers to uniting with Black workers meant that people couldn't be unionized. I think those days are over.

Our jurisdiction is only private hospitals, and we have a strict industrial approach to organizing. We organize top to bottom, everybody who works in the hospital. That puts us in a better bargaining position. We even have our first doctor, actually a dentist who punches a time clock and is on an hourly rate.

We've been around awhile now, showing people that unionization works. The idea is no longer so strange. People think, "Well, maybe." We've made gains, and winning is now on the agenda. After six years we now have over 3,000 members in hospitals and nursing homes, mostly in small suburban places. We're now going after the Boston giants. It's a very different constituency. Our members now are suburban, white, small institutions, limited resources. In Boston it's a thousand people in service and maintenance jobs, and a population that is Black, Hispanic, Italian—everything. It's a different struggle, and a lot more exciting. When a thousand people all of a sudden join a union, people feel a lot more powerful. It will make a real difference to the union and the city when the big ones are organized.

The response of women I organize is, "I'm not a women's libber *but.*" And then they support a lot of the aims. They don't want to be identified with some of the individuals. They keep their distance because they believe in wearing bras and they love their husbands.

I'm excited about CLUW. My reaction to other women's groups is that they haven't organized much around issues that affect masses of women. My interest is in getting lots of women active in all different levels of the union. Making it possible for a few women to rise up and become George Meanys is important, but more important is getting masses of women involved with unionism. CLUW can also help shake up the unions around women's issues. My priority would be to develop leadership training for women members. Unfortunately, small locals like ours can't do it.

The labor movement in Boston is predominantly male. It is also dominated by the construction trades, so you can imagine how many women participate. Women are a new thing in Boston.

The union has a lot to offer. Hospital workers suffer the indignity and disrespect of being unknown and unseen. Doctors, administrators, even RNs, treat them like they're not even there. The union asks them what they want, what they need. It's a first for them. They get involved in an organization with other people. That's also a first.

The union is a whole new world, a way of getting away from their homes, asserting themselves, feeling involved in productive labor. They *make* the time to get involved in the union. Some of them have struggles in their marriage over it but they usually resolve it for the better.

At St. Elizabeth's hospital, we tried to get the hospital to fire their union busters. The women got up and addressed national officers of the AFL-CIO. They spoke at public meetings and they talked to Catholic priests and bishops about how the hospital abridged their rights. These women had never spoken to more than five people. Suddenly they were addressing hundreds.

Most workingclass people don't have any sense of their own power. Women have it even less than men. When you unionize hospitals, that changes. The women feel: "Do I really *deserve* to be treated with respect and to be paid well?" When they start to unionize, they say, "Yeah, I *do* deserve it."

Most men, in proportion to their numbers, get involved in organizing. The men don't have to go home, make dinner, deal with a husband. The men have less trouble saying, "Yeah, I deserve it." They have more experience with public speaking, being asked what they think, doing collective thinking. They are more comfortable about filing grievances and confronting authority.

We're looking for a Black organizer, an experienced one, but there are very few. Labor is weak in dealing with issues of special interest to Blacks and in training minority leadership. It's weak on women's issues, but it's even weaker on minority issues. Black workers can be organized by a white organizer, but it's even easier with a Black organizer. They don't want to join an all-white union and who blames them?

Having role models for women is important, and one of the good things about our union is that, compared to other unions, we have some. It's very important in organizing. Women like to be organized by women. It encourages them to say, "If Nancy can do it, I can do it too."

HELLAN DOWDEN, LEGISLATIVE REPRESENTATIVE*

In some ways I'm a lot less threatening than a lot of men are. People understand I'm not building my own power base. I try to be sensitive to that and to men who don't have much experience working with women. If I got mad at every chauvinist comment made to me I'd go crazy. You won't change people that way. Humor helps. "Why offend them with style when you can offend them with substance." That's my feeling about it. Being taken seriously is the biggest problem. If you're ugly you're seen as, "Oh, you're doing this to make up for your ugliness." If you're good looking, it's, "This is just a fancy way to get laid." Either way you lose. So you do the best job you can. You'll be recognized for that.

I came to California from Columbus, Ohio, in 1968 and, with a degree in sociology, I went to work for the Department of Social Services. I was active in the union and I got fired for organizing welfare recipients. After a year in Oxford, England, I returned and became very

*Hellan Dowden is legislative representative for the SEIU in Sacramento, California.

active in the anti-war movement, the womens' movement, and tenants' rights groups. I met some SEIU staff on a political campaign and later I went to work for the union. On my current job in Sacramento, I have a staff of two other lobbyists, a research person, and an intern; and I represent about 180,000 members in California. I've always been the breadwinner in the family because my husband's been in school.

When I first came to California I went to consciousness raising groups, and for a couple of years we talked about, "It's just terrible" and all the rest. Marriages started breaking up over it. In most cases they came back together again, only stronger. Many of the women had never been away from their husbands overnight, except to stay with their mothers. These women were in their early thirties like me. The women's movement gave a lot of them confidence. I realized that we had to leap from that into the "man's world." Once you get the support, the strength, and you get your head together, then export it. It was no good having women pat you on the back all the time and tell you how right you are. It didn't affect the problems.

The union is open and receptive to women, but you have to build a constituency within the union. You can't get out there totally unprotected. As an organizer, that's what you do anyway. You build a cadre of women that support you. Then you can deal with their issues. When most workers are women, who will they elect to negotiating committees? Women. Once on negotiating committees, women can go up into staff positions, and then become union officers. In many big unions, negotiating committees and officers have always been men. They're locked into it.

We need special programs for women. Men have had their own programs. After all, who's been putting on all the workshops? The men. I'm not as much into assertiveness training as I am into *Roberts' Rules of Order*. Women have to teach other women about things like running a meeting. We also need to develop role models for women. Women don't have leadership experience, so they tend to have a very charismatic style. That's okay, but it's very individualistic. They may just blow their own horns instead of moving other people up.

Some women need to be organized by women. Others think women aren't competent. They have all the same prejudices as men. Some men organizers turn me off. Lots of them organize women very much on a sexual politics basis. When I started organizing, I'd go to the hospital library and read the RN journals to learn their vocabulary. If you're not organizing around being a big handsome man, who comes and pats you on the butt, you'd better know what you're talking about. Women respect that.

Sometimes it's more difficult organizing women. They don't have the institutional background that men have. So you have to build on the involvement they do have, like being PTA or church activists. Men go out after work and have a drink together. Women go home to their families. They are more home-centered. You have to get through their individualism and get them to see themselves as a collective.

We organize women by taking them to the State Legislature and to the County Board of Supervisors. We get them to work in political campaigns. It's another level of understanding, letting people use their free time to work for the union. We have lots of talent out there in the hospitals. If management's not going to take advantage of it, let the unions do it. A woman who has raised a family by herself has the strength to go out and be a strong advocate for the union.

My staff takes a kidding. I always say, "The reason I hired you guys is that you've got the greatest legs." If anybody asks me how I like having men work for me, I say, "Oh, they make wonderful coffee." We all get along very well and work as a team.

JUDY BEREK, LEGISLATIVE REPRESENTATIVE*

I come from a union family so I was always pro-labor. When I was asked to go on the union staff as an organizer, I was unsure because I was supposed to be a trained scientist at the hospital. But, as they say, the employer makes you a union person. We had negotiated a "technical specialist" classification. I was qualified for it because I had a masters' degree, but the director's reaction was, "You're a nice girl, Judy, but you're much too young to be in the highest classification."

The union got me into the classification after a big fight, but that was sort of the kicker. I decided to go with the union. That same director then told me: "How can you go with them? You are a scientist." I was supposed to play with my test tubes the rest of my life. The fact is I was good cheap help for them. They also saw the union as being Blacks and Puerto Ricans, so they couldn't understand why a nice Jewish girl like me would get caught up in it.

I first became a technician through on-the-job training, so I'm typical of lab technicians over 35 and atypical of those under 35. Lots of people moved up into technical jobs in the past, but they can't any longer because now they need the formal education and the license. The work is infinitely more complicated now, so the formal training is necessary to some extent. But there's been an over-reaction and a rejection of apprenticeships and training in the hospital. An awful lot

*Judy Berek is a legislative representative for District 1199 of RWDSU (Retail, Wholesale and Department Store Union), now merging with the Service Employee's International Union.

can be learned on the job, and learned better. The only licensing with any flexibility is New York's. They let you take X number of years as a trainee, then if you take the exam and pass it, they give you the same license they give someone with a two year degree. From there, if you work more, you get something equivalent to a four-year degree.

We're locking people out through formal education requirements. And we're locking out a lot of women and minorities. It's the white male establishment gaining hold of occupations they had left to women. It's easier for them to get formal education, and it shuts the others out. The more formal education you require, and the less you go by on-the-job training, the harder you make it on women and minorities.

The union opposes some of the stringencies of formal licensing, but we favor licensing to some extent because we have to protect the public. If someone does a blood test inaccurately, it can kill you. If someone does an x-ray incorrectly, it can expose you to terrible radiation. It's like a doctor prescribing the wrong medication.

I faced more age than sex discrimination in the hospital. I was a strident person and I didn't pay any attention to the more subtle forms of discrimination. If someone was discriminating against me, unless they told me point-blank, I never noticed. Even as an organizer I was much more aware of age than sex discrimination. I was 24 but I could pass for 18. I had long hair that I wore in braids, although not when I went out to represent the union. In retrospect I know that, because I was female, it was harder to get that top classification. If I had been a young man, they would have wanted to give me recognition, raise my salary, and push me up. And they wouldn't have treated a young male the way they treated me.

This union's position on sex discrimination is very good. That isn't to say that nobody inside the union discriminates, because some of them do. They'd like not to, but they do. They're more likely to ask me to go for a xerox than a man in a comparable position. I'm also more likely to offer to do it than the guy is, which is the double edge. But there's always a blind effort in the union to give people a chance, without asking if they're male or female. So people who deal with the union get their sexism battered down.

In the union, women can make the time to become active rank-and-file leaders but it's hard to make the time to come on staff. We have lost good staff people to their children. It's mainly the women with medium sized kids, that they can't leave with baby sitters or that can't take care of themselves.

I got bored being an organizer after about four years and we talked about what else I could do. I love the union but there's a limit to the number of grievances you can handle without getting bored. I was moved into this job and I was given absolute free rein. The primary issue I work on is funding of the health industry. If they cut back the funds, we lose jobs. I went to the state capitol with a hospital disclosure bill, to get hospital books open to the public, and that has been a constant thread throughout.

We got involved in the legislation to clean up the nursing homes and to reorganize the home health care system. If profiteers are bad in hospitals and nursing homes, you can imagine what they'd be like in home care. We support licensing of health care occupations but we oppose licensing that's very restrictive. We support continuing education but we're against requirements that are unnecessary, restrictive and discriminatory.

Then we get involved in all the women's issues: ERA, maternity disability, health insurance payments for pregnancy, even the redefinition of bank credit for women and the extension of collective bargaining for household workers. We are part of the coalition against the death penalty and part of the fight to maintain medicaid abortions in New York.

Pregnancy disability finally got the support of the AFL-CIO. But it was always the first thing dropped every year in discussions of changes in the workers' compensation law. They'd say, "These are the 20 changes in the law we want. Well, let's bring it down to 19," and maternity disability was the first one out. When you get into the final compromise meetings, the women's movement is not always inside to push on women's issues. That's why we need more people inside.

The major concern of the service workers is money. They still don't make enough. Money and access to education. Most hospital jobs are dead-end. There's no automatic moving up because each new level requires formal education. Our younger members are very much interested in that. Our social workers earn good money and they have lots of other interests. As the money eases up a little, other things are emphasized. Now it's better work shifts. Lots of people get only one weekend off a month, and there's a big push to get it down to every other weekend. It's very expensive. The hospitals resist because they have to increase staff to do that. Shift work is also a big problem. The new contract lets people with seniority bid for better shifts, so that helps.

Hospital workers are exposed to all the hazards of industrial work, plus some. They have all the problems of construction work and all the chemical hazards of the chemical industry and all the hazards of the laundry industry. And there's been nothing, virtually nothing, done. Nobody cares about it except the union.

Stress is a health hazard. One study showed that doctors had the *lowest* levels of stress in the hospital because they make the decisions. The others see things that are wrong but have no power to change them. Part of wanting to move up is wanting to influence the decisions that affect you and the patients. A nurses' aide does what the nurse tells her. She figures if she becomes a nurse it'll be better. Once she's a nurse, she finds she can only do what the doctor tells her.

Top supervision is overwhelmingly male, and there's nothing we can do about it in collective bargaining because the "promotion by seniority" clauses only cover the bargaining unit—which excludes supervision. It's a morale problem for the entire industry. More women are studying hospital administration but the male still gets promoted to lab or social service director faster than the female.

I think the University of Minnesota is the only school of health services administration where the class is half women. That's good, but it takes years of cranking out classes like that to make up for all the years when 5 percent of the class was women. It will take some real affirmative action suits to get women into administration. I don't think the problem will go away by itself. It is not an industry that reforms itself.

The only hospitals with female hierarchies are run by nuns, and they can be viciously anti-union and racist. We had a strike in a nursing home run by nuns. They were so bad we were going to appeal to the Pope because it was a Papal order of nuns. They give women administrators a bad name, one they don't deserve.

The union made a big difference to service workers. Wages are the biggest change—and more self determination. In the first organizing drive, people made $28 a week and had no fringes. Now fringes have gone from zero to about 20 percent of all compensation. We have health benefits, pensions, training benefits, you name it. People feel they have some say about what they do, that they are represented and they're not in the pits. That's the biggest difference, having something to be proud of. When the jobs were the lowest paid jobs in society, they were shit jobs. Now they're valuable jobs and the people are valuable people.

We have training and upgrading funds so our members can go to school. They can get tuition reimbursement and go to school at night, or they can go to school full time, if they're accepted in a training program, and get 85 percent of their salary paid until they finish. That's not bad. We even put someone through medical school. If there isn't enough money in the fund for everyone, the decision about who is to go is made by seniority.

People get involved in many things through the union—educational, cultural, political activities. Our members get holidays and vacations now, so they have more times for themselves.

The oldest division in 1199 is the drug division. Its members are overwhelmingly white male pharmacists. They organized the rest of us. Now the union has four divisions. The hospital division, which is by far the largest, includes the skilled maintenance workers and all the unskilled people, the aides, orderlies, housekeepers, and so forth. The service workers were the first ones in the hospital to organize.

Next in age is the guild division—the technical, professional, and clerical hospital workers—the practical nurses, lab and x-ray technicians, social workers, psychologists, pharmacists in hospitals. The newest division is the registered nurses. When we had just a few, we told them that if we got a thousand nurses, we'd set up a separate division for RNs, and we did. The RNs are the largest classification in the hospital, but the largest bargaining unit is usually the service unit.

The technical people didn't want to be in the same unit with the service workers. A lot of it was racial. In the early sixties, the service workers were almost all Black and the technical, professional and clericals were almost all white. That is no longer true. Now there are Blacks in all classifications. But back then it was just snobbery. The union breaks that down by bringing everyone together in the same organization, but where we don't have the RNs organized, the class system is still strong.

We have a few thousand RNs now. That's a very small proportion of the total, but we haven't been working on it long. The women's movement has helped that to some extent. The RNs identify less with the doctors and the institution than they used to, and they're more aware that professionalism doesn't conflict with unionism.

The clericals are in the guild division. They're white and they're also white collar workers, so they identify more with the technical than with the service people. Clericals are very important during a strike. In places where they're unorganized, they provide a real army of strikebreakers. Normally they wouldn't do service work if their lives depended on it, but when the service workers are on strike, they go in and do their jobs.

The initial aim of the union was to organize the service workers. I don't think anyone thought of the others as being oppressed. But it became obvious that service workers couldn't have much strength unless the other groups were organized. They needed the technicians especially because the hospital can't operate without them, and nobody else can do their work. The supervisors can do maintenance work to some extent, but the doctors can't do the technicians' work.

I can remember when clericals thought they were working just for pin money. That's changed. It wasn't so much the women's movement as the economy. They came to depend on those wages. And as we negotiated things like health insurance, people saw that the wife's job was the best insurance the family had, so her job became more important. The more you see your job as essential, the readier you are for organization. If your job is important, you want to make it better.

I don't think any job in a hospital is as demanding of your time as working for this union. I took a salary and a benefits cut when I came here, but I haven't been sorry. I've seen an enormous change take place in the hospital. And we have a union. That's the biggest thing. It's something that's yours to be proud of.

Eight

LABOR LEADERS (FEMALE)

The women sit and watch the game rather than playing on the field. We need more women leaders to bring them in.

More than half of the 700 top leaders of SEIU at the time of this study, including paid and unpaid officers, were women; six of the 45 members of the International Executive Board (13 percent) were women; one of the nine vice presidents was a woman; and 20 percent of locals had a woman president. "Most of the women are presidents of smaller locals," one staff member commented, "although a woman is a principal officer of our biggest local." An estimated 40 to 65 percent of the union's members are women, with the more reliable estimates falling nearer the top of the range.

In doing this research, we helped assemble the names of women SEIU leaders, and then we obtained questionnaire survey responses from 74 of them, well over half those polled.* Of these, 58 percent were from locals of under 5,000 members (the usual cutting point for representation on the Executive Board), compared to about 30 percent of all members who belonged to these smaller locals. Thus, women leaders were almost twice as likely as the average member to come from the smaller locals.

These leaders were asked what they thought accounted for the lower participation rates of women in union leadership, as compared with men. Of the ten leading factors chosen, at least three related to family issues: "family responsibilities," "lack of adequate child care,"

*The group is highly educated: 73 percent had at least some college, 45 percent were college graduates, and fewer than 10 percent did not finish high school. The California women were most likely to be college graduates.

and "husband's objections." Probably "long hours" and "late hours," from among the top ten chosen, were also family related.

That family life affects union participation is suggested in the biographical data on the women leaders themselves. Only 37 percent of these women were currently married (compared to 57 percent of women hospital workers surveyed); 32 percent of them were divorced or separated (compared to 18 percent of workers); and 45 percent of them had no children (compared to only 14 percent of workers). Almost all the women leaders with children had at least one child old enough to care for young children.*

Thus, most of the women leaders were currently unmarried and, while a majority had children, most of them may not have had acute child care problems at the moment since, in most cases, children were old enough to care for themselves. Without husbands or young children, union participation is easier to manage. Those who are heads of families (*with* children but *without* husbands) may be more highly motivated than others to pursue union careers: certainly they are less vulnerable to "husband's objections" about union activities.

Factors seen by women leaders as being *important* or *very important* in accounting for the lower participation of women than men in union leadership.

		Percent of women leaders responding
1.	Family responsibilities	94%
2.	Lack of leadership training opportunities	86
3.	Lack of adequate child care	81
4.	Not involved enough at lower levels of participation, which provides experience for leadership and staff positions	79
5.	Long hours	79
6.	Husband's objections	79
7.	Lack of information about opportunities	78
8.	Lack of self confidence	71
9.	Late hours	69
10.	Lack of support from men	68
11.	Don't want the responsibility	63
12.	Lack of support from other women	62
13.	Lack of interest on the part of women	61

*Among those with children, 67 percent had no children under age 16; 82 percent had at least one child over age 16, and only one of those who had *no* children over age 16 also had a child under age 2½.

14.	Positions don't open up very often	61
15.	Fear that supervisors are hard on union activists	56
16.	Lack of encouragement from union officials	55
17.	She feels she can't handle the job	49
18.	Reluctance to compete with men for positions	46
19.	Having to relocate	46
20.	Don't like the nature of the work or duties	46
21.	Wages and benefits aren't good enough	44
22.	Feels it's not an appropriate role for her	36
23.	Discrimination against women in the union	33
24.	Women don't feel the same drive as men to move up the ladder or to achieve positions of power	32

Only one of the ten leading factors has to do with the *attitudes* (or consciousness) of women themselves—"lack of confidence." The factor *least* often chosen is also attitudinal—"women don't feel the same drive as men do to move up the ladder or to achieve positions of power." On the other hand, "husband's objections" and "lack of support from men" are among the leading ten. These women leaders apparently think male attitudes are a greater barrier to the participation of women than are female attitudes.

Two of the top ten have to do with opportunities—"lack of leadership training opportunities" and "lack of information about opportunities." Two of the top ten have to do with hours—"long hours" and "late hours." Almost at the bottom of the list is "discrimination against women in the union."

On another question put to these women leaders, 65 percent *agreed* that "women in the union have an equal chance with men of becoming officers and staff for the union." (On the other hand, 35 percent, or more than one in three, *disagreed* with the statement and felt women did *not* have an equal chance.) At a more personal level, 63 percent *disagreed* with the statement, "I have been discriminated against in the union." Thus, the great majority of these women leaders feel that neither other women nor themselves are discriminated against in the competition for union leadership.

While most women saw insufficient encouragement of women as an important problem, 76 percent *agreed* that "The International union is attempting to get women more actively involved in the union," and 71 percent *agreed* that their local was trying to do this.

They also saw support for women as increasing in the union. A substantial 85 percent *agreed* that, "men in the union are more supportive than they were five years ago of women taking officer and staff positions in the union." And they also saw the attitudes and aspirations of women as improving: 89 percent *agreed* that, "women are

more willing to stand for elected office than they were five years ago."
· As for personal aspirations, 69 percent said that, "one of my personal goals is to hold a higher position in the union." Concerning support for these aspirations, 72 percent said, "men would rather have men as officers and staff in the union," and only 18 percent said that women would prefer men.

The perception that males prefer other males as union leaders seems somewhat contradictory to the view that women are not discriminated against in competitions for union office. Perhaps this "preference" is seen as an expression of biased attitudes which are not strong enough to result in discriminatory acts. These women apparently see two contradictory strains in the attitudes of males: a bias which favors men, and a desire (at least on the part of many male leaders) to involve women much more in union activities.

A similar point is raised by the fact that 69 percent of these leaders *agreed* that, "In my role as an officer or staff person in the union I have encountered special problems because I am a woman." Some of these "problems" result from the biased attitudes of males, but others undoubtedly result from their special family responsibilities, and from the difficulties women experience in functioning in a male milieu and operating by male rules. More information is needed about the precise nature of these problems.

As for the value to the union of having women leaders, 99 percent *agreed* that, "It is important to have women organizers in union organizing campaigns which involve women workers." With respect to women's activities in the union, 71 percent *agreed* that, "There should be more separate activities and conferences for women in the union (while a surprisingly large proportion—29 percent—*disagreed* on this).

Questions concerning separate women's activities within the union also need further exploration. When they are *substitutes* for mainstream activities, separate activities may lead to the further segregation of women. But when they are *supplementary* to them, they can provide crucial support and information networks. *Substitution* can occur at conventions and mixed meetings where women attend separate women's sessions *at the same time* that men, in other sessions, discuss regular union business. But when such separate sessions are held at *other times* (when regular union business is not under discussion) they can, as *supplementary* activities, help balance the strong networks that male leaders have created and the separate activities they have carried on over the years.

Substitution can also occur where women staff are assigned to women's activities within the union, or to other traditionally female roles, rather than being integrated into the union's mainstream activities, especially those leading to top union offices.

Very often *institutional* forms of discrimination are invisible—to women and men alike. Often they have to do with rules-of-the-game, rules made by men that inadvertently (or deliberately) penalize women. These may include requiring unnecessarily long or late working hours of union staff, or extensive travel, or transfers to other locations. They may include inadequate leadership training, inattention to family issues and responsibilities, or to the difficulties involved for women in being "token" members of male groups; or they may include organization rules that favor male (or incumbent) leadership.

Strategies aimed at reducing these institutional forms of discrimination might include: chartering more new locals for newly organized women workers, so women aspirants to union office will not compete with established male leadership; establishing new forms of proportional representation in locals where established male leadership presides over a majority of female members; giving more representation on the Executive Board (and at other policy levels) to smaller locals, where a disproportionate share of female leaders apparently work. At a different level, they may include efforts to involve *families* in social, cultural, community activities sponsored by the union, activities that bring the family into the union rather than taking the woman out of the family; or giving specific attention to the child care needs of members (at union meetings and activities) and staff; or making special efforts to listen to and act upon the problems women identify as barriers to union participation.

≈

THE WOMEN—IN THEIR OWN WORDS

TOP LEADERSHIP
Women on the Executive Board are accepted very well. There's no putting them down. You can imagine trying to put down Elinor Glenn. She tells *you* what to do. Rosemary is the same way. Where women are heads of their locals, they're very outspoken on the Board.

Women are obviously not equally represented on the Board. If they're half the members (or more) of the union, they probably should be half the Board, but they're less than 15 percent. That's because they're new to leadership and because so few of them are presidents of big locals. Most Board members are officers of large locals. The Board is really controlled by the old building service locals. They're about half the Board and about a third of the members. Until recently, they've been the largest locals in the International.

A lot of the big locals are mixed men and women. In many cases the leadership is still male even though the membership is changing underneath them. A man may have founded the local and been

president of it for 40 years. Underneath him he may have a membership that has become 80 percent female.

We don't charter a lot of new locals, and we organize mainly
through existing locals. Most young women in leadership are from the
newer locals, which tend to be small even when they're growing very
fast.

The women leaders are mainly in hospital and public employee
locals, where the new organizing has been done. If there isn't any
established leadership, it's easier for women to come in and get elected.
About half of our members in health care and public employment are
women. Building service is about two-thirds women. An incredible
number of young people also head locals now. Women are attracted to
union work.

LOCAL LEADERS

We have 15 people on staff in our local. At one time half of them
were women, now we have only four. We have a democratic way of
picking staff. It's done by a committee of members and officers, and
there's a tendency to pick the "best qualified" person. Many times they
pick a man with academic qualifications over an experienced women
from the rank-and-file. That's probably the way the labor movement is
going: professional business agents, people with advanced degrees in
industrial relations. We're trying to correct that and weight it so the
women with experience will have a better chance. And we're building a
women's committee in order to get more leadership training for
women.

We take the easy road and rely on volunteers to do a lot of union
work. These volunteers tend to be men. So we wind up with male
stewards and delegates even where members are 75 percent female.
The women don't volunteer. That makes it even more necessary to go
out and find the women.

Our local got an award for doing the most for our women
members. That's wonderful, but it's a reflection of the state of the art.
In fact, we are critically down in the number of women playing
leadership roles. I don't have the answers. I'm trying to build up
women stewards so they will rise from there. You can't really bring
them in at the top. A lot of times people are like shooting stars. They
flare and do a lot and then they die.

FAMILY ROLES, ONE VIEW

Women are very qualified for union leadership. But they have to fill many roles. My two children have taken a beating behind this job. They more or less raised themselves. It's fortunate that I had two very independent kids or I couldn't have done this. Even when I'm at home, my job takes a lot of time. I have to call members, and think about what I'll do tomorrow. I'm still dealing with the job when I go home, and I sometimes become very irritable. It's very difficult to have a husband on this job because you don't have time for it. The marriage takes a beating also. And it's not only women. In fact, a lot of men labor leaders are divorced.

A CONTRARY VIEW

Child raising *doesn't* make it harder for women to get involved in the union. The men have two jobs too. They moonlight. It has to do with how the individual feels about being a trade unionist. Sometimes women restrict themselves because they believe they can't do the things men do. As a trade unionist your time certainly isn't your own. There's an awful lot of travel involved. I find that women don't reach out and take advantage of some of the things that are there. Women have to be more aggressive than a man, and they certainly have to make noises to be seen and counted, but the opportunities are there. You have to discipline yourself. You're pretty much on your own. People find that hard to do.

CONTROL

A lot of men feel threatened by women. At meetings they say, "Oh, shit. . . . Oh, pardon me, lady." That's typical. It's a put-down and a fear that they'll be shown up, that the women will know more or do better. It's hard to give up power. Men have been the leaders, and it's threatening to have a woman up there.

I have a problem with one man on my negotiating team. He wanted us to strike, but we didn't. So he has decided that I prevented the strike. He had this sort of power struggle with me. I hate to label it "macho" because that's not fair. He wasn't comfortable with me being in that role. He always tried to be dominant, and it produced a lot of tension. It's happened before. Maybe it's not resentment. It's a feeling that men should be in control. It's, "What is she doing putting herself up as an expert?" Most of the men I deal with are wonderful. Some aren't.

SILENCE

I walk into county meetings where there's two women, and we say to each other, "Gee, guys, it's good you could come." I don't like to go to a meeting with 22 men and myself. I feel awkward. You have to force yourself to say anything because they're all talking. And you have to talk loud. And you have to get your words out fast. And you have to sound decisive and not like you're waffling. By the time you think of what you want to say, they change the subject. You have to train yourself to that level of discipline and assertiveness.

Women are socialized not to be dominant. So you have to unsocialize yourself. Your parents or society may not have done it consciously—put you down, made you more moderate and soft spoken—but the result is that you just sit there in silence. You have to undo that. That's why I started working with women stewards, trying to get them into negotiations so they'll know what to do.

DEALING WITH PREJUDICE: COMPETENCE, FITTING IN, MUSCLE

When I first started it was difficult, being a woman and being Black, and running a local as big as this. The men have accepted me and helped me. They are beautiful. They want me to move up.

I have trouble because I'm a woman, but I simply ignore it. And I have trouble because I'm Black, and I ignore that. I don't have a problem. *They* have the problem. I just pray to God they'll learn how to deal with their problems.

One of our female reps works in a blue collar unit, all male. The men like her. She plays poker. She likes to cuss and she smokes, sometimes cigars. She fits in well.

Being a woman, you find dealing with management a little awkward at times. They never give you credit for knowing your jobs. It's like, "Here's that dingaling lady again, making trouble." But you find out where they're coming from, and you deal with it. Many men don't take you seriously until they think you have something worthwhile to say. Then they listen to you.

I'm a Black woman and that's an obstacle. But if women take a direct approach to their vocations, and if they have goals and time tables to work toward, they can achieve almost anything. Women want to be treated like Dresden China, yet they want equality. It can't be done that way. You can't powder puff your way through a negotiating session, and earn people's respect.

In our union, the female staff has just tried to show competency. We haven't really started to campaign on women's issues yet. We know some males still don't like us around, but we are forcing them to deal with us, by our own individual performance, not by collective action. A women's caucus on the job wouldn't have worked here. We'd have all been out on the street after a few months.

There was a small local in Pennsylvania, all men, all middle-aged and over. Very conservative. They had a tremendous backlog of grievances and wanted me to help. We met at a Polish American club, all men. I felt out of place. They handed me this stuff to do, and the president of the local said, "You know, there are two places for women in this world, in the kitchen and in the bedroom." I'm very defensive about that. I've come across too many situations where that's a factor. It takes me more time to develop credibility with members than it would for a man. But I have developed a good rapport with them, really the strongest.

Some men in the union try to appear very pro women's lib. But when you have a beer with them, it's all there, all the prejudice against women. The sexist remarks: "I tried to get her into bed tonight." They appear gung ho for women's lib but in the actual job setting, it's not there. You have to recognize that, and either dismiss it or fight it. Or both.

The unions have been run by rough, tough men because the movement started the hard way, in the streets. Most people don't picture women in that role. My own father has been a unionist from Day One, but God forbid a broad should work for a union. Women sitting in smoke filled rooms? Hell no. A teamster official comes into the plant. You're being paid minimum wages and he's wearing diamond rings, but he's rough. You might join his union because you think management will be scared of him, just as you are. That's changing. The women know how to handle themselves and they're developing their own muscle.

It's hard for women to take leadership. Everyone she works with is scared. She's got to be awfully strong to lead a gang of scared people. The men test you, try to scare you, make you run off. You have to stand your ground.
Females at the top usually have a male in their background. Maybe

10 or 15 years from now we'll find one that doesn't. It's a crying shame that the only sponsors you can get are males. The men have sponsors too, of course—other guys who bring them along. Female support is becoming more important now, and women are making it through political clout.

STRENGTH IN BEING A WOMAN

It's easier for women to work with women in the union. One night I was going to meet some members, and my husband said, "What group are you going with?" I said, "Oh, the Red Cross." He said, "Yes, and you're going drinking afterwards, right?"

There wasn't any problem with that. Like some women said, it was easier on their husbands knowing the field rep was a woman. We were freer to go down to Taco's and drink two pitchers of peach margueritas after the meeting. I'm married to a political man who is really conscious, and yet that's still there, that suspicion. And it's there in a lot of people. It's easier for us to get together when we're all women.

I had meetings at my house where I'd stop and put my baby to bed. It makes for a good relationship with people I represent. It's funny. You go to a meeting and people come up and give you a big hug. There's affection and a feeling you're all moving in the same direction.

JOB SATISFACTION

I like servicing members. It's a thankless job though. They look you up when they need you and become the best of friends. Then they may forget you. Still you know when you go home that you saved the job of a woman with four kids. That's the best part of the labor movement. People would otherwise be at the mercy of management. A member may have credit problems, so you take five minutes to call a finance company that's trying to repossess her car. You assist her with family problems. Maybe she needs somebody to talk to her husband or son. There's no limit to what you can do for members.

I like being a business rep, arguing, fact finding, staying on top of what's going on, comparing things. People get pushed around, and I like telling them their rights so they can defend themselves. Guess I'm kind of a rebel. People are scared for their jobs, and their superiors ride the hell out of them because they know they're scared. I enjoy helping people, backing management to the wall, seeing the low man come out on top.

The first six months on this job were totally miserable. I yearned to be back in the hospital taking care of people. I guess I'm an old softie. I wanted to get a contract at the hospital so our people would never be crapped on again. We got the contract, but I kept going. Now I feel I do more for people working for the union than I did in nursing.

Nine

THE UNION

You know, O. J. Simpson's mother was a member of our union.

There's a deeply troubled society out there. It's up to each one of us to help turn it around.

John Sweeney, president, SEIU

GEORGE HARDY (RETIRED PRESIDENT, SEIU) DESCRIBES A LIFE OF LABOR

I started back in the depression days. There were no jobs around. I was a radio operator on the ships and I travelled all over the world. I tried to form a union for radio operators, and I was black-balled and couldn't get a job. In the thirties there was no work around, and it was horrible. The city appropriated five million dollars and we got one week's work a month. Pick, shovel, cleaning. I had blisters all over my hands, but I lived on that.

Then I got work as a janitor. They had shapeups, like on the waterfront. I'd work extra in every place I could, *this* building and *that* building. It was an education for me because I got to know most of the janitors. At one shapeup I was ready with my organizing group. We barricaded the alleys and the streets and wouldn't let anybody get into the shapeup. We wanted a union. Even elderly workers, if they wanted work, would have to kick back to the bosses. The women, if they didn't put out, didn't get the work. If a woman wanted to work steady she had to shack up with the foreman. Horrible conditions.

The employers ran everything. They hired vicious goon squads to break your head open if you asked for anything. We had a nice bunch of young men, and we said, "We are going to have a union." We felt nobody had ever given us anything and, by God, we won't get anything out of life unless we fight for it. It's 47 years and I'm still fighting, harder than I was then. Our unions are a lot better. We don't have to meet in basements any more.

I don't know of any other thing that is more important than workers organizing. They used to say, "Hey *you*, c'mere. Hey you." I don't think that expression is used any more. We abolished it. We also abolished spittoons in the industry. We refused to clean them. It's degrading to ask an elderly woman to clean spittoons.

The hospital workers right now are in trouble. The American Hospital Association has hired these so-called labor advisors to tell them how to maintain a union-free environment. The Catholic hospitals have been doing that too. They hire supervisors to keep the women from joining the union. But the women need unions. In nursing homes and some hospitals, workers are making minimum wage.

The service trades have more accidents than any other division of workers in the country. The young women in the hospitals have to lift the patients and their backs go. They're never able to fix them; I don't give a goddam what doctor they go to. My wife had back problems. She was a waitress and hurt her back, and even the best specialists in the country can't fix it.

We have so many poor people today. In our industry, half the families have to work two jobs, the husband or the wife. The wife goes to work and the husband comes home, and they pass like ships in the night. They get together maybe on their day off. You take our membership, the Blacks and the minorities. If you could see the struggle they're going through. They know what it is not to have education, so they're striving to put their children through college. If they get them to go, it costs maybe $4,000 a year. How can they afford it? And the women. I'm glad to see that more and more of them are becoming electricians and getting skilled, high-paying jobs. It makes me very happy to see this. I always like to see people who are poor get a break.

We had a committee from the auto workers and ourselves to help with the problems of the Black ghetto in Watts, California. This was before the riots. We put our money together, we had a little office, and we were trying to get them some transportation. An amazing thing. I never forgot it. Everything around our offices in Watts was burned out, but here was our little office, not a hit. It brought tears to my eyes, to think that they really knew we were trying to help them, we weren't just bullshitting.

I can't stop telling about the exciting life I've led in the labor movement. In my day I'd find that the workers were always being short changed. Our leaders were not the best in the early days of labor. Most of them drank too much. Most of them were uneducated. But the labor movement moved in spite of the leadership. We also had some great leaders.

I wouldn't have gone into any other profession if I had an opportunity, as I look back now. I don't want to be a lawyer. I don't want to be a priest. I don't want to be nothing. I want to be a labor leader. I've had the most exciting life. When I look back at all of the years. An enjoyable life. When I go to bed I sleep soundly. I know that I can't do all that I want to do. But I've helped a hell of a lot of people. If it wasn't for the union they wouldn't be helped. I look at the children and I look back at my life, and I know that without the union none of the kids would ever have broken out. This to me is the labor movement.

I don't think anybody can make a better America but the labor movement. If the leaders of corporate America were labor leaders they'd all be in jail. They're unjust. They exploit their workers and cheat their customers. They all steal money, and they put up bribes for everyone else. I've never seen a millionaire executed. And as long as there are no millionaires being executed, sent to the gas chamber, I'm against capital punishment.

INSIDE THE ORGANIZATION

Women are outsiders in most organizations. Or they sit in the balcony, the back seat, the bleachers. In any case, they do not (usually) have a clear view of how the organization works, where it came from, where it might be going, who its principal actors are, or where power is located in it. They either stand outside the forest, or they cannot see the forest for the trees. The advantage of their perspective, of course, is that, standing among the trees as they do, they get a close-up view of their general condition that others miss. Both perspectives are important, close-up and distant.

Because women need a better view of the larger picture, these notes on the union and its history are included here. The notes are introductory rather than definitive. They suggest what information might be useful to those seeking more central roles in the union—or to those wishing to press "women's issues"—or to those simply wanting to know more about the union.

IN THEIR OWN WORDS

THE OLD DAYS*

Back in the thirties none of the other unions wanted janitors. The AFL especially looked down on them: "They're unskilled and they shouldn't be in craft unions." We wanted them, so in the thirties, we went after health care and the public sector. School janitors, city hall janitors, hospital janitors. No one was organizing them and they were terribly exploited, still are. AFSCME was still a small Wisconsin-based civil service group. We started organizing hospitals on the west coast on the heels of the big general strike in the thirties. Now we've got the whole Bay area, and about 28,000 people employed in an association of hospitals.

We organized at the bottom, and gradually our people said: "Hey, everybody above us needs to be in the union too." Our janitors spent their dues money to build up the other sections. They had to overcome the fear people had of belonging to a janitor's union, and that's still a problem.

Breakthroughs in hospital organizing were also made by Leon Davis of 1199, (retail-wholesale), and Jerry Wurf (AFSCME) deserves credit in the public sector. Organizing was already focused on municipal and county hospitals, but Wurf helped bust it loose. We did it in Chicago, Detroit and California. Since the sixties, we have moved pretty fast. The major growth came after George Hardy became International president in 1972.

In 1943 the union had about 50,000 members, mainly in building service. Now we have about a million members, and the real strength of the union is still in two locals, the Chicago flat janitors, who work in apartment houses, and the New York building service group.

Elizabeth Grady, one of our early union women, represented the bathhouse attendants. The baths were like the old Roman baths, with swimming pools and showers in them. They were found mainly in the midwest, in Milwaukee and Chicago and such cities. Elizabeth Grady became an executive board member of the union in about 1940, so we had a woman quite early, but she died in the fifties and we didn't get another woman on the board until the early seventies.

---

*Most of the material in this section comes from International officers and staff, especially Sylvia Kassalow, June McMahon, Dick Murphy, Bob Welsh, John Geagan, Stephanie Keener, Leonore Stoffel, George Hardy.

The Building Service Employee's Union was chartered in 1921 and its first president was William Quesse. The union's name was changed in 1968 to the Service Employees' International Union.

In New York the men and women once had separate locals. The women cleaned the offices, and the men did the heavy duty cleaning, running the floor waxing machines, climbing the ladders. Now they're in the same local, our biggest, which has about 60,000 members. There were pay differentials between light cleaners and heavy cleaners until fairly recently. In the unionized parts of the industry, they've been wiped out.

The union's founders were predominantly Irish Catholic and we still have a lot of Irish leadership. George Hardy was born in Canada and he was one of those people like his predecessor, David Sullivan, who put the union together in the big cities during the thirties. The leaders had themselves worked as janitors. George Hardy was a janitor, a school janitor, a theater janitor. He can talk about it for hours. People out in the field love him. His father founded the union on the west coast. Pop Hardy was a legend and died a young man. He was an International vice president and he would have been International president had he lived.

After the war, George and his father got rid of the corrupt gangsters in the union. They got a bus and went all over the country organizing the rank-and-file dissidents. A guy named George Scalese, who was the right hand man of Al Capone, had taken over the union for a few years in the late thirties and ran it out of Chicago. Some of the stories from that period are incredible. George and his father turned the union around. In New York State, Thomas Dewey who was district attorney, helped clean it out. When the good guys took over in the early forties they moved the union's headquarters and treasury to Milwaukee because it had a reputation for being a very honest city and having honest police.

This union has a reputation for doing a lot with women. It's really George. It started with him. He's got some very deep convictions about that. They come from the fact that his father was black-balled in San Francisco as a labor organizer, so the only income in the family came from his mother who was a laundry worker. They lived in tents as migrant workers. From that very visceral feeling, "My mother supported us," it was equal pay, equal rights with him from day one. I don't think he understood what the hue-and-cry over women's lib was all about. It was simply his mother.

In the forties he took on Franklin Roosevelt to get equal pay for women janitors in our contracts. When he became president of the union he integrated the male and female locals, expanded the board and put the first women on it. From there he put women on staff in the field research operations, and encouraged locals to hire women. It really changed the face of SEIU. The law had a big effect on this change, no question. But mainly it was *him*.

George was in the general strike in San Francisco. He tells great stories about that strike in our organizing workshop. The whole city was shut down. George uses this story to psych up the workshop. His job was to close down the barber shop, and if they wouldn't do it, he was to throw the barber's pole through the window. Now he's got the barber's curse. A bald head.

BACKDROP: THE HOSPITAL INDUSTRY

Hospital work is a women's industry. That's why it's one of the lowest paid in the country. It's been low wage, low status since its inception. What's interesting is how it is changing. In places like San Francisco, for example, where SEIU has had every hospital organized for ten years and been in the field for 35 years, the contracts have gotten very good. In an unorganized situation, people are at the minimum wage. The difference in wage rates between our better contracts in the big northern cities and the small non-union towns in the South is immense. Twice as much. The industry dictates that.

In the last 20 years the health care industry really exploded. In California, for instance, it's the fourth largest industry in the state. It's a labor rather than capital intensive industry, and it employs a lot of minorities because it's low wage. In California the only people that are paid less are farm workers.

The city and county hospitals serve the community. State hospitals have a special function. They are what some people call "nut houses." Besides the public hospitals, there are two other kinds of hospitals: non-profit and proprietary.

About 7,000 hospitals in the U.S. are non-profit—the Catholic, Methodist, university hospitals, and so forth. They are community-based and run by boards of directors, but they are not public. They can't show a profit on the books, so they often hide it in the budget under "undistributed reserve." The "profits" are supposed to be plowed back into services, but they aren't.

At one hospital in Washington, D.C., for instance, I bet there's at least two million dollars sitting in bank accounts. They're non-interest accounts because the board of directors of that hospital are bankers. They bank the money and don't pay interest. It's awful, scandalous. There's no regulation of profit.

Then there are about a thousand hospitals that are run *for profit*, owned by doctors or bankers. Proprietary hospitals, businesses. Almost all the hospitals in New York City are organized and in general the SEIU has the proprietaries. Historically, this is how things were divided up. In New York the proprietaries are a small part of the whole scene, but the wages in them are much higher than in the other hospitals. The owners save money in lots of other ways. They only take patients with insurance or the ability to pay. They don't get patients dumped on them like public hospitals do. The non-profits are about the same as public hospitals in most places, and the proprietaries are just money makers.

THE INTERNATIONAL UNION

The SEIU is one of the largest unions in the AFL-CIO. About a third of its members are in health care and about a third are public employees. The balance are in building service, gas workers, industrial, public events (race tracks, ball parks, stadiums). Race track jobs are among the highest paying we have. People work five hours per day and make terrific wages. They're political appointments most of them. They're not covered by the National Labor Relations Act, so it's a closed shop. The jobs are our jobs, political jobs, very closely guarded jobs.

The International level of the union has two principal officers, the president and the secretary-treasurer, and nine vice presidents who are elected at large by the convention.

Most of them are presidents of large locals and have a substantial political base. Being International VPs doesn't change what they do in their locals. It only means they come to board meetings, make policy, and get assignments to do certain things with other locals.

Then we have a 34 member executive board, most of them elected at large by the convention. They superintend the policy of the union, and they're paid, but not much. All of them have local union jobs, and use them as International reps essentially.

Any local with more than 5,000 members can have a seat on the board, so when the board meets, we're meeting with 70 percent of the International union. The board meets twice a year and conventions and elections are held every four years.

The International has a national legislative person and a state-level political action person who works mainly out in the field. We recruit a lot of our International staff from outside the union, but we make a real effort to bring in people from the ranks. Local staffs usually come out of the ranks. Our stewards' training program is pretty good now and it turns up leadership that can become staff.

We also have *councils* that work on legislation in the states and carry on mutual aid between locals. The council is not a big structure in SEIU and it's a creature of the local unions, not the national office. We have 20 research people in the field, all paid by the International. That's a big feature of this union. Sometimes they take assignments from councils, but essentially they're called on by the locals.

The International worked hard on the hospital cost containment bill, trying to put a cap on hospital spending and trying to provide room under the cap for decent wages. We have been deeply involved in national health insurance, medicare, health planning, health training. We worked hard on ERA. At the time of the extension, they didn't want labor out front, so we worked but kept a very low profile. We lobbied on pregnancy disability. We're especially interested in minimum wage legislation because of the low wage people we organize— not that we tie our contracts to the minimum wage but a few are written that way. Then we share the general interests of the labor movement— workers' compensation, unemployment compensation, food stamps. When we good on strike, most of our people are immediately eligible for food stamps. Sometimes they can exist only because of the food stamps.

LOCALS

In the SEIU, locals have an enormous amount of power. We don't have any really small locals. They are all a thousand members or better, so they can afford to underwrite staff. Locals have almost total responsibility for negotiations, administration of contracts and servicing. They engage in a lot of mutual aid so it's a healthy, dynamic structure. If they request staff from the International, we may send people in. Per capita dues to the International are very low, the lowest in the AFL-CIO, so the International does not have a big pile of money.

Gradually we've gotten minorities and women integrated into local leadership. People are less afraid and more friendly with women leadership. They find the women are good workers and good union people, so they work together. Exposure has done the education job.

ORGANIZING

At the International we design front-end organizing campaigns. We identify large areas of the public sector that need organizing and we initiate drives and open up new areas. When locals are in place, they do the organizing, with underwrite money from us. But it's a local-oriented effort.

A lot of our locals just didn't organize. They were sitting with a few thousand members, and the leaders were getting re-elected, so they were comfortable. Why organize? Today they are very actively organizing under the same local leadership. Hardy did it. He preached about it all the time. He prodded our executive board to do it, lectured them, shamed them, anything he could. He got incredibly high when he was victorious. You made his day by calling in the morning and saying,

"We won an election for seven food service workers." He'd run in and put it on the chart.

Sometimes he drrew the line. There was a question about organizing the hookers, the Coyotes. George finally said "no." He was getting sick of looking at the expense reports: "Man is not made of wood— $20.00." That was the end of the local. Shut it down.

Hardy loved organizing. He developed an organizing manual, the most complete one around. He went around personally and taught the staff how to organize. He'd go through the book, from page one to page 100. He did this all over the country, a week at a time, every year. Himself! He also set up classes in how to price a contract, collective bargaining, and he sat there as a student and as a teacher. One person *can* do it.

He went out his first year as president and spent the whole organizing treasury. He'll tell you that. Spent $2 million the first year and we didn't gain a member. He says, "I could have thrown the money down the sewer and at least had the pleasure of seeing it float away." He spent money so we could grow. Finally we did.

Organizing big hospitals these days is almost impossible. It's the effort and money it takes to organize. The resources against you are immense: the industry itself, the way it operates with third party payers, a lot of pressures on costs, and a lot of resistance to unions. People may gave you a PR answer to this, but the bottom line is a lot of frustration.

Nursing homes? Some unions won't organize them. They could any time they wanted to, but it undercuts wage rates in an area. You could have a practical nurse in a nursing home who can't get more than $3.00 an hour and you're bargaining for $6.00 an hour in a hospital down the street.

FIELD NOTES FROM WOMEN ORGANIZERS

The union has three strikes against it: lack of union consciousness, lack of organizing rights in some hospitals until 1974, and women workers with no history of organizing. RNs are among the toughest people to organize. I've organized engineers and other professionals so I have some experience. The RNs have ideas about "professionalism," so they hold themselves above the other workers and feel they are much more important. Professionalism is like a lead weight around their necks, and around the necks of all employees. It divides people, separates them into small classifications. Everyone feels, "I'm more professional because I went to school for six months, and I take care of *this*, not *that*."

It's very tough convincing them that this is a *job*, that the hospital has millions in the bank, and that their voice can only be heard through a contract that spells out their rights. It has to do with women's position in society, the way they're treated, and the general lack of respect for them. RNs are a microcosm of women's position. But it's worse for them because a lot of them still think they've made it. "How dare you talk about organizing a union? We're not waitresses." It's the lone ranger mentality. Solve all your problems by yourself. That's why a lot of them make less than factory workers. That's changing as women become more militant and more conscious of what their real status is.

Low wage jobs with high turnover are the hardest to organize. With people coming and going, how can you organize? It happens that women get these low wage, high turnover jobs.

In a hospital, you're working in a place that takes care of people. It's difficult to know who you're fighting against. A lot of times people think the problem is *themselves:* "I can't get along with Mary or Pete," or "I can't get along with the RN's." You have to be very tuned in to the way people perceive their job, and you have to be careful about explaining the union to them. They don't know about unions. People in factories know what a union is, and they know that the boss is no good, and that he's trying to take money off them. In the hospital, people don't see that everyone is making money but them. You tell them, *"The Wall Street Journal* says the drug companies are enjoying the biggest boom in history." They say, "What does that mean?" You have to explain it.

In organizing hospitals, I always get in touch with the women first. The men will follow women in anything. You find out who is the most vocal woman in the hospital, somebody also with a sense of humor. That's your lead person, your publicity. I always tell that person the truth, let her know the odds, the limitations. I talk to her outside the institution, in a restaurant maybe, and get to know her and her likes and dislikes. Two or three times I'll do that. Then I'll slowly approach her about the union. "What do you think?" I let her do the talking. It's more difficult to get a man to go into a restaurant, so you find out his habits. At one hospital, a man parked his car about two blocks away, so we struck up a conversation with him near his car.

I always have a floor chart of the hospital showing exactly who is who and on what shift, before I go in to organize. Then I go in with a male organizer. You get there early in the morning—if it's, say, dietary—and go around saying "Hi" to people. The men will speak to a woman a little quicker than they will to another man. The men are much more afraid than women, so we approach them a little different. Eventually they'll speak.

When you help someone, word gets out. People call and say, "Can you help with *my* problem?" It's a lot of work, but I go and help them, especially if it's a disgruntled former union member. Those people are the worst in an organizing drive. They hate all unions and they talk against them. Employers like to hire them because it's the surest way to keep the union out. So if I come across one, I bend over backwards to help him.

Because of the fiscal crisis in many cities, everyone is very fearful. They don't know whether their institution is going to close or cut back on services. In southern California, it's like organizing in the South. A lot of migrants there don't know about unions, and a lot of them don't speak the language.

Most men like a sort of tough and rough union image. You need a different image when you organize women. You have to be more concerned about interpersonal communications. You need to talk to people in small groups and have their concerns discussed and understood. You have to put more stress on the product of peoples' work, like patient care.

When I organize I make special efforts to get women involved. That doesn't necessarily mean addressing issues like child care. It means making meetings easier for them to attend, and providing child care at those meetings. Some issues are different for women. I'll be very honest with you. Issues come up around organizing that the union has not been in shape to really confront yet. We haven't nurtured these issues. I hope there will be a time when we will.

In the first hospital I organized, the workers were afraid of losing their jobs, so we sneaked around corners and talked. That was hard. Finally I decided, "I can't do this. I'm going crazy. What are we sneaking around for? I'm not having an affair with these people. I only want to organize them!" I decided that the only thing to do was attack management in some fashion, and bring them out in the open. I did and it helped a lot.

My son and I worked long hours talking to people in the hospital. The guard they'd send after me had a gun and he was always shaking. I told him he shouldn't have a gun in his hand, he might shoot himself. They towed my car away a couple of times. "Get this woman out of Long Beach." But I loved it. It was good to see people rally, when at first it was so hard to pull them close. Finally it got so they weren't always towing my car or sending for the guard.

When we organize, we try to focus on the technical workers. If you can organize *them*, they'll get the rest for you. They're respected and listened to by the others. We organize nurses by targeting a group within a certain classification and telling them what you can do for them. In my experience, clericals are the hardest to organize. The boss gives them a little here and there. If the secretary is a couple of minutes late, she won't be disciplined. Clerks like to say, "My boss is an important executive and is well-known in the media." That makes her happy even though there's no compensation for her in it.

People say women are harder to organize than men, but the fact that they are so exploited can make them easier to organize. It's safer to say that younger employees, men and women, are harder to organize. They're new to labor and not very educated in unionism. The older employees see the need for a union.

Some women say they can't join the union because they need permission from their husbands. That is a cop-out. The same woman when she's in trouble will say, "I'm in trouble and I need the union."

I say, "You couldn't join last month because your husband wouldn't let you."

"Well," she says, "It's my money, and I can join if I want to."

The chief problem women workers talk about is time. They're responsible not only for their work time but for time at home. In organizing that makes it very difficult to hold meetings or talk to the women.

Organizing is a matter of selling yourself. If I *believe* in you, then you can sell it to me. If I *don't* believe in you, I will be turned off, whether you're man, woman or child. People don't know beans about what you are selling them. So they have to believe in *you* in order to be sold.

The biggest hesitation about joining the union is the strike issue. They think they can't strike because of the patients. You assure them that this is a responsible union and that you're not going to ask them to leave their patients high and dry. You tell them they will vote on whether or not to strike, and that if a strike is called it will be orderly and emergency care will be given in the hospitals. Assuring them the union is responsible is the best organizing tool I have.

LEGISLATIVE NOTES

(FROM DICK MURPHY, LEGISLATIVE DIRECTOR)

The major national issue we've worked on was the coverage of non-profit hospital employees by the National Labor Relations Act. When we finally got it through, it was the first change in the Act in 30 years. We've added more than 75,000 hospital workers since then, in our union alone.

Our union had the bill introduced in Congress in the late fifties and every year thereafter we had it re-introduced just to keep it alive. I was up on the hill in 1970 and wandered into Frank Thompson's office to talk to Duffy, his counsel on the labor committee, about the bill. He then talked to Thompson and they decided, "Let's hold some hearings." The hearings were held without any major opposition at all from the industry. They never thought anything could happen on the bill. Duffy was a marvelous strategist. When calls came into his office he would say, "This is not controversial legislation. It covers a lot of poor people, deprived of their rights under the National Labor Relations Act. Nobody seems to be actively opposing it."

Thompson put the bill on the calendar and it passed the House. No problem. When it went to the Senate, Andy Biemiller, the AFL-CIO man, called up and said "Don't bring it up." He hadn't expected us to get it through the House, and he was afraid of all the amendments that might be added. It would attach to the labor bill, he thought, and we'd lose all kinds of stuff. So we had to drop it.

In January of 1972 I asked Hardy to go directly to Meany for permission to go ahead with our bill. Meany said, "Go ahead, but we'll need clearance from all the unions that have hospital workers." There were seven unions and all saw this as a great chance to organize the 1.7 million hospital workers who were not covered by the law. So, with AFL-CIO backing, we went ahead full blast.

During the Congressional hearings, they had nuns up there testifying, "There's going to be blood in the operating rooms. They'll go on strike and pull out the plugs as they leave." We assured them that any time we went on strike, even for recognition, we'd warn the hospitals well in advance. Taft said, "How about a ten day strike notice in the law?" We said "fine." The bill finally passed the second reading in the House by a close vote.

Funny things happened. After the bill passed the Senate, and was ready for the President's signature, they couldn't find the papers. They had been signed by the majority leader, the Speaker of the House, and others, and they were missing. After a two day search they found them in a Senate chamber drawer.

The President has to sign the bill in ten days. If he doesn't sign by then, the bill doesn't become law. The final expiration day was the *Friday before the Monday that Nixon resigned the Presidency.* We knew that Nixon would sign it, but at two o'clock on Friday afternoon, I got a call saying "I got bad news for you. The American Hospital Association got to Weinberger at HEW and asked him to get the President to veto it. I'm going to do whatever I can, but it looks bad."

I could have died. I was at home first of all. I had to use my neighbor's phone for outgoing calls, and kept my own phone for incoming calls. I didn't even have time to go to the office. I called everyone, the AFL, the Laborers, the Teamsters, Taft, Nixon's guys. Nobody could get through to the President. Nixon was on the west coast in San Clemente. At 6 pm I finally got a call saying Fitzsimmons, the Teamster president, had gotten to Nixon and that he had agreed to sign it. Amazing! Bernstein and Woodward in their book, by the way, say that Nixon was raving drunk in the White House that Friday. He was actually in San Clemente and that was the last bill he signed as President.

Ten

PERSPECTIVES ON THE WOMEN'S MOVEMENT

The women's movement and the labor movement are exactly the same movement. Equity on the job. That's it. We support the women's movement wall-to-wall.

I don't see that women's lib has changed anything in hospitals. There's not that many men's jobs that women want. Lower paid women want to know where the next rent check is coming from. Period.

We asked hospital workers what they thought about the "women's movement," or what they call "women's lib." Some supported "lib" all the way, some opposed it all the way. Most had mixed responses, some strong reservations, and a sense of being untouched by the movement.

Many of them thought that, by disturbing traditional sex roles, "lib" makes men respect women less and "respect" is apparently an important word to them, respect from employers and from men. Many thought that "lib's" main interest was in getting women to work at "men's jobs" and even to "become men." Their objections to doing "men's work" included the belief that the work is not respectable or "ladylike," that it is heavy and dirty work, that women are not qualified for it, and that women should not work among men. It also included the conviction that certain jobs "belong" to men, almost as if they had historic property rights to them, and that men need the jobs to support their families.

Many other women felt that "lib" had done a lot of good and that, "if a woman can do a man's job, more power to her." But, they often added, women should not be *expected* to do "men's work." Almost all agree with "lib" about equal pay when men and women do the same work, and equal opportunities when they want the same jobs.

Their scepticism about women doing "men's work" is based on both myths and realities. The reality is that the men they know usually perform heavy physical labor, in the mines and steel mills of Pennsylvania, for example. Women do not envy men those jobs. The *myth* is the assumption that all (or even most) men's jobs are physically demanding and risky. In fact, most men's jobs (even among blue collar workers) probably entail less risk and physical stress than do the jobs of women hospital workers.

Reflecting their concern about being "pushed" into men's jobs, 52 percent of the hospital workers surveyed said they *agreed* that, "more and more, women are expected to do work that should be done by men." Perhaps even more significantly, among the women leaders polled, an astonishing 41 percent *agreed* with the statement.

Even more surprising, 51 percent of women leaders *agreed* that, "The women's rights movement has caused men to treat women less courteously or less respectfully," compared with only 27 percent of women workers. The difference may be explained by the fact that women union leaders work with men on non-traditional jobs, while hospital workers still work in a women's world.

On another issue, 20 percent of workers and 16 percent of women unionists *agreed* that, "Women are getting jobs for which they are not qualified, just because they are women." In interviews with these women, however, no mention was made of any personal experience with women getting jobs for which they were unqualified.

On the more positive side, 55 percent of workers and 86 percent of the leaders *agreed* that, "The womens' rights movement has helped women get better jobs and better pay." While these responses are definitely positive, especially among leaders, it should also be noted that almost half of the women workers *disagreed* with the statement. Opinion, then, is quite evenly divided among these hospital workers on the effects of the women's movement on jobs and pay.

Also on the positive side, 48 percent of workers *agreed* that, "The women's rights movement has encouraged me to stand up more for my rights." Perhaps this is the most positive response by workers found in the survey, for it indicates that almost half of the women workers perceive the womens' movement as having a positive impact on their own personal lives.

On more general issues, 83 percent of workers *agreed* that, "Sex discrimination in this country is a serious problem" (65 percent of them *strongly agreed*). And 94 percent *agreed* that, "The Equal Rights Amendment will have a positive effect on the lives of women."

Hospital workers have had very little personal experience with the womens' movement, their information coming mainly from hear-say and the media. Women leaders have had much more contact, through both college and work experience, and some of them came to unionism in the first place through contact with feminist ideas, at least. The movement's impact on hospital workers may also come, therefore, through interaction with these women leaders.

The indirect impact of the women's movement on hospital workers has probably exceeded the direct impact. That is, the movement has "opened the eyes" of many workers, encouraged them to stand up more for their rights, and exposed them to the feminist views of women union leaders—thereby encouraging them to stand up to employers and to unionize. The *direct* impact of the movement—through the issues raised by it—has been less substantial. This subject will be discussed in later chapters.

THE COALITION OF LABOR UNION WOMEN

CLUW brings a new constituency of millions of women union members to the women's movement. It also brings a new concern for the 80 percent of employed women who work in *non*-professional and *non*-managerial jobs—workingclass women. CLUW was well-known to the women union leaders surveyed, but because of its relative youth, it was unfamiliar to most women workers. Of hospital workers surveyed, however, 89 percent *agreed* that, "There is a need for an organization which brings women together from many different unions to work on common concerns." Since this is CLUW's main purpose, support for its goals are a good deal more pervasive than knowledge about the organization.

Among women leaders surveyed, 85 percent *agreed* that, "CLUW has made union leadership more sensitive to the concerns of women union members" and 76 percent *agreed* that, "CLUW has helped get women more actively involved in their unions." Asked what two activities CLUW should concentrate on, the one most often chosen by women leaders was "education and training," followed by others as listed below:

What two activities should CLUW concentrate on?

Activity	Percent of women union leaders selecting the activity
Education and Training	47%
Pressuring union leaders to use their influence to help elect, hire, and promote more women within their unions	30
Bringing union women into contact with each other	29
National legislation and policy	26
Research on the problems and needs of working women	22
Giving support to union organizing drives	21
Pressuring unions to work more aggressively on the enforcement of sex discrimination laws	12

Thus, the highest priorities for CLUW, as perceived by these women union leaders, relate mainly to facilitating the participation of women in union leadership roles.

≈

THE WOMEN—IN THEIR OWN WORDS

ROLES AND RIGHTS
We had a big fight at our Thanksgiving table because my sister refused to give money to the midget baseball team. One of the little boys had told her, "the coach says there ain't no girls on the team so there ain't gonna be none." My sister said, "If that's how your coach feels, he ain't gonna get no money from me." All the men in the family thought that was dumb. The women thought she was right.

I don't see doing dangerous work. My father works for the telephone company. He has two women under him now who have to climb telephone poles. The first day at work one lady was upset. She had broken one of her long fingernails off. You have to be prepared for that kind of work. If you want to be a complete women's libber, you have to settle for looking and acting like a man.

A woman could get hurt, lifting heavy boxes, getting on a scaffold, fighting fires. The real hard work—and running the country—should be left to men. You've got to let a man feel he's a man. He'll lose respect if you dominate him and do things he should do.

Coal miners don't like the fact that women are in the mines with them, and coal miners' wives don't like it either. Women working on construction, I can't see it. Women are more fragile than men. Their whole chemistry is different. Why should they do a man's job and keep him from making a living for his family? They're getting carried away, competing with a man for everything. It would be like a man trying to have a baby.

If I wanted to be a truck driver, my God, what kind of stamina would I have to have? Would I be able to pop pills like they do and drive all night long? If a woman can do it, give it to her, but not just because you *have* to put women in that job.

I'd like to hear what the women's libbers have to say. They're doing a lot of good, but they may be doing some wrong too. We're told that in factories a woman has to lift heavy things now, whereas before she didn't. If you're paid as much, you have to do what men do.

I'm not saying I'm not as smart as a man. I just can't handle wheelbarrows and things like that. In a hospital, women can do anything a man does. There's not much heavy work.

I'm not a women's libber to an extreme point. I can do many jobs as well as a man, but not all of them. I wouldn't go into a coal mine and work. Thank God I'm too old for the draft. We have a nurse up in surgery that's leaving the hospital. She's going to drive a diesel truck from L.A. to Phoenix. I told her, "Are you sure this is what you want to do?"

She said, "I've always wanted to do this. I went to school for it, trucking school, and I'm ready to leave here now."

I said, "Who's going to ride with you?"

She said, "Me and my Doberman."

If she can do it, wonderful. If a woman's got the brains to drive a diesel or work on a car, why not? The men's jobs pay more, and money is hard to get these days. You can't save anything. All you do is make ends meet. I think it's a challenge to work against the man. I like it, and I like to beat him. I really do.

My husband came home and said, "We've got a woman working in the foundry."

And I said, "How do you feel about it?"

"She's doing her job."

It's a free country, so why not go all the way? Let the world know that we are capable.

The positive things about women need to be stressed. Women may demonstrate their emotions more, but that's not a weakness. That's a strength. Women need to hold onto their unique nature and their special attributes and not apologize for them. You don't have to be tough. You don't have to run a mile in four minutes. That's not important. The women's movement was apologetic in a way. They initially grabbed onto qualities that were defined as male, "Okay, if we adapt these qualities, if we're aggressive, if we're tough, if we do this and that, then we'll be better off." That was the wrong direction. It would have been better to say, "Listen, this is how women are and isn't it wonderful? We're strong and we're worthy of recognition and we can do all *these* things."

A lot of the resentment against women's lib comes from the sitting-at-home type of women. I support my family so I can't stay home and play house. I've got to work every day, and I want a chance to make as much money as the men make. I like the freedom women are getting and if I wasn't such an introvert, I'd be marching with the women.

One mistake the women's groups made was being a little elitist about housewives. They should have given them recognition along with the women who get on the corporate board of directors. They encouraged women to get out of the home, but many women, for very valid reasons, couldn't get out of the home, or chose not to. They should have been told, "You can go out and do these other things, but if you choose to be *this*, a housewife, you're no less a woman."

It's not true that women are fed up with housework chores and want to go to work. If women go to work it's because they need to work. I'm certainly not fed up with *my* kitchen. I have a marvelous kitchen and I love it. And my family would love to have me there instead of telling them to get a TV dinner from the freezer.

RESPECT

Men aren't courteous to women like they used to be—opening a door when she gets out of a car, bringing flowers or candy. The men won't get up on the bus and give you a seat. They say, "Godamit, you belong to women's lib." I say, "I don't belong to no women's lib. I got to set down and rest my bones."

Once upon a time if a man swore in front of me, I wouldn't go out with him. Now they call you anything. When a person treats me like that, shove it. I'm against it, 100 percent.

A friend of mine stood in line for gas, but it was self service and she couldn't pump gas.

She said to the man, "Would you help me?"

He said, "No, you do it yourself."

She almost cried she was so mad. Women are nuts. They try to keep up with a man, but they can't. Going out in coal mines, factories, or road work is not for women. They think they can show off, listen to that foul language, and do filthy things. Then they get mad if the man won't help them pump gas.

The women say, "I'm working and bringing home as much money as you, and you must hear me." If she wants a pair of shoes, she buys them. The Mexican man, the Black man, the poor man, they all need a woman to back them. If he doesn't have support from some woman, he's had it, baby. Forget it. They can't make it without the woman. Now he respects her. He's afraid. He feels like now she's got a good job, and she's going to school, and she's going to get away from him. This is the poor man's attitude. "I need this woman and she's going to get away from me. She's the mother of my children. If she could just stay here. I'm getting older and I'm not making much money. We can pool our resources and live together."

Without her help, he can't make it. That's why you find all the alcoholics and drug addicts. They feel sorry for themselves if they don't have a woman.

Some women say men treat them with less respect now. What do they mean by "respect"? Having doors opened? Is that respect? I'd much rather that a man listen to me than open a door for me. The men are listening to women more, and looking at them differently. More and more they want women to have some kind of life of their own. They say, "Okay, baby. I'm proud to see you've made it." He knows she's entitled.

If you give respect, you're going to get respect, whatever you are. Maybe men don't open doors for us, but that stopped a long time ago. The only time they did it was when they were courting. After you got married, you got into that car the best way you could.

CONSCIOUSNESS: THE MUTUAL IMPACT OF THE LABOR AND WOMEN'S MOVEMENTS

When we organized a home for retarded people, a young woman counselor with a master's degree in psychology told us that the union gave her, for the first time in her life, an understanding that she could change other people's attitudes and lives. She was a graduate in psychology and she had never learned how to change people! She got people to vote for the union, hang in there, and not be intimidated by management. It was the best thing that ever happened to her, she said. It raised her consciousness.

The union changes your personality. Women become more assertive, they don't let people walk on them as much, and they know more about what they want. The next step is to link that up with the question of women in general, and that's only a matter of time.

Even though they might not think of themselves as feminists, a woman of 18 today is a thousand light years away from where I was at 18. And it's because of the women's movement. My kid sister at 18 is not a political person, but she's going to be a doctor. When I was her age, I'd say, "I am going to be a lawyer," and everybody snickered. My mother would say, "You should be a teacher."

The women have opened their eyes. They don't have to be dominated any more. They can take care of themselves and their families. Before, if a woman's husband died, the poor woman was lost. She wasn't able to work. Women are no longer so shy and they'll complain if something's wrong. They're more aware of their own strengths.

The women's movement changed how I think about myself. Now I think the sky's the limit. Ten years ago I hated being a woman. It seemed like the guys got all the good jobs. Women today don't put up with the shenanigans their grandmothers, or even their mothers, put up with.

Women can try to raise male consciousness, but it works better to change practices. You can hate me as much as you want, but by God, I'm going to get paid the same as anybody else. I don't care particularly if somebody likes me or not, but I do care that I get the benefits that are coming to me.

In the hospital, people don't talk about women's lib. If they do, they think it's for old ladies. Most of the people I work with are young and don't follow those things. They say, "That's for ladies that sit home and do nothing." They don't think they're union ladies. They don't think that those organizations are for them. I don't know why.

THE COALITION OF LABOR UNION WOMEN

The women's movement says, "Women have the right to be bankers and capitalists. Let's have women own Chase Manhattan so they can invest their money in South Africa." If that's what the women's movement is about, I can't give it much support. CLUW is an indication that the women's movement has become more concerned about workingclass women.

CLUW does not posture itself so stridently that its recommendations are ignored. It's been immensely successful in winning acceptance from the powers that be, which is important. It's difficult to operate in an adversary situation all the time.

It gives people with something to say a chance to participate in the labor movement. It also has the broader job of identifying with rank-and-file women and giving them a chance to be heard. Its leadership is well-respected, and it has a good track record with labor, but in my opinion about half the CLUW board should be rank-and-file. Maybe women from the ranks wouldn't worry about their jobs being jeopardized if they spoke out.

One thing I was happy about at the last CLUW convention was that older women who had been involved in unions in the early days got up and spoke about their struggles. The feeling of having continuity of history really helps me, makes me feel less isolated.

I'd like to see CLUW get more into national child care availability. A major problem that working women have is getting decent child care. I'd like to see federal money and corporate profits put into child care facilities at the work place, so women could see their children or nurse them if they wanted to.

Sometimes you feel like a voice in the wilderness. You feel people are tired of listening to you say it over and over, and that nobody else is fighting. You really need an association like CLUW to get you across those bridges. It's hard to do it by yourself. Doing it in groups, and building consciousness in groups, is the way to go about it. That way you avoid the elitism that is so disastrous, not only to the person but to what we're trying to do—build a trade union society that *everybody* can function in. Sometimes when people do it all on their own, they turn into what they were fighting against. They have this attitude about being better than other women. "I made it. Why can't they? I'm superwoman. They're going to let me into the club because I'm wonderful."

Eleven

WOMEN'S ISSUES DISCRIMINATION, SEGREGATION, COMPARABLE WORTH

They treat women as if they were coming out of religious orders, without family, children, or husband.

The problem I see is that management treats women equally as crummy as they treat men.

Looked at one way, all issues are women's issues. Looked at another way, almost none are. Most women union leaders apparently feel that the truth about this lies midway between the two extremes and that "women workers have different problems and concerns than men workers" but that many problems are common to both sexes. Yet about one in every seven women leaders we surveyed denied that any special women's issues exist or that their women members had any concerns other than those of male members. Interestingly, some of these women were the most stridently "feminist" in their belief that women can do anything men can do, if they try hard enough; what they apparently lack is the feminist sense of the handicapping practices of the male marketplace.

Many problems exist, of course, without being recognized for what they are. Viruses make us sick but they cannot be seen; the moon pulls at the tides but its action is largely invisible. In the workplace, health and safety issues often fall into this invisible category: for example, radiation exposure may be imperceptible but nevertheless very lethal.

Or, people may experience extreme stress from rotating shifts or demanding schedules yet be unaware of either the stress or its cause.

Some problems may be visible yet not perceived as problems because they are *undeveloped*—not pointed out or talked about enough, or not easily solvable. Simply naming the problem—"sexism," "discrimination," "harassment" helps people recognize these issues when they see them, and talk about them with others. Still, most of our maladies and problems already have names and are already high up in our consciousness levels, and while it may not be advisable to ignore what is unseen and undeveloped, it may be even more inadvisable to ignore what is most highly visible to us.

If we wish to comprehend how workingclass women feel, if we wish to organize them or recruit them to feminist or other causes, or if we wish simply to support them as they pursue their own goals, then we should hear what they say about their jobs and their lives. Unions organize workers by listening to the issues they raise, and they survive by continuing to listen and to act on what they hear. Similarly, women's groups organize and survive by listening to their constituents. And women rise to union leadership positions by responding to these problems and in this way creating a base of support for themselves.

To learn more about the priorities of hospital workers, we asked them what they "most dislike about their jobs," and the women most often chose: "scheduling of hours"; "trying to work and raise a family"; "not enough time off"; "staffing" (not enough people to do the work); "the way I'm treated"; and "wages"—in that order. These responses are suggestive, not definitive, of their priorities. The women *leaders* surveyed chose essentially the same issues (for hospital workers), but gave top rating to "the way they're treated," and put "trying to work and raise a family" in fifth place.

Many issues interlock, in particular, staffing and scheduling. The hospital does not hire adequate staff, so the staff on hand works harder, longer, more irregular hours, which creates more turnover and absenteeism, and more staffing and scheduling problems.

DISCRIMINATION AND SEGREGATION

Since job discrimination has been the highest priority issue of the women's movement, it is astonishing that only 21 percent of the hospital workers surveyed identified "discrimination because I am a woman" as a *sizeable* or *great* problem—compared with 72 percent who felt the same about "not enough staff," and 24 percent and 36 percent who felt the same, respectively, about "discrimination because of my age" and "discrimination because of race." This also contrasts with the

83 percent of women who *agreed* that "sex discrimination is a serious problem in this country," but who apparently see that it is a problem for others, not themselves.

Whatever experiences women may have had, sex discrimination obviously pervades hospital life. Sex segregation (one form of discrimination) is almost total and, as with racial segregation, not only are men and women separate, they are very unequal. The discrimination is *institutional* rather than *individual,* directed at women as a class rather than as individuals, so women are less aware of its presence and its impact on them personally. Women work in segregated occupations, so they seldom compete with men for the *same jobs,* and thus seldom experience discrimination against themselves as individuals.

Some women *have* experienced discrimination in competition with men for the same jobs; one woman, for example, felt discriminated against in competition for a chef's job, another woman felt men were given preference on some jobs in pharmacy. Such instances are rare, however, since women and men usually do not seek the same jobs.

Hospital workers are aware that discrimination against women on "men's jobs" exists: 98 percent, for example, *agreed* (and 75 percent *strongly agreed*) that, "There should be more women in the higher positions here at the hospital, such as doctors and administrators." They recognize discrimination at these levels, and they disapprove of it, but most feel they are not touched by it, and in fact, their perceptions have some validity. Even as a class, most hospital workers are not affected very much, directly, by exclusion from "men's jobs" in the hospital.

As an example (a semi-mythical one): Nancy Aide is a nursing assistant, a non-professional. She has never dreamed of becoming a doctor or an administrator. Advanced degrees are required for those jobs. She is a high school graduate. To qualify for these "men's jobs" she would have to spend long years in college. She lacks the interest, perhaps the academic record, and almost certainly the money for it.

She knows about other "men's jobs" in the hospital—blue-collar jobs that do not require college training. Some of them are highly skilled and require long apprenticeships; some are unskilled (ambulance driving, maintenance work, security guards) and require less training. Many, but by no means all, of these jobs require strength and physical risk-taking, so she wonders if she would like the work. She thinks she might try for one of them anyhow, even though the hospital tries to keep women out, because she needs more money. The unskilled blue collar jobs pay a little more than she's making, and the skilled ones a lot more. *The problem is she likes nursing*—what she is doing now—and does not really want to leave it. She might try for practical nursing, but what she really wants is better pay and hours, a lighter work load, and more respect, rather than a different job.

If Nancy Aide decides to become a practical nurse or an RN, she will remain in a "woman's job." If she decides to try for a "man's job," she might make it, and she might be better off as a result. But not many others can follow her, for the number of accessible "men's jobs" in hospitals are finite, and even if all these jobs were shared with women, *the vast majority of women hospital workers would still be exactly where they are.*

It appears, therefore, that one high priority sex discrimination issue—the exclusion of women from "men's jobs"—has rather limited meaning to women hospital workers, whatever its applications to other workingclass women may be.

Registered nurses are something else. As "professionals," they are (or should be) in line for top level "men's jobs," but various forms of discrimination by the hospital and professional schools block their way. Some RNs aspire to these "men's jobs," but again the reality is that most RNs want to be what they *are*, nurses, not doctors or administrators. They want mainly what other hospital workers want, improvements in their jobs. In addition they want more control over the work they do and an enlarged scope of practice.

The exclusion of women from men's jobs in the hospital is not a negligible form of discrimination, however. It is real, present, and obviously in need of legal remedy, but it is not the leading issue for hospital workers.

The women surveyed thought that women can more easily and advantageously move into professional than into blue collar "men's jobs," but their fears that "men's" jobs may be too physically demanding are often unfounded. In Penn hospital, for example, one woman decided to become a "maintenance man." No woman had held the job before, and some of her coworkers felt it was "no place for a woman." As it turned out, the job was far more rewarding, easier, pleasanter than the women's jobs she had left in the dietary department. And the men on the job were far more receptive and helpful to her than any of her coworkers had predicted they would be. Breaking the barriers in this case, however, is more symbolic than real, since the women who might be affected are relatively few. Penetrating such jobs can, nevertheless, serve women's interests by showing them how arbitrary and permeable the barriers between male and female jobs can be—and by opening better jobs to some women.

"Equal pay for equal work" is, of course, a basic sex discrimination issue, one from which the "equal pay for work of comparable value" issue flows. That women should be paid the same wage as men for doing the same work, does not, in retrospect, seem a very revolutionary point of law—any more than did the earlier principle that women should actually be *paid* for the work they do. Still, in the long search for equity, getting legal guarantees on equal pay has been a large step forward, one that was hard fought for by unions. Equal pay, however, is not often at issue in hospitals now. In most places, it has been achieved. Orderlies (males) and nursing assistants (females) were among the few cases where any dispute arose over equal pay. In any event the pay difference (in favor of orderlies) was small and it has been ruled illegal by the courts under the equal pay law.

"Sexual harassment" is another form of sex discrimination about which there is growing awareness. The term has been used rather loosely, however. In popular usage, it has been applied to a broad spectrum of male behaviors, from physical threats and reprisals to off-color jokes, but it is more precisely defined by the Equal Employment Opportunity Commission guidelines. These guidelines establish three criteria for determining if alleged acts of sexual harassment are unlawful:

One, if submission to the conduct is either an explicit or implicit term or condition of employment; Two, if this is used as a basis for an employment decision affecting the employee; Three, if it substantially interferes with work performance or creates an intimidating, hostile, or offensive work environment. Both unwelcomed verbal and physical acts can constitute sex discrimination under Title VII of the Civil Rights Act. Employers are responsible for the actions of their supervisory employees or agents and in some cases for the acts of others when the employer or a supervisory employee knows of or should have known of the behavior.

Given the rising concern about sexual harassment, it was surprising that in our interviews with hospital workers and union staff, the issue (as defined by these EEOC guidelines) was seldom raised as an important one to women. Perhaps it has not surfaced yet or perhaps it is simply not a common or serious complaint in hospitals. Studies show that, in some settings, many women say they have experienced sexual harassment (as they define it) "sometime during their working life," but in the hospital, at the time of this survey, the issue did not compare in severity or extensiveness with other women's issues. Nurses, in particular, talked about unwelcomed advances from doctors, but they were usually far more concerned about issues such as wages, staffing, scheduling. Since the immediate supervisors of hospital workers are often women, sexual harassment may be less pervasive in hospitals than in offices and more integrated work settings. For those women affected by it, of course, sexual harassment can be an extremely serious issue, posing physical danger as well as threats to job security.

A variant of sexual harassment (and of the control males exercise over female subordinates) is more often raised by hospital workers. The issue might be called "sexual favoritism" or the power to grant favors to responsive women and deny them to unresponsive women. In this case, the woman being favored may not define the behavior as harassment, or even find it objectionable, but coworkers are likely to object, as they do to other forms of favoritism.

The problem originates in the male's power to reward responsiveness in women, rather than (as in sexual harassment) to apply sanctions to *un*responsiveness. In cases of sexual favoritism, coworkers may blame the woman more than the man, and they may even charge her with being active rather than passive in the exchange of favors. Whatever the case, the woman does in fact respond to a sexist balance of power: the superior authority of males over females, and the job favors such authority can bestow in exchange for sexual favors.

In cases of sexual favoritism, the redress women may seek is not through the law (since the law does not cover such behavior) but through union rules that reduce the authority of supervisors to grant favors to subordinates.

One approach to women's issues looks at the rules of the marketplace (and its rewards) and says they should be applied impartially to women and men. A second approach agrees that rules should be applied impartially but challenges the bias in the *rules themselves*, a bias based on the fact that the rules are designed in the first place by men, and seldom take account of the special needs, interests, aptitudes of women. The redesign of jobs, work hours, workplaces, etc. are sought in an effort to accommodate these special needs.

An example of job redesign that "fits the job to the worker," rather than the other way around, is found in AT&T's efforts, under duress, to make it easier for women to climb telephone poles by adapting the climbing tool to women's physique and by burying more wires underground.

In the hospital, the redesign of rules would, among other things, take account of the problems involved for women (in time, energy, physical and mental health) in trying to both work and raise a family. The intersection between work and family life was especially important to the women included in our survey—only 21 percent of whom were "never married" and only 14 percent of whom had no children.

Redefining women's issues begins with an inquiry into how women perceive their problems and proceeds of necessity from one work site, one occupation, to another. We have looked at hospital workers in two work sites (and women union leaders from around the country) and, while we may assume the issues are common to other hospital workers (since they were shared by women in two very different work sites), we can only be certain by also asking the others— as unionists do in defining *worker* issues. Women in other occupations or industries (clericals, waitresses, retail workers, etc.) may raise different issues, so it is necessary to look at each of them case by case. This study may offer some guidelines about how that might be done.[1]

To say that women may have different preferences, aptitudes, and life conditions from men does not at all mean that different rules should be applied to the two sexes, or that women should be "protected" by law against conditions to which men are exposed. Women have already experienced the discrimination imposed by separate rules, and they have rejected it in favor of decent rules, devised *by* and *for* both sexes, that apply to both sexes equally.

Thus, a complementary set of issues to those of job equality might add this dimension: Yes, women should be treated equally, but they also have special problems that need attention, problems that flow largely from their need to both work and raise a family. Attending to these special needs should not result in discriminatory treatment of the sexes, as in the case of "protective legislation." Instead, whatever benefits flow from addressing these needs should be available equally to both men and women.

Of course, in two-parent households, family duties should ideally be shared by working wives and husbands, but until they are, women will continue to have special needs in relation to those duties.

≈

THE WOMEN—IN THEIR OWN WORDS

SEXUAL HARASSMENT (NOTES BY WOMEN REPS)

The grievance I had yesterday was strange. A woman's husband initiated it. The woman's supervisor liked her, went to lunch with her, that kind of thing. When that ceased, he got busy writing her up, harassing her, staying on her back. I filed a grievance on it and won, but sexual harassment is almost impossible to prove.

Occasionally you hear about sexual harassment by doctors and to a lesser extent by supervisors. You find different levels of harassment. One level is simply language, people being treated disrespectfully. One way people cope with stress is through sexual overtures in conversation. Doctors, nurses and other staff talk a lot about sex to relieve tensions on the floor. They play verbal games with each other. Women complain about not liking that, but sometimes, when they get into it because of stress, they are a party to it.

I've heard complaints about winks and being invited on dates by doctors when the women didn't want it. Sometimes the women consent to that, but a lot of times they don't. I haven't heard much about sexual harassment and I didn't experience it myself when I worked in the hospital. I find a lot of confusion about what sexual harassment really means and about when it's serious and when it's not.

The very structure of the hospital encourages sexual harassment. People are undressed and people are in bed. There are men in high offices and women in low offices. In California we had this terrible case of a physician sexually abusing *patients*. The women in the operating room were so frightened they didn't report it right away, so they were fired for it. Hospitals are like other places except that sex is treated with less secrecy. You're down to basics and it's very hard to maintain Victorian illusions in a hospital.

Doctors can be a pain in the ass. Some have very arrogant attitudes and don't know how to keep their hands where they belong. It's a joke how some people get their jobs. Many a nurse has been promoted because of the doctors she slept with. That disturbs the morale of the nursing staff. The good nurses resent it. Women can advance three times quicker, and get treated better, if they're friendly with the doctors. This isn't right. Women are stepped on because they are women. It used to be worse. You can go to the union with it now and control it more.

"MEN'S JOBS"

Pharmacy. We have about 40 people in pharmacy and only about five women. All the top jobs are held by men. I like working in pharmacy because I am constantly learning about new medications. But I have to go into something else. I don't have a chance here. The problem is the new male supervisor. He says, "Females are no good as pharmacy helpers." The last female he hired as a pharmacy helper was in her late fifties and about four feet tall. There was no way she could handle the trucks, so she's going to be out. That's why he hired her, to meet his quota and get rid of her. There are no female pharmacists in this building.

Physician's Assistant. Compare a nurse practitioner and a physician's assistant. One's a female, and one's a male. The nurse practitioner has a lot more education, her responsibilities are greater, and she has to rotate shifts. In most cases, the practitioner is paid less than the physician's assistant. It's an open and shut case—discrimination.

Apprenticeships and electricians. I tried to get into the electrician apprenticeship program. The guys laughed right in my face.

"Ha, ha, you don't want this. A woman, no way."

I asked the supervisors, "Is there some written rule?"

He said, "No, but they won't let you. They'll put your application in the trash can."

That really made me angry. I went there six or seven times, but they wouldn't even let me apply. I'm serious about it. My kids want to go to college. Unless a rich man comes along and marries me, I've got to make more money.

They have other apprenticeships in the hospital—sheet metal, refrigeration—and they're better paying jobs, but there's no women in them. The ambulance drivers and custodians are also male. They make more than the licensed vocational nurses. The men are fighters, and they're demanding. That's why they get more.

Maintenance "man." When I started in dietary, everybody said, "She always has a smile on her face." The longer I was there, the less I smiled. People were fighting and screaming and I was going crazy, so I applied for a job in maintenance. They had only men there.

Everybody in the hospital was excited. They couldn't believe I was applying for this job. A lot of women—and guys too—were pleased. "If you can do the job, go for it." Some women thought I didn't belong there, but they didn't say much.

I got the job, and I can't say I've had any problems with it. I was a little afraid at first, afraid I'd have to do heavy lifting. But I found that if something was too heavy for me, somebody would help me, just as I helped them.

Maintenance is a lot quieter than dietary. You work on your own most of the time and nobody screams at you. Even if I make a mistake, they just point it out to me calmly and explain the right way. I was trained on the job for a few weeks, but most of it is simply common sense.

The work isn't hard. We do preventative maintenance every day. We go into every room, check the air conditioners, clean the filters. We check the refrigerators in dietary and if something's broken we get it fixed. We do linen and garbage pickup, but usually the same man does it every day. If he's off, I may do it. The laundry bags are pretty heavy, but whenever I ask for help with them, I get it.

I do a lot of pickups in the van. Each morning I usually have a pickup. Then I'm supposed to check the temperatures on all floors and in the water coolers. Then I usually make a run to the lab at another hospital, come back and have lunch, then make more pickups. I like driving because it lets me move around on my own.

In winter, we plow the snow from the parking lots and we shovel the sidewalks. We all share in that job, and we have snowball fights. Nobody is standing there telling us what to do, so we have more freedom than we have inside the hospital.

I myself am not a women's libber. I'm not doing this job because I want a man's job. I'm doing it because it's a good job. A lot of men's jobs I wouldn't want. The women who think this job is for-men-only don't know what they're missing.

Being the only woman in the department makes me feel important. A few other girls think they might apply, but the guys don't like them. I get along fine with all the men. They like me and I like them, so it works. They're all very nice. We joke and have fun. I like fixing things, making repairs, and I've learned a lot. When something breaks at home now, I can fix it myself.

I was a cheer leader in high school. Some girls were more intelligent. They went to college and got nursing degrees, so they feel they're above me now. They feel they can order me around, but they don't have the authority to do that. When I pass one of them in the hall, it's always, "Don't talk to her, she's in maintenance." But if they have a problem in their department and need something fixed, they're the best of friends again. They shouldn't be that way. I could go to college and be a nurse too, but I'm doing what I like.

Administration. There isn't one woman hospital director in California. Women will usually be head of personnel, but the real policy makers are men. The exception is the nursing department, but these women don't have that much influence, and they haven't been exposed much to feminist ideas. Some good women are qualified for the top jobs, but they never get them. Our chief has been here 30 years. She's had a hell of a way to go just because she's a female. She should be paid more and treated better. Women get roughed up when they try to get into higher administration.

If a male nurse has it together at all, he'll rise into administration faster than a female nurse. Nursing wants to have a lot of men visible so they can recruit more male nurses.

Certain departments employ almost all women but are supervised by men. That was a big issue with ward secretaries. The unit managers had to have college degrees in hospital administration, so the jobs went to men. The ward secretaries were all women, Black and white, and they were all being supervised by white men.

I don't necessarily feel discriminated against because I'm a woman, but as I look through the hospital hierarchy, I see the hospital is run by men. I don't feel people come down on me because I'm a woman, but I *am* a nurse, not a doctor or an administrator. The department heads are generally men. The Board of Supervisors in the county are all men. They run the whole show. So in the total picture, hospitals are certainly male dominated.

COMPARABLE WORTH

Woman is only matter. The male principal is better and more divine.

Aristotle

Anti-discrimination activities have reduced discrimination in hiring, promoting, training, paying, and sex stereotyping of women, but the gains for some workingclass women have been limited, and for hospital workers they have been minimal. Perhaps measures seeking to upgrade women's jobs—especially "comparable worth" and "scope of practice"—will be more helpful to hospital workers than affirmative action and other efforts to move women into non-traditional jobs have been.

Scope of practice pertains to the virtual monopoly doctors have on most high level skills, while comparable worth applies to the employer practice of under-evaluating women's jobs (relative to comparable male jobs) and assigning lower "market" rates to them. Nancy Aide, for example, may perform work of comparable skill, effort, and responsibility to that of a male machine operator who works for the same employer. But she is paid less than he is because of biased evaluations of her job, or more likely because the employer feels he can pay her less (the "market" wage) and get away with it.

Comparable worth is a rising issue. In our survey of women leaders, for example, we asked what the priorities of the Coalition of Labor Union Women should be. Comparable worth was chosen more than twice as often as the second place issue, "child care"—and even more often than "ERA," "social security reforms for women," "getting women into non-traditional jobs," and "enforcement of anti-discrimination laws."* It is significant to note that about ten times as many women chose "comparable worth" as chose "sexual harassment."

The union has pursued comparable worth, but the principle is relatively new and its potential still largely unexplored. Moreover, it is applicable only in places (usually large systems) where "men's jobs" exist with which "women's jobs" can be compared. At Penn hospital, for example, it may have no applications at all. Employers at Penn operate no establishment other than the hospital, so only male and female jobs within that hospital can be compared. But, very few

---

*Respondents were asked to check only two items: 49 chose comparable worth, 21 child care, 19 ERA, 15 social security reforms for women, 12 getting women into non-traditional jobs, 12 enforcement of anti-discrimination laws, 5 sexual harassment, 5 occupational safety and health, 4 comprehensive health coverage, 1 abortion rights.

comparable male jobs exist within that hospital, and among those few that are comparable, no substantial wage differentials exist. *

Cal hospital, on the other hand, is part of a giant county system, containing vast numbers of male classifications with which female jobs might be compared. Comparable worth has been raised repeatedly in collective bargaining at the hospital, in an effort to correct wage differentials, but legal action against the county has not yet been taken, as it has in some other places.

Comparable worth, which the Supreme Court has ruled is covered under the Civil Rights Act, can go far in reducing the stunning inequities between the wages of males and females doing work of equal value, but it cannot achieve total victory over the major issues that trouble women workers. In the case of hospital workers, for example, even where comparable worth is applicable, it does not address any of the non-economic issues. Hence, staffing, scheduling, time-off, career opportunities, conditions, etc. would remain unaffected even by a total elimination of pay inequities based on the principle of comparable worth.

≈

THE WOMEN—IN THEIR OWN WORDS

ELINOR GLENN

The unions are just coming to understand a slogan that's been emerging in the last five or six years, "equal pay for work of equal value." It's a new slogan for the women's movement. A clerk in a liquor store, for example, gets much more money in many cases than a clerk on a hospital ward. Yet the ward clerk has a much more responsible job. A laborer can get $500 a week and the laundry worker $125 a week, using the same education and skills. One is male, the other female and third world.

There's no reason to encourage our women to think only in terms

---

* Local 585 (to which Penn Hospital workers are affiliated) was involved in a comparable worth case with the County of Washington, the final settlement of which stated: "An extensive review of the salaries being paid all employees will be conducted to ensure that the salaries in each job classification are based on a reasonable assessment of the skill, effort, responsibility and working conditions of the position." The local was included as a defendant in the case, even though the union neither initiated nor condoned employer wage practices. The self-perceived role of the local in the settlement was to press for stronger comparable worth language in the settlement and to instruct its staff to oversee the proper enforcement of the settlement.

of non-traditional jobs—climbing up telephone poles or driving a caterpillar. Many women want to be nursery school teachers and nurses. They may prefer that work. Why should they be penalized monetarily for doing "women's work"? Maybe there's a social or cultural reason why women like to do these jobs: mothering, nurturing, working with children, sick people, old people.

In the hospitals, one could say, "Well, if we get more men to be nurses then the wages will go up." That proves the discriminatory pattern of the job. Why should wages go up only when men come in? And why should women leave a profession they like because it is paid a discriminatory wage?

We're policing the apprenticeships to see that women are encouraged to enter them. But that will not seriously impact the millions of women workers who are underpaid for their work. Those millions are not going to be operating engineers or lumberjacks. They are going to be in the mainstream of women's work. When we seriously commit ourselves to fight for comparable worth, the whole pattern of sexism and wages will change.

HELLAN DOWDEN

In 1973 the Governor of the state of Washington had those jobs in state government that were held predominantly by men or by women evaluated. This study (the Willis Study on Classified Staff) indicated that the state had two separate pay systems—one for men and another for women. None of the women's jobs were paid as much as the poorest paid male job of the same worth.

When results of the study became widely known, I was working as a field representative in Palo Alto. We decided in light of the study to investigate the salary setting practices of the Palo Alto personnel department. We found that the city had hired a consulting firm to establish salaries based on a combination of job evaluation and market wage rates. The job evaluation gave point ratings for job content, such as "problem solving," "accountability," "working conditions." Market rates were set by surveying bench-mark cities for pay rates.

Our findings were similar to the Willis study. Technical, maintenance, and operation jobs of similar point ratings were close in salary—diverging from 2½ to 5 percent. But clerical jobs with the *same point ratings* as the technical, maintenance and operations jobs (men's jobs) were from 14 to 21 percent below them in salary.

The pay differences were due to "the market standard of pay," where jobs are benchmarked to similar jobs in other industries or cities. The system perpetuates the low wages of women and is inherently discriminatory against them.

The union recommended that the city stop using the market system in such cases, but the city refused. We filed charges against the city with the EEOC and later in the Federal Court. We have used this suit as leverage to gain equal pay for work of comparable value through collective bargaining, and, after arduous battles with the city, we have won agreement for upgrading the wages of clerical workers.

The local also filed suit against the County of Santa Clara for discrimination based on the market standard. As a result, we were able to negotiate a study of all clerical positions with the following goals: One, promotional opportunities for all levels of clerical classes; Two, expansion of career ladders to administrative classifications; Three, validation of job duties, qualification and selection processes; Four, educational/work opportunities to acquire relevant qualifications so that clerks can promote to male dominated classes.

Our approach in Santa Clara County was to upgrade the pay for classifications mainly occupied by women *and* to create a bridge to better paying male dominated classifications. To fulfill these goals, the County was mandated to hire a team of analysts to study all clerical positions within the county. The union demanded and won the right for a clerk of our choosing to be hired to work on the study. The going wasn't easy. I can remember one occasion when after constant stalling and delays on the part of the county, the clerks locked their phones in their desks and proceeded to sit-in at Board of Supervisors' meeting until issues surrounding the study were resolved.

As a result of the study, many positions received pay increases, half of them held by minority women. Most increases were achieved by reclassifying positions and creating differentials for various skills. For example, we said that using a typewriter was "machine operation." Whatever men might think, typewriters do not grow from the tips of women's fingers. They are machines and women should be compensated for knowing how to operate them.

Many exciting programs resulted from this study. Some involved use of seniority to transfer into higher paying maintenance and operations positions. Others involved paid time off, similar to what professionals received, to upgrade skills for higher paying positions.

Twelve

WAGES, BENEFITS, CHILDCARE, FAIRNESS

"When am I going to get more money?" That's the first thing they greet you with. They don't even get to the second and third problems. With the economy a shambles, it's a rear guard action, not an offensive battle, and money is the bottom line.

Most women work because they need the money and, though many of them say they would work even if they did *not* need the money, probably few would do so if their employers stopped paying them. In that sense, the paycheck *is* the bottom line.

Money figures in the shortage of RNs: one survey of nurses in Florida, for example, found that conflicts with doctors and insufficient control over work were only minor sources of dissatisfaction.[1] Leaders of the nursing profession, the study concludes, are troubled about issues of authority, but the average RN has more pressing problems, and the preferred solution to them, by a two to one margin, was found to be higher pay.

To discover what value hospital workers in our own survey attached to wages, compared with other issues, we asked them which they would prefer: a 15 percent wage increase (roughly the cost-of-living increase for the year)—or other job improvements which we specified.

About two-thirds of the women preferred a 15 percent wage increase to *any other job improvement.*

The only improvements that as many as *a third* of the women preferred to a 15 percent wage increase were: "improved fringe benefits" and "more staff."

Following these were "more vacation and personal days" (preferred by 32 percent), "more opportunities for promotion" (24 percent), "more control of schedule" (19 percent), "better treatment" (18 percent), "better supervision" (13 percent), "less tiring work" (11 percent), "safer and healthier work place" (11 percent), and "more interesting work" (7 percent).

As for equity and the "fairness" of wages, a surprising 75 percent of the women identified as a *sizeable* or *great* problem "wages not being fair compared to what other employees in the hospital make." This compared with 64 percent who gave the same response to "wages not as high as I could earn elsewhere"; 50 percent to "wages not high enough considering the work I do," and 41 percent to "wages not high enough to support my family."

Thus, the "fairness" of their wages was a serious problem to more women than the absolute level of their wages—that is "wages not high enough to support my family." Again, the women indicate a central interest in equity and the fairness of their treatment. Among the strongest feelings about wage inequities were those of ancillary staff in relation to RNs. At Cal hospital, for example, the aide's starting salary was 42 percent of the RN's, and the LVNs was 61 percent of the RN's, yet the aides and LVNs were responsible (they claimed) for training the RNs and doing much of their work.

Hospitals (and other employers) try to minimize discontent about wage inequities by imposing a rule of silence and secrecy on employees. In non-union hospitals, where virtually everyone's wage rate is different, workers are often warned against comparing their rates or paychecks with others. When such information is concealed, workers may be unaware of discriminatory rates and inequities.

Unionists also claim that hospitals, instead of paying decent wages across the board, set up numerous small job classifications, each with separate wage rates, to satisfy individuals or groups of workers who demand more money—an approach, the union says, that has the effect (perhaps a planned one) of dividing workers and setting them against one another.

The union has progressively raised the wage rates of its members across the board. It has also attempted to equalize pay rates *within* classifications, create a more rational and equitable classification scheme, set seniority rules for wage increases (and movement into higher classifications), and end the silence about pay rates and inequities. Also, by raising the rates of low wage workers across the board, it has made them more equitable in relation to other wage rates. Yet complaints about inequities persist and will probably be relieved only after general wage rates rise to acceptable levels.

The priority given by unions to wage rates is obviously more than mere "economism," as is often charged; it is quite clearly in this case, and in most other cases involving workingclass women, a response to the genuinely felt needs and priorities of the women themselves. It is for this reason that both the labor and women's movement have focused on economic issues, but in different ways in each case. Unionism seeks mainly to raise wages across the board, and reduce classification inequities. Women's groups on the other hand have sought mainly to desegregate the higher paying "male jobs" and to reduce discrimination in hiring, firing, compensation, etc. But, as we have seen, these anti-discrimination strategies have limited applications for hospital workers. The newer issue, "comparable worth," which has been raised mainly by unionists, may reduce wage discrimination more significantly than other anti-discrimination strategies have.

The low wages (and benefits) of hospital workers are women's issues in that they result largely from sex segregation and the undervaluation of "women's work." The "fairness" of wages may also be a women's issue in that inequities and divisive classification schemes are apparently associated more often with low-wage women's jobs than with men's occupations. Wages, benefits, and fairness, then, are major "women's issues," which flow largely from sex discrimination and segregation.

Everybody had a different wage rate in that hospital. People had been there for years and weren't making what the new employees made. Many old timers were outraged and wanted this changed. As an aide, I was making more than one of the PNs, even though I started years after her. We had a cleaning lady that was making only fifty dollars a week because she'd started in the old hospital years ago. She got a cost-of-living raise with the rest of us, but it never went up to anything she could live on. That's one reason we insisted on getting a union. The rates were unfair and much too low.

The ward clerks handle charts day-in and day-out and have to *know* what the doctor says and what he writes, but we're paid only half as much as the medical secretaries. That's not right.

The RN's pay is not a particular source of aggravation to me. It just pisses me off that I'm training nurses and I don't get paid for it. Maybe it's just an ego thing.

There are 144 classifications at the hospital. Now what's the reason for it? Very simple. If they paid them enough money they wouldn't need 144 classifications. The only way you can get a decent wage sometimes is to get a special inequity classification for your job. That keeps other people busy writing classifications. And it keeps people fighting with each other about who gets one penny more an hour. It breaks up the unity of the negotiating team. It creates a pecking order that is very bad, workers fighting workers instead of fighting management.

FRINGE BENEFITS

Fringe benefits were more often chosen than any other option in preference to the hypothetical 15 percent wage increase offered in our survey. Also, 75 percent of those surveyed identified "pension won't be adequate when I retire" as a *sizeable* or *great* problem (a proportion equalled only by responses to "wages not fair"), while 61 percent responded similarly to "health insurance doesn't cover long illnesses."

Asked what benefits they would most like to receive or improve, women at Penn hospital most often chose "pensions and the retirement system" and at Cal (where pension gains had been greater than at Penn) women most often chose "health insurance."

The union has improved health benefits through bargaining and through support of national health insurance, but benefits remain limited, even though the hospital worker's business (an unusually hazardous and stressful one) is health care.

As for pensions, many women reach old age without means of self support. If women remain housewives, they earn no pension credits at all, and those who work only part time earn only minimal credits. Women face the loss of pension rights when they quit their jobs (as they often do) before their pensions are vested under national law. In hospitals, worker turnover is high and the loss of pension rights is considerable. In general, hospital workers are unclear about what their pensions will be or whether they will have any at all.

Pensions and other benefits have been kept on hold by the priority given to wage increases. As one union rep put it: "If you're negotiating for $3.50 an hour and hitting your head on the wall to get that, you can't worry about pensions. We're trying to change that by getting the national industry pension fund negotiated into our contracts."

Women are more likely than men to work part time or intermittently, so they are more likely than men to profit from improved pension eligibility terms and better protection (in their contracts and in the law) against pension credit loss when they leave a job.

As for pregnancy disability benefits, before the issue was covered in the contract, pregnant women were usually asked to resign their jobs. The union, in this case, took important initiatives in collective bargaining even before the Supreme Court decision requiring pregnancy to be treated as a compensable disability, with paid time off the job.

Aside from these issues (health care, pensions, pregnancy disability) a host of unexplored benefits issues pertain to the special problems of working and raising a family—as, family members who are disturbed, addicted, alcoholic; children with learning disabilities or school problems; marital discord; aged parents or relatives for whom women must care; budgeting and consumer problems. Such issues are "personal" problems but, like health, they also greatly affect the workers' ability to function on their jobs. Some unions offer community services and referrals to public agencies on such problems, but in most cases these "women's issues" are neither identified nor brought forcefully to the union's attention, though they are suitable issues for negotiations as well as for union-sponsored community services programs.

In our survey, women were asked what benefits they would most like to have. Of the twelve items on the list, the four that were *least* often selected were: "education assistance programs," "holidays," "good, inexpensive child care centers," and "free legal assistance." Health insurance was selected more than twice as often as these four issues combined. Also high on the list were dental, optical and prescription coverage, vacations, pensions and sick days.

The meager benefits received by hospital workers, like their low wages, derive largely from the segregation of women into under-valued jobs, and they are, therefore, also women's issues. Moreover, some benefits are of specific concern to women and are also, in that sense, special women's issues. These include pensions, child care, and other benefits relating to family responsibilities.

CHILD CARE

Child care, usually for children from about age two to five, is an issue of obvious concern to women who work and raise families, and while the issue has been raised forcefully by union women and other feminists, its progress in legislatures and at the bargaining table has been less than spectacular.

In the case of hospital workers (at least those currently employed), our survey found that, contrary to expectations, the issue was not assigned as high a priority as some other issues, and in fact "good, inexpensive child care centers" was among the least often chosen benefits women said they wanted to receive or improve.

Perhaps with further development, the issue might become a more desired option to these women. However, rather few of those surveyed had young, child care age, children at home: only seven percent had children between the ages of two and five, and only 12 percent had any children under the age of five. Of those *with* young children, many had apparently already solved their child care problems, and probably would not be working if they had not. Very likely the most desperate child care needs are found, not among employed women, but among those whose child care needs prevent their employment. Hospital workers may also find it easier than other workingclass women to solve child care problems by working different shifts from those worked by husbands or other adults in the family, thus permitting an adult to be home at all times.

Union leaders often mentioned child care as a restriction on the participation of women in the union, a problem which in some places had been eased by providing child care at union meetings.

Child care may not be the highest priority issue to women surveyed, but it is certainly, nevertheless, an issue of overriding concern to those women who do need it, as well as to unions seeking to assess and address women's needs. In any case, the issue needs more attention and development, not less. In this context, it is worth noting that many other countries not only provide abundant child care facilities but also operate numerous summer camp facilities so that working mothers can have total vacations from child care responsibilities during summers.

≈

THE WOMEN—IN THEIR OWN WORDS

It would be a good idea to have child care centers, but I myself don't have that problem. My mother lives with us so we have a built-in baby sitter.

I feel very positive about my child care arrangements. I feel that my husband's taking a very active part in raising our child and that he cares for her when I'm at work. He's as much a parent to her as I am. He feeds her, diapers her, bathes her, takes her out on the bicycle. Besides, this hospital can screw up putting a nail in the wall. I don't know if I'd trust my child to a center operated by the hospital.

I don't think the hospital should be responsible for my child care, but they should make it easier for us to get to work. They should say, "OK, you have children. What is the best shift for you? Do you want to rotate or do you want to work steady?" Women could take care of their families then, and the hospital would get better staffing.

The administration at Cal is looking at child care, not for the purpose of helping women, but for the purpose of helping themselves. They want to see if it can recruit evening nurses. Their biggest need is at night, so if it could recruit for nights, that would be a big payoff.

Child care has been explored many times, but the problem is bucks. It's very expensive providing child care to thousands of employees. Everybody agrees it would be good, but the county doesn't have that kind of money. Federal support is needed. It could make a big difference in absenteeism.

We union reps push child care, but the women don't. We think it's necessary and we think the women haven't taken a good look at it. Having child care at the job site would allow closer family ties. The mother would not have to worry about her child and could see her during breaks. We've had it on the bargaining table for the last six years, but where's the money? Child care is a basic issue. Many of the problems I deal with have to do with workers being late for work because they don't have good child care. Some women spend close to half their income on baby-sitters.

At Penn, issues like child care are not discussed. People feel so held down and intimidated by supervision that they're struggling for basics, just to get the union in. Later they'll move beyond that. It's hard to get hospital workers, who are down in the gutter and making only 30 cents above the minimum wage, to all of a sudden jump to the tree tops.

A hundred hospitals nationally operate child care facilities. For ten years we've tried to get Cal hospital off its ass and provide child care. We have six programs in other hospitals. Some are for the children of patients, some for battered children, and two are for children of employees. We haven't convinced County yet that it's in their own interest and could reduce the high turnover of nurses.

I wish we did more to push bargaining on child care, but there's a lot of problems with it in terms of location and employer resistance. You have a real high cost demand that gets a lot of resistance from hospital administrators, who are a bunch of bastards on most issues anyway. How do you play it off with other demands? That's what it always comes back to. Then there's the matter of time and location. One women's hospital has a day care center, but it doesn't open until 8 am, so what happens to women who start work at 7 am?

The potential for bargaining on child care is greater in other industries. The telephone company, for instance, has its own child care center now. The industry is predominantly women, fairly high paid, and can afford to trade off some other things and put money into child care. They've satisfied other basics. Hospital workers need it more but can afford it less.

Or you could take an area like San Francisco, where almost all hospitals are organized and we have a lot of strength. We might win it in collective bargaining there, and then spread it around. That's how you make headway in collective bargaining, start where you're strong. In the East, it might have to be legislated.

In California we've worked on legislation requiring that state buildings with more than 300 workers provide child care facilities. Government should be a model for the private sector. A national health program could do the job. That's the main direction we should go on the issue.

Thirteen

HOURS OF WORK: SCHEDULING AND REDUCING THEM

My mother was 83 years old and she was dying. I told the supervisors I wanted to go home to see her. They made me work that Christmas day. I said, "I'll work Christmas, but then I'm going home whether you like it or not. I can get another job, but I can't get another mother."

Hospitals stay open 24 hours a day, 365 days a year, so they must be staffed at times when most women want to be home with their families—afternoons, evenings, weekends, holidays. Given a choice, hospitals indicate a preference for assigning employees to work at any time and without any advance notice, but workers quite naturally resist such arrangements. They claim that hospital scheduling, even as it is, disrupts their personal lives and that, by driving out workers and causing absenteeism and turnover, it also harms the patients and the hospital. They insist that scheduling is used punitively by supervisors and that decent schedules could be assigned without adding to hospital costs.

Since it directly affects family life, the scheduling of work hours is a special women's issue, but it is not yet a highly developed one. The only major issue affecting the hours of work that has yet been advanced by women's groups is "flexible scheduling"—that is, scheduling which makes rather minor adjustments in work hours and allows women to start work an hour earlier or later, or perhaps work four-ten shifts (four days, ten hours a day) to suit family needs. Such "flexitime" may have many applications in offices, and perhaps even in hospitals, but it does not begin to address the serious issues of hours, scheduling, and time-off confronted by hospital workers.

Shift work, for instance, is a high priority issue for women who are required (rather than who choose) to work afternoon or evening shifts. Most women, given a choice, prefer to work the day shift, even though other shifts offer premium pay.

Other serious issues include: rotating and changing shifts, rotating and changing days off, requiring week-end and holiday work, working a seven-day week, insufficient advance posting of work schedules. They include the desire of many women for regular and fairly-compensated part time or temporary work. And they include issues of time-off the job—sick days, personal days, vacation time, leaves of absence. These are women's issues because they affect a woman's ability to both work and raise a family. The union has addressed most of them in collective bargaining, but progress is slow and some problems seem intractable.

As an example of the worst abuses, let us return to Nancy Aide. She is new to the hospital and has an extremely disruptive schedule. She knows only two weeks in advance what her hours will be. This week she works seven days: three on the night shift, two on afternoons, two on days. On one or more days she may be required to put in overtime hours. For this overtime, she will be allowed compensatory time-off, but the hospital will probably resist giving it to her. She will get only one weekend off this month. She can count on working Christmas, New Year's, Thanksgiving, and other holidays. She will not know much ahead of time exactly when her vacation will start or end. Her social and family life will be disrupted. She will be unable to go to school, schedule classes, train for a better job. She may become exhausted and eventually sick from the stress of working such long and difficult hours. If she takes off the sick days she is entitled to, the hospital may harass her for absenteeism.

Predictably, Nancy Aide and other hospital workers assign a very high priority to issues of scheduling and working hours. Asked what they *most dislike* about their jobs, the women surveyed put scheduling in third place. Moreover, about four in six women identified "no time for leisure" and "harassment for using sick days" as *sizeable* or *great* problems. And about a third gave the same response to "not having a steady, permanent shift," "having to work more than five days in a row," "not enough time to spend with my family," "work schedule interferes with my family life," and "working evening or night shift."

≈

THE WOMEN—IN THEIR OWN WORDS

ONE: SCHEDULES

THE SEVEN DAY STRETCH

Lots of times, we work seven days and get two days off. There's no need for it. Even factories only put in five days. By the fifth day you're tired. The sixth day you're bitchy. The seventh day you can't move. And we don't get overtime pay for it. When the union came in at Penn we asked for time and a half, just like all the factories get, for over five days. The hospital refused, but they gave us time and a half for *over* seven days.

WEEKENDS

I don't insist on having every weekend free. On weekends I don't have to pay a babysitter; my husband's home with our little girl. I'd rather work four days, ten hours a day. It would give a lot of mothers more time with their children. They could send them off with breakfast at least one day a week.

The contract at Penn states we must get at least every third weekend off, so that's all we get. We wanted that in the contract because some people weren't getting *any* weekends off. One person was getting all of them, and the other wasn't getting any.

Because we were bad kids and got the contract, this year they're not giving us the weekend before and after our vacation. The RNs get them but we don't. I'd like to tell them where to shove those weekends. People say, "I'd rather have my weekends free than get more money." So let's hire some part time staff, the way other hospitals have done, to work weekends. The full timers could work Monday through Friday.

COMPULSORY OVERTIME

Sometimes they say you *have* to work overtime. I refused one time, and we kind of got into it. I usually get home at 5:00 pm. He wanted me to work til 1:00 am!

I said, "I can't stay."

He says, "Well, you'll have to."

I said, "There's no law in the world that says I have to leave my children alone, unattended and hungry until 1:00 in the morning. I won't do that. Whatever disciplinary action you have to take, go and take it, because I cannot do it." He found someone else.

A man can grab a bite to eat and stay on. A woman has to go home and provide meals for everyone else.

SHIFT WORK

Shift work is hard on some women, but others like to work afternoons while their husband works days. It's easier to take care of the kids. The day shift is loaded. They tramp on one another's feet. That's one reason I don't like it. There's too much confusion. To me the four to twelve shift is good, quieter. Going to work, there's not so much traffic, and leaving there's no traffic at all. Some people don't like the strain on their social life and family life of working afternoons. Most activity is for daylight people.

It's very dangerous working nights at Cal. A lot of women have been raped here. They need more lights and security. On days I'm treated more like a woman. On nights I was treated like a man.

On days they said, "You're a woman. We won't make you walk all over the place with all these kooks around."

On nights the guys said, "Well, hey, you're a woman. We all get paid equal, so you're going to walk around this place by yourself just like we do."

I said, "What if somebody jumps out, takes my money, and beats me on the head? They ain't bopping no man. They're smarter than we think they are."

So I'm a lady on days and a man on nights. You can't wear a dress on nights, you have to wear pants. But they go after the ladies even if they wear pants. On nights nobody was here to talk to. The halls were empty, nobody around. You feel like you're in a twilight zone. A woman could have a nervous breakdown. Half the time I was depressed. If a woman can work nights and leave her husband in an empty bed by himself, she's a strong woman. I can't go without sleeping in my bed.

STEADY SHIFTS

I'm lucky. I have a steady daylight shift. But anybody hired now has to rotate, usually three shifts. How can you sleep when one week you're on days and the next on nights? And how do you arrange your family life? You can't plan anything. The hospital doesn't care.

Management wants to keep changing shifts, then when they're short, you've already agreed to work any schedule they give you. Some people were going to school, but they were told, "You have to work any shift." Our people said, "Hey, I'm almost graduated. I already paid my fees for this quarter." They had to quit their jobs so they could finish school.

At Penn we don't have steady shifts, but we're trying to get it down to where people can be shifted at no more than one week intervals. We want steady shifts, no rotations, and we also want to choose the shift. Most people want days. Women go into nursing because of that. They think it'll be easy to work and raise a family.

Here in California we don't rotate shifts, like they do in most hospitals. The union fights that because it's too devastating to private lives. We do have rotating days off, which is really rough.

POSTING THE SCHEDULE

They change the schedules all the time. They can change our days off and our shift with only two weeks notice. The supervisor makes up the schedule six to eight days in advance but she posts it only two weeks in advance. She says that's all the contract requires.

I work the same shift all the time, but I never know far enough in advance what days I'm getting off. I go on a two week vacation after this week, but I don't know what day I go back to work. I have to keep bothering my head nurse to tell me when I have to return. She has the schedule made up but I can't see it.

In hospitals without labor agreements, sometimes you don't know when you'll be working *next week*. That's one of the first things people want, to have the schedules posted well in advance.

SOME UNION COMMENTS ON SCHEDULING

It's very hard to get the hospital hierarchy to change. Part of it is that nurses are not willing to challenge the authority of the institution or males at the top. If women have complaints, they quit rather than fight. They don't like working nights, they want decent hours, so they go into real estate.

Women usually don't like to go out at night by themselves. It's one hidden reason for the staffing problem. Most women won't work the swing shifts. In Canada, what they do is, while people are in training, they give them jobs on the pm shift or on weekends. That helps with their staffing, and people get the money to continue their training. We're not quite that hep in this country.

In my spare time I'm working on computerized scheduling. We'll tell the computer the jobs available, the preferences of people, and their seniority. It would give them a permanent schedule, if that's what they like. They can change if they want to.

The union has done a lot to correct scheduling. Prior to the contract, management could change schedules without any notice. Now the contract requires that the schedule be posted, and that they give employees at least 14 days notice of any change.

Many people now work a steady shift. Our big problem is bargaining for weekends off so women can be with their families, and for choice of shifts so they can accommodate their hours to child care. The real issue is how to gain control of scheduling so as to schedule for the needs of individuals, rather than the needs of the hospital.

In the hospitals it's hard to allow flexible scheduling. What you have to do is four-tens. We've done this with clerks—four days a week, ten hours a day. So they get three days off a week.

The hospital could bring the family in on the late shifts and weekends to help care for patients. Those things aren't that far out. In Europe, the family stays with the patient, participates, gives them care. In pediatric units, the parents stay at night. There's a nurse available, but the family is with the child all night.

Many patients are well enough to be sent home at night or on weekends. It's a little more difficult for us at Cal hospital because we have a gun-and-stab-wound club on the weekends, so we keep busy with emergencies. In some private hospitals, the physician admits patients and does his thing early in the week. Then he has only a few patients in the hospital over the weekend, and some wards are only kept open five days a week.

Treating ambulatory patients in out-patient clinics rather than hospitalizing them can also permit staff to go home nights and weekends. We've moving in that direction more and more.

TWO: SICK TIME AND PERSONAL DAYS

Sick time and personal leave are pressing women's issues in the hospital. They are also hotly contested issues since hospitals do not hire enough staff and, hence, try to limit the amount of time the available staff takes off.

Penn hospital, as an example, allows 15 days a year sick leave, for either personal or immediate family usage. This gives a worker only slightly more than one day per month, a figure well below sick-time allowances in most male industries. Despite this meager allowance, the hospital routinely harasses workers when they take the time off. The hospital may even charge a worker with taking excessive sick time and fire her, despite proofs of sickness she may offer. Such punitive hospital practices put "harassment for using sick days" high on the list of women's issues, and four in six women surveyed identified it as a sizeable or great problem.

≈

One girl is scared to take sick days. The other day she had an infected toe, but she didn't miss a day. She could hardly walk. I'd almost rather they didn't pay us for sick days. Then maybe they wouldn't harass us. I know people who took only two days off in a year and they asked them for a doctor's note.

I filed a grievance for an LPN. She called in and said her baby was sick, so she was taking a sick day. Our contract says if a family member is sick, you're entitled to sick time. They told her she couldn't take a sick day, only an absent day without pay, because the baby was not seriously ill. Who's to say how sick a baby is? We won that grievance. She had to wait a good while for her pay because they would not bend.

At Penn we get two days a year for "personal leave," for our own use. It should be for something that comes up unexpectedly. But you must request it five days in advance in writing. Nine times out of ten it's turned down. They say they don't have adequate staff on that day.

Before my mother passed, they treated me kind of ill. I told them I wanted to go home. My mother was 83 years and she was dying. They told me that if my mother didn't die, I would have to bring a doctor's statement to back me up. I had time on the book, okay? But they made me work that Christmas day. I said, "I'll work Christmas but then I'm going home whether you like it or not. I can get another job, but I can't get another mother." I got home on the 26th and my mother died on the 29th.

One girl was fired for missing excessively. She had a doctor's excuse, but the supervisor didn't believe her. Now they have a health nurse. If you call in sick, she's supposed to find out if you're really sick. A woman I work with hurt her back on a patient. She missed 18 days and they harassed her about coming back to work. Eleven of those days she was in traction *in our hospital* from that patient. They knew she was sick, and they knew she did it on the job.

There are exceptions, people that miss work excessively. You see them out Saturday night, and they're sick Sunday morning. Some people won't work over five days. They call in sick. We have a nurse that always calls in, but she's an RN so they don't harass her.

I'd like to see more women supervisors. The men are not as

sympathetic as they should be about sick time. What's more, some men in the union don't sympathize either. I know one of them that takes management's side on sick leave. He thinks we take too much time off. He doesn't understand. He's never been a woman. People are down on him for that. Women have to take care of sick people in their families. We're the family nurses.

SOME UNION RESPONSES

Our contract at Penn says that sick leave can only be used for illness. We are not happy about it, but it is the best we've been able to get. We side with our members who want to use the time for personal reasons. But that's not what the contract provides.

Right now most grievances are on attendance, maybe eight out of ten. The state Supreme Court in California rendered a decision on a union class action case that involved an employee who was fired for attendance. The decision was disheartening. The court said that an employee is hired to function at a certain job and if the employee does not make herself available to function, then management has the right to hire somebody that will function in that job.

Management at Cal has started a big campaign to eliminate people with attendance problems. We were always successful in winning these cases, but not now. One employee was terminated after ten years of county service, with a record of commendations as long as my arm. She went three days over her 100 percent sick time, and management took the position that they no longer wanted her services. This is the attitude management has taken since the court decision came down.

That is the biggest problem within the county system. Certain people deserve time off. If I become emotionally ill and have to take off six months, I should still have my job when I come back. If you lose seniority and job security, then what have we got? You can make a thousand dollars an hour, but if you don't know you'll have a job tomorrow, you're dead. That has really hurt us. In private industry, we don't have this attendance problem. People are given whatever time is necessary, but they don't take off as much as public employees.

Some employees think that because they have 12 days on the books, they have a right to use them as they please. That's illegal. The rules that govern these employees are county laws, and if you take a sick day off and you're not sick, you're breaking the law. You're in big trouble for that. Generally the lower you go on the pay scale the bigger the absentee problem. When there's a problem at home, they go home. And they have *many* problems at home. The skilled people are more likely to quit. The less skilled are more likely to take time off.

They're tough even on educational leaves. I represent many members on requests for leaves at Cal. The leaves are supposed to be granted but they aren't. I sit down with management, but they won't listen. I know the person is honestly trying to go to school, but can't also work and take care of a family, especially if she has 30 patients to work with instead of ten. She needs a leave. I tell them, "You say you're an equal opportunity employer and you want to see people promoted, yet you're not giving employees a chance to better themselves."

THREE: REDUCED HOURS

Hospital workers complain that they work long, hard hours and need more time off. Asked what they most disliked about their jobs, the women surveyed ranked "not enough vacations, personal days and holidays" in third place—only behind "my schedule" and "trying to work and raise a family" (all of which are closely linked). And, as previously noted, four in six women surveyed identified "no time for leisure" as a sizeable or great problem.

In many European countries, the law requires that employees be given four weeks or more paid vacation. In the United States, the law is mute on the subject of vacations. Lengthened vacations are of special importance to women, along with all other time-off issues, because of family demands on their time.

One way to reduce the hours of work is to increase vacations, sick days, holidays, and other time-off periods. Another is to reduce the work week. In general, unions and workers have preferred the first to the second option. (They have also preferred early retirement, or time-off at the end of the work life, to the reduced work week).

A third option is part time or temporary work. In the past, hospitals hired many part timers and substitutes, but they use relatively few of them now. Unions have also sought to reduce the marginality of the work force in low wage industries by reducing the number of part time jobs. But where unions have achieved some success and stability, the merits of "reduced time" jobs might be explored further, including the following questions:

What has been the experience of part time and temporary workers in hospitals?

Can a regular "weekend shift" be created, or regular substitute jobs, to fill in on holidays or for absent workers?

Can "reduced time" workers be regularized and provided with pro-rated benefits, security, and an open option of moving into full time work?

Can they be organized and unionized? If so, by what methods?

In Germany (and elsewhere) union women have raised the six hour work day for all as their principal demand, and rejected proposals for increases in part time work: "Part time work is only a last resort . . . a way of exploiting the female working power." Yet they acknowledge that it offers to many women with families the only option available to them. In their view, shortening the life-working time, through early retirement, is not a solution for women with families, since children are already grown before the solution takes effect. Nor do longer holidays provide the solution, they say, since family members do not vacation at the same time—nor shortening the work week to four days since schools do not operate on a four-day week.

On the other hand, they say, shortening the work day for everyone would give the family more time together and also bring more employment to the unemployed: it would give men and women what they really want—a chance to live in a real partnership and divide responsibilities in family and working life. The working life could be opened for women and the family opened to men in this way.

The demands raised by German unionists in this connection include: that unions and employers discuss the shortening of work hours, giving preference to shortening of the work day, that legislation curtail overtime hours, that incentives be given to shorten the work day, and that models of the short work day be introduced—first in industries that require heavy manual work or health risks.

THE REGISTRY

Nurses who do not want full-time jobs turn for temporary assignments to the "registry," a private employment agency similar to office temporaries or substitute teachers, or even union hiring halls. Through the registry they can determine when and how long they will work, and they can schedule work to suit personal and family needs. They can also, in California at least, earn a higher hourly rate than they would on full time jobs. The great disadvantage to nurses in the registry is that they receive no benefits, accumulate no seniority credit, and have no union representation. Yet the totally flexible schedule of the registry obviously offers many women ideal working hours and makes it easier for them to both work and raise families.

The registry is nevertheless frowned upon by the hospital because it is expensive and does not provide steady workers, and by the union because those participating in it are very difficult to organize. In view of the registry's popularity with nurses, however, unions might consider either establishing their own registries (hiring halls) or organizing those that already exist.

Some women talk about the need for reduced hours.

≈

I've been working all my life, so I wouldn't want to stay home and do nothing but routine housework. If I could get out of the house at least three days a week, it would be fine. But now, working full time, I'm tired. I'd like to be able to work when I feel like it. If I didn't want to work today, I wouldn't have to go in. That would be the best way.

With my family and all, I don't see myself working full time for long. I wish I'd gone on for an RN. It's not that the RN pays more or is more interesting. It's just easier to work part time if you're an RN.

There are so many people asking for part time. A lot of them want Saturday and Sunday work. Some regular help wants to go on part time too. If they could do it, it would make it real nice for the full time employees. They could work out the staffing to suit everyone.

SOME UNION RESPONSES

Our focus hasn't been on part timers. The reason, frankly, is that with part timers you have to deal with specialized issues. What kind of hours, benefits? They always try to cheat part timers, and then they start to cheat full timers.

Years ago, a lot of women worked part time. That affected wages in health care. Women worked weekends to supplement their husbands' checks. They didn't go out and beat the doors down about a raise. A lot of people come into health care while they're going to school. It's temporary, and it sustains them for a time. That person's not going to make much of a rumble either.

More flexibility and shorter hours are needed. Invariably, even in our contracts, the part time people get screwed out of benefits. Work needs to be done on that. It impacts women more than men. "Why hasn't this been done?" Among other reasons, it's the male domination of unions, and just not paying attention to those issues.

We've got to be real creative with women workers. In Palo Alto, for example, we have women who do job sharing, not in hospitals but in other places. We've had nursing attendants work four hours in the morning and go to school to become LVNs in the afternoon.

The nurse registry is going to make nursing much more of a cottage industry. It's the rent-a-nurse idea. The RNs register and work the hours they want. In some ways this will hold nursing back. If women are in the same hospital full time, they can be organized as units, and they can fight for better working conditions. The registry makes it much harder. Maybe we should organize the registry.

Fourteen

STAFFING

There's loads of tension in hospitals because they're under-staffed and loads of scheduling problems. The males who run the hospitals are responsible for the under-staffing. The women are victims. The patients are victims.

Two thirds of the human and mechanical errors reported at Presbyterian-University Hospital in Pittsburgh in 1978, according to the *Journal of the American Medical Association*, occurred during the 90 days that the 16-bed intensive-care unit was "suboptimally staffed" with nurses.

Paula Span, *New York Times*, February 22, 1981.

Another surprise in this study was the appearance of a giant "fourth dimension" in the issues raised by hospital workers. If wages, benefits, hours are three dimensions, then "working conditions" or the "quality of work life" is this towering fourth dimension. So large is its scope (if taken to its far borders) that it relates to other issues much as outer space does to the finite bodies it contains. It is, in the final analysis, a "democracy in the workplace issue" and it encompasses virtually all decisions and behavior within the workplace.

These issues may become more visible as bread and butter issues are settled. In this case, however, hospital workers still need bread, but they clearly indicate that bread is not enough. Unfortunately, these issues, like so many others, tend to fall by the wayside in collective bargaining because they lack the urgency of economic issues and because management insists they are exclusive management prerogatives and, therefore, non-negotiable.

The most important of these issues is "staffing." In both hospitals surveyed, workers complained bitterly about staff shortages and about the fall-out from those shortages: stress, increased work load, physical fatigue, chaos, poor patient care.

Staff shortages also affect the scheduling of work and the amount of time-off workers can get. They strain human relations (supervisors and workers, RNs and others, patients and workers, women and their families). They increase health and safety risks by increasing the speed, stress, and fatigue of work.

Most of the women surveyed were acutely affected by staff shortages, or so they said. Indeed, 72 percent of them identified "not enough staff" as a *sizeable* or *great* problem.

Beyond that, 63 percent gave the same response to "going home tired," 58 percent to "hard to work all day, then go home and do housework," 40 percent to "doing the work of two people when someone doesn't show or calls off," and 28 percent to "not able to take my breaks."

Asked what they *most disliked* about their work, women ranked staffing only behind problems of scheduling, working and raising a family, and time off. A third of them said they would prefer more staff to a 15 percent wage increase.

Staff shortages exist among both unskilled and skilled workers. They result much less from a shortage in the *supply* of workers than from a shortage in the *demand* for them. Unskilled workers, of course, are in abundant supply, yet acute staff shortages exist in both hospitals.

At Cal, management attributes its real inability to hire and keep RNs—not to the wages, hours, conditions it offers—but to the misguided policies of the nursing profession and nursing schools. Yet Cal does little to train its most natural labor supply (its own employees and community people) for jobs where labor shortages exist. Almost all the RNs it *does* train go elsewhere to work.

One large-scale study of RNs found that the loudest complaint voiced was that "nurses aren't able to care for their patients as well as they want to because of staffing problems."[1] Those with most direct patient contact complained most about under-staffing: 25 percent of the team leaders, and 21 percent of the staff nurses said they were badly under-staffed, but only 18 percent of the head nurses and supervisors, and 8 percent of the administrators.

Staffing is an important women's issue because the stress it causes is reflected in the quality of home life as well as in the quality of worklife; it is a women's issue because women cannot easily go home and sleep off their fatigue. They have another job to do.

≈

THE WOMEN—IN THEIR OWN WORDS

We never have enough help, so the load is heavy. The hospital is just saving money on hiring a full staff. People have to do their own work plus someone else's. It's especially bad in the summer months. People go on vacations and there aren't enough substitutes. I miss a lot of my breaks. Sometimes I'll run in the back and gobble down my lunch because I'm so hungry I can't stand it. After work I'm usually exhausted. My doctor says it's mental fatigue from all the work they push on me. If you're off sick, they're after you: "Why did you take off?" They *make* you sick.

We schedule too many patients in the clinic. We have maybe 100 patients, maybe nine doctors, and very few nurses and aides. We're always giving bulk care. We don't have time to treat people as individuals. Some patients have to sit on that bench all day. They have an appointment for 10:00 but maybe 19 people are scheduled for 10:00. You hate to see sick people hanging around all those hours. It keeps you running at top speed.

One nice thing about our unit is that we can be more flexible with time. If somebody says, "Can I come in later?", they can say "yes" because we are pretty well staffed. It's really appalling in other areas. Here you have a little energy left at the end of the day. It's not a constant hassle. The job doesn't drive you nuts, so there's not much turnover. I don't see how some women on the wards manage, they work so hard. Well, they don't stay around. Or they get terribly frustrated and can't give good care. The absolute best you can do on those wards is mediocre. And there's no job satisfaction in that, none at all.

More people are quitting at Cal than are being hired. We're always short. They should hire more people. They have the money for it but they won't do it. The union has gotten them to hire more in dietary and other places that have shortages and high turnovers. We've also gotten them to hire more floaters to fill in when people are out. But it's a constant struggle. The turnover of technical people is very high, especially in x-ray. Right now the only techs that apply are foreigners.

SHORTAGES OF SKILLED WORKERS AT CAL:
MANAGEMENT VIEWS

There's a critical shortage of RNs in all southern California. Nobody knows why. Nationwide and in California, we have more graduate nurses than are needed, but only 50 percent of them practice nursing. The shortage involves the academic programs that turn out nurses, and the expectations engendered in nurses. Yesterday's nurses were strictly bedside nurses. They were committed to patient care.

Today the nursing academy is involved with philosophies about holistic care—one nurse, one patient, on a psychological and sociological level. My perception is that the nurse's role is to take care of the *medical* needs of patients. We have other professionals to take care of the non-medical needs. Our nurse educators are floundering for an identity. They're looking for more roles for nursing. That's fine with me. I tell them I will support nursing in any direction it wants to travel, so long as they provide me with the means to care for patients.

We need good typists badly, but we rely on the community schools to train them. We don't offer typing classes. The county is not in the education business, even though the medical center is an educational institution. Maybe we should be.

The further down you go on the professional ladder, the less acute the shortage is. We just ran an attendant's exam and 400 people applied in one day. Most of them qualified, and we hired about 100 of them. There are plenty of trades people, plumbers and electricians. And the quasi-professional areas—that require a business or administration background—get millions of applicants. We have them coming out of our ears.

STAFFING AT CAL: UNION VIEWS

Staffing is a symptom of the anger and frustration people feel. The morale of the workers is very low and the trust is very low. On any given day you find about 20 to 30 percent of your work force out, either sick, on vacation, or something. They should hire with that in mind and they don't. The hire the bare minimum and in some cases below minimum. The poor guy who comes to work every day gets the shaft. Instead of taking care of ten patients, he's given 30 to work with. The hospital ends up paying a lot of overtime when they're short of staff.

Then management tells us they can't grant time off because of staffing. It's difficult even to get vacation time. We have personal time (three days off each year) plus a compensatory day when they work a holiday. They accumulate this time, but they can't take it. I'm constantly facing grievances against supervisors who will not grant time off. To get away with it, they have to prove they don't have adequate staff. We're winning a lot of cases at the second level, if we can prove there was adequate staffing. They win by not hiring enough staff. Then they have an excuse for not granting time off. They lose in the long run because people quit or take sick time.

It's very difficult to deal with staffing if the primary thrust of the union is to develop a contract in the usual way. It has to be dealt with in a much different way. I haven't seen it successfully resolved to everyone's satisfaction. Employers won't bargain about staffing.

Fifteen

HEALTH, SAFETY, STRESS

The aides say the hospital is trying to kill us off. It sounds funny, but if the doctor says, "Get this 300 pound patient out of bed," you move him if it kills you.

Hospitals can make the sick healthy, and they can also make the healthy sick. The hospital is filled with communicable disease, hazardous devices and chemicals, radium, x-rays, cat scanners, infected hypodermic needles, dangerous gases, drugs.[1]

Hospital work is physically and emotionally demanding, injuries are common, and the heavy lifting required in nursing (a "lady-like" occupation) may exceed that of many macho jobs, perhaps even construction and mining. Yet hospital workers do not regard health and safety as being among the most disturbing features of their work: asked what they *most disliked* about their jobs, for instance, the women surveyed put health and safety in 12th place in a field of 14 issues.

The union has examined health and safety issues, tried to alert members to them, and taken steps to reduce the hazards, but workers still give the issue a low priority because so many dangers are invisible to them.

Stress may be the greatest health hazard in the hospital. Of women surveyed, 60 percent identified "emotional stress" as a *sizeable* or *great* problem—compared to only 24 percent who felt the same about "lifting and bending," 13 percent about "cuts, bruises, burns," 15 percent about "catching disease because of work," 9 percent about "falling down" and roughly 5 percent about "dangerous chemicals, gas, tools, machinery."

One doctor, writing of her counseling experience with absentee women, reported that colds and fatigue were just as important as menstruation as causes of absences. "More women have respiratory infections than men, but this is related many times to their close association with young children. Fatigue as a source of absenteeism is the most interesting of the three categories. Here we find true tiredness, much of it due to the two full jobs carried by many women— i.e. home and children, and work. It is a cover for boredom and frustrations as well. The job may be monotonous, too busy, or not busy enough."[2]

Such fatigue, in its advanced stages, has another name, *burnout*, described by another writer:

"Hospital employees who are undergoing the burnout process gradually begin to manifest a variety of behavioral, emotional, cognitive, and physical changes. Many of the first symptoms of burnout are physical—increasing levels of fatigue, easy tiring, sleep disturbances, low levels of energy, changes in appetite, lowered resistance to infection, or a variety of physiological dysfunctions such as gastrointestinal disturbances and headaches. In many cases, the major physical consequence of burnout is chronic fatigue at the start of a work shift. . . . Perhaps the most dramatic effects of burnout occur in an employee's psychological functioning."[3]

SHIFT WORK STRESS

Studies have linked shift work to an assortment of ailments, but especially to sleep disturbances and the inefficiency and fatigue that result. Shift work can disturb both the quantity and quality of sleep, so that people sleep less, and less restfully. The stress of shift work is traced to disturbances in the body's natural 24 hour "circadian" rhythm which controls pulse, body temperature, the flow of urine, and other body functions. The rhythm is disturbed when people sleep odd or irregular hours, or try to sleep when others are awake, making noise, having fun.

A study of nurses and food processors, confirming European studies, showed that shift workers have significantly more trouble adapting to work schedules than day workers do.[4] Those who rotated shifts had most trouble, followed closely by night shift workers. Rotating shifts were significantly associated with digestion trouble, leg and foot cramps, colds, chest pains, menstrual problems, nervousness, wheezing, alcohol consumption, inadequate sleep patterns, use of sleep-inducing medicines, use of stimulants, fatigue, less satisfying domestic and social life, less satisfactory psychological health, and less satisfactory work performance. Rotating nurses were found to be significantly more confused, depressed, and anxious than other nurses.[5]

Studies have also found shift work to be associated with ulcers, constipation, irregular eating, poor diets, and the consumption of too much coffee, tobacco, alcohol—and marital problems and divorce. Yet at least one in six Americans is a shift worker (not counting those who rotate shifts), and more than half of RNs rotate shifts.

Some workers who must rotate shifts (as air controllers) prefer rapid rotations, every few days rather than every few weeks. In France it is believed that less damage is done to circadian rhythms by rotating shifts than by rigid late shifts.

The damage of shift work is often cumulative and long-term. As one union safety person put it, "I'd bet money that within 15 years you'll see ulcers, colon and kidney problems, nervous disorders, all kinds of physical deterioration due to the continued abuse. But it's like asbestos: you'll have to be able to count the bodies or no one will believe it's harmful."[6]

≈

THE WOMEN—IN THEIR OWN WORDS

INJURY

In an eight hour day, an aide lifts about 3,000 pounds—incredible. She gives maybe 20 baths in a morning, and lifts more than a man in an auto assembly plant. That's why her back goes. The hospital thinks it's a matter of lifting the right way. That helps, but it's not the answer. A person who lifts 20 people a day will have problems no matter what she does. She needs help, more staff.

Women fall on wet floors in bathing areas. In food service they fall over things, cut themselves, burn themselves on sterilizers. They get stuck with needles and glass that's thrown into the laundry. In the psychiatric wards, they are attacked by patients.

I hurt my back in neuro lifting a patient. Nobody likes neurology. Most patients are paralyzed or in comas. It's the heaviest load a nurse can have. I wanted it because people really need me there. I injured myself and I stayed off about two months. They sent me right back there, and I hurt myself again. Then I stayed out for three and a half years.

We are short staffed and we have to lift really obese people, but we're not trained for that. We also have a lot of elderly people to lift. If it's going to be a geriatric floor, they should get more help and train us in moving people around. We used to have a lifting law for women. Now we don't have it. The first thing county said was, "We can't have protective laws for women, so women will have to do what the men do"—like push a 600 pound x-ray cart. They use it to punish women.

DISEASE

You don't always know what patients have before you x-ray them. One patient I x-rayed should have had a mask on. I saw his films and he had TB all over him. We go with portable x-rays to patients in isolation wards and we're not compensated for that. People used to be paid for working in hazardous areas, but not any more. One tech got spinal meningitis in the hospital. One got TB. Hospitals are full of people with cancer, and some people say it's caused by a virus and that you can get it through exposure. People get jaundice all the time, people who work in renal, with kidney problems. You're exposed to all kinds of disease.

We had this patient, Willie. He was the nastiest little thing. He used to make duck sounds and bark like a dog when the nurses made their rounds. He had hepatitis and I had to give him injections. I was very careful, but my gloves made me a little clumsy and I stuck myself with the needle. About four weeks later I had hepatitis, but I didn't bark like a dog, thank God.

OTHER HAZARDS

Radiation is dangerous. If we do what we're supposed to, we shouldn't have any problems. But some things we can't control, or even know about, like the tube may be leaking radiation and we won't know it. We wear radiation badges and they give us a reading once a month. We could be dead by the time we get it back.

People in surgery worry about gas leaks from the anaesthetics. In dietary they worry about leaks from the microwave ovens. In house-keeping the detergents have some very harsh chemicals in them, and sometimes the housekeepers break out in rashes. The patients do too. They get rashes all over their backs from the sheets washed in these detergents.

People get toxic reactions from the gas used in sterilizers. Admin-istrators like to talk about all the protective gear they'll give the workers, but they never talk about changing the kind of gas used so workers won't need protection. They try to put everything on the workers. If they were throwing poison darts at the workers, they'd say, "Well, let's give them a protective shield. If they forget to use the shield, it's their fault." Stop throwing the darts, I say.

The gases released in operating rooms affect the ability of women in there to have children. It also affects the men. Their wives have trouble having children, or the children they bear have problems. These workers go in there every day. The doctors only go in when they operate.

SICK ENVIRONMENTS

Medical records has a toilet that leaks. The ceiling gets wet and all sorts of human waste spills around. Once every two or three months, the ceiling gives way and the place smells like shit. They don't fix it.

I have been at Penn for seven years and the air conditioning has never worked. The supervisor comes up and says, "Shut the window, the air conditioning is on." So we shut the windows. Two hours later, the patients can't breathe, so we have to open the windows again. It's so hot in there you can't move. The offices of top supervision are very cool. The kitchen, the hottest spot, has never had an air conditioner.

We have fire hazards. The contractor told us we'd have a serious problem if the old wing ever caught fire. Pediatrics is over there. It's ground level so you can push the children out the window. But we're on the third floor and the building is literally falling down. It's a fire trap. The roof leaks. Patients take showers in their beds when it leaks. Management couldn't care less.

Cal hospital is over 50 years old. We don't have lounges for employees in many wards. The cafeteria is too far, so people have to eat lunch on the ward. They don't have a place to take a break, smoke a cigarette, prop up their feet and say, "God, I'm tired." The building is not air conditioned and it's a horrible heat sink. This concrete monster heats up and you'd think it was Auschwitz.

It used to be we couldn't even take a phone call from a sick child. I was a big instigator in changing that. My daughter is asthmatic and several times she called to tell me she was sick and needed medication. They put the message in my mailbox without telling me. I didn't find it until late afternoon. I raised so much hell they changed the rule. You were like a prisoner in there, no messages in or out.

Shift work is dangerous for women. Muggings. Rape. There isn't enough security in the parking lot. Management is absolutely oblivious to these dangers.

STRESS

The doctors keep after you in x-ray. They want you to do their patient immediately, but we don't have the staff for it. That gets to you, dealing with all that pressure, spinning your wheels all the time.

I wish there was a better way to make a living. I'm tired of getting up every morning and coming in here, wrestling with these people. I like the hospital work, but I get so tense and so tired. If I go to school and get educated a little more in nursing, maybe I can get out of this.

There's more stress in hospitals than in other places. That's why there are so many industrial accidents and workers' compensation cases. Even if you had enough help, which you don't, you are in crisis 24 hours a day. People are ill, they are dying, children are being born, patients are screaming, relatives are asking questions.

I like the mini intensive care unit because there's less stress in there. I don't have Tom, Dick and Harry breathing down my neck, and I don't have to cope with the chaos out there. I get to know my patients better because I have the same ones every day. I can't stand the floor, it's bedlam. I might go up north or leave California. The chaos gets to you. When you leave here each day you're fit to be tied. I'm getting older now and I can't handle it. I get migraine headaches if I get overly tired. At the end of a seven day stretch I have a tension headache like you wouldn't believe. I come home and my two days off I'm sick.

People on the floors complain about stress constantly, the stress of overwork, headaches, tension in the neck and back, digestive problems, bad tempers, constant running. Too much is happening, and you don't want to screw the patients and your coworkers by leaving. You see the need, so you bust your ass. If you're on the floor, a patient hits a buzzer, and you have to respond instantly. An endless series of responses are required. In housekeeping you can pace your responses to some extent.

Dietary and housekeeping complain about stress too. It's disrespect mainly. Supervisors treat them shabbily, wag their fingers in their faces. One dietary worker wanted a day off to see her doctor. Her supervisor *called the doctor* to find out if she really had an appointment.

STRESS, PATIENTS

People burn out from stress. A patient that dies. A patient that is very sick and in danger. In the emergency room, a few minutes can make all the difference. The nurses that work in there go berserk sometimes.

A lot of mental stress comes from dealing with chronically ill patients too. You're trained to make people better. There's no way you're going to make patients in renal better. You'll only fend off the inevitable. They're not going to get their kidney function back, regardless of what you do. It's real tough being a chronically ill person, and sometimes they project their frustration and anger on the staff. You have to deal with that, because you'll be taking care of them for many years. It takes energy, a lot of creative thinking, a lot of charity. It takes a heavy toll.

It's disturbing working with patients who are very ill. You walk around all the time feeling sad and depressed. Some cases affect me more than others. A person that is old and has been sick a long time, it's understandable. They will eventually die. But when it happens to a young person it's very depressing. I try not to let it get to me because I can't do anything about it. The stress comes more from doctors, trying to keep them off your back.

People think, "How horrible for a doctor to have a patient die." Well, nurses are with that patient day in and day out, while the poor person hangs on by the fingernails. They're the ones that are shattered when the patient dies. And it's not just people in patient care. Dietary workers get to know patients too. They deliver trays and some of them develop a better relation with patients than nurses do. It's a class thing, or cultural thing. The patient finds it easier to talk to someone in a blue uniform than a white one.

I love the patients here in oncology. Most of them are very nice, and most of them come back until they die. They may go years before they die. I hate to see the young ones come in, it's too soon for them, they haven't had their chance yet. But I can't get too attached, I can't let it bother me too much, it's too painful.

TROUBLE WITH PATIENTS

Very few patients cause us any stress. The stress comes from caring about the patients, wanting to help them too much. Of course, if you're in this hole and knocking yourself out because you care about those patients, when they give you trouble, it hurts. Most of them appreciate what you're doing, and that's the only appreciation you get.

Oh, you might get an old lady that doesn't have anybody. She gets in the hospital and doesn't want to go home, so she has all these fake ailments, and these hurts and complaints, and she's forever ringing the bell. That type of patient bothers us, but you just go in and explain to her, "Honey, you're not the only one here. Please don't ring the bell unless you need us." But all she wants is company. They don't bother us.

Patients don't have to be grateful for what I do, but I'd like them to be polite and say "thank you" once in awhile, or maybe they just never learned manners. When you're working your ass off and somebody's real crabby to you, it doesn't make it any better.

At times there's a lot of stress dealing with patients' families. Upon discharge, you find patients' families that don't want to take them home. Or they may not have equipment at home that the patient needs. You contact social services and make arrangements to have them meet and talk. The families can be nasty and troublesome.

There's stress because of the types of patients we care for at the Cal clinic. There's a lot of abuse with drugs and alcohol in the county facilities. Some of the patients are very belligerent. It's hard to take care of them when they're cussing you out.

The patients are very sick and they're constantly ringing up the staff. It would be all right if we had enough staff. The nurses don't like the type of patients we have. Our patients are usually poor. A lot of them live on the street and the police bring them in. They're dirty. They come with maggots and lice, and they are very abusive verbally and physically.

Some patients want to jump on you. I've had that happen to me in the emergency area. There have been shoot-outs. There's been incidents of nurses getting stabbed and beaten up. It never hits the newspapers so no one knows what we go through. In emergency we try to x-ray patients and we have to call security half the time to make the family leave the room. If you say too much to the family, they want to jump on you. There are gangs that follow their people to the hospital.

In the alcoholics ward, you feel, "All this work is futile, it's not doing anything for them." They take it as a joke. They come back drunk the next day, and the day after. It's upsetting. One man lunged at me. He was really wild. But I jumped back. They told me, "Hey, don't be afraid. Every time he comes in here he's violent." I was really scared.

The women can be worse than the men. They're demanding, they want to come to the hospital like a hotel. If they don't get their way they call you all kinds of names. They get upset, start running around, chasing after the other patients. When I first started I was afraid of drunks, but if you let them know you're afraid, they try to dominate you, abuse you. It really gets to you, like working in a prison or an asylum.

PHYSICAL SYMPTOMS OF STRESS

Hospital workers suffer from ulcers, high blood pressure and various heart conditions brought on by stress. If doctors examined the health of health workers, they'd be appalled to find out how bad it is. They're given x-rays regularly but not general examinations. And they're never given tender loving care, yet they're expected to give it to patients. Most of the girls usually work until they get sick.

How about a 20 year old with an ulcer? From the stress and tension. No matter what this girl did, to her supervisors, nothing was right. They didn't like her, so they picked on her.

A doctor once talked to us on stress. He said, "If your body is tired, you're sick." I work seven days and I have to go home, clean my house, cook, shop, all that. I'm physically exhausted. Plus having my supervisor on me all day.

SOME UNION RESPONSES

We are getting more and more into health and safety. In x-ray, for instance, people can get time off with pay when the doctor in charge thinks something is wrong. Our union is like 50 steps ahead of other unions on OSHA issues. We wanted to go from 50 to 100 and applied for an OSHA grant. But they wanted the unions that needed to go from 1 to 50. They got the grants.

It's more dangerous to work in a hospital than to be a fire fighter. Once you've injured your back in a hospital, you're done for. You can never find another job in hospital work. People are afraid to bring up these injuries, afraid they won't be able to get another job in the health industry. We have to look more at nurses in operating rooms; there's been a large number of birth defects in children of operating room nurses.

The x-ray techs sometimes leave their badges on their desks because they're afraid if they get too much exposure they'll be forced off their jobs. The physicians with the shortest life span are radiologists, and it's probably the same for x-ray techs. One orderly who worked around x-rays was refused a radiation badge. We hit the ceiling, grieved it and won. How come they think a tech can be exposed to radiation, but not housekeepers and orderlies?

In a survey we made, we found one woman that wanted a coat to put on when she had to go into the freezer three or four times a day. It's a simple request, but it's a real struggle getting it out of the hospital.

People can't get help when they need to lift someone. The new lifting machines can help a lot. The union tries to tell them, "Hey, wait a minute. If that patient is too heavy to lift, wait for someone to help." But there is this philosophy, "Oh, no, the patient is more important than I am."

The law used to require hospitals to have a safety committee. But the committees are a joke. They're all run by the administrators. When I was a business agent, we had a hospital safety committee and we really made it work. The hospital doesn't take responsibility for educating people and our members don't know enough about the potential dangers. We need more education of stewards and more knowledge about the chemicals and other dangers people are exposed to.

I don't know what we can do in the state legislatures. It's an area where the union's been rather weak. Every time you bring up OSHA regulations, the business community screams about how costs will go up with protective measures, and you get your head beaten in.

There's a lot of rage, buried, suppressed rage. Our people are pissed off at management for giving them more than they can do physically. But they also feel, "I really want to get it done." So they go home exhausted.

What is common to everybody is the feeling of powerlessness. The union gave them some dignity and a sense that there is something they can do to change things. In unorganized hospitals, the situation is desperate. In organized hospitals it's not good but it's much better. The struggle to get more power and control for workers isn't won overnight.

Sixteen

SUPERVISION AND "THE WAY WE'RE TREATED"

Respect and dignity is the number one issue. If people had it, they'd have better wages and conditions and a say in what goes on at work.

In the hospital all the roads lead to supervision, for it is the control center where most decisions affecting the daily lives of hospital workers are made. When workers complain about supervision, however—as they do often and vigorously—they usually refer less to formal decisions about wages and hours than to the behavior of supervisors, their poor human relations, the indignities they inflict on subordinates.

The hospital hierarchy, of course, includes doctors and administrators along with immediate supervisors (who are often head nurses), but since friction only occurs when two parts are in contact, and rubbing each other, most dissatisfaction is with immediate supervisors. Complaints charge that supervisors harass workers, ignore what they say, "treat them like dirt;" they charge that supervisors are incompetent and lacking in the skill and the will needed to do a good job and to "get things done" and "change things;" they charge that supervisors can't lead, can't work with people, and won't help out in time of need.

Asked what they *most disliked* about their work, the women surveyed put "the way I'm treated, lack of appreciation, respect, dignity" in fifth place, in a tie with "wages" and behind only "scheduling," "trying to work and raise a family," time-off, and staffing.

On this *most disliked* list, "supervision" followed right after "the way I'm treated."

Almost half of those surveyed said that "too hard to change things" was a *sizeable* or *great* problem—and 43 percent gave the same response to "superior doesn't know enough"; 35 percent to "job not considered important"; 31 percent to "supervisor not fair"; and 29 percent to "supervisor doesn't solve problems."

Disrespectful treatment by supervision is a women's issue, much as other issues afflicting sexually segregated low-wage workers are women's issues. Women in the hospital are a servant class and are treated with the characteristic disrespect shown that class. Top policy makers in the hospital, those with real authority, are almost all males, while those at lower levels are mainly female, and those at the top (it is claimed) push female subordinates harder than they do males, demand more of them, expect more submissive behavior, confer less respect on them. Women perhaps also resent disrespectful treatment more than men do, since having respect and being respectable appear (also in other contexts) to be dominant themes with them. Respect is a women's issue, then, because women apparently want more of it, and get less, than comparably situated males do.

The sexist nature of the issue is obscured (as noted previously) by the presence of a buffer between workers and male policy makers, the immediate supervisor, who is often an RN. But immediate supervisors make few of the rules about which workers complain, and when these supervisors behave badly it is often because they are treated badly by those above them. If they fail to "change things," it is often because those above them do not allow change. These supervisors are like sergeants in the sense that they follow orders from above and represent those in higher ranks.

Complaints about poor supervision and disrespectful treatment are rarely covered in union contracts. Both workers and unions seek greater control over the behavior of supervisors, though it is not a highly developed issue. To date, management resistance and the problems involved in mandating good human relations have made progress on the issue difficult.

≈

THE WOMEN—IN THEIR OWN WORDS

Women are victimized by supervisors more than men are. There is definitely discrimination against women, especially by male supervisors. The women's concerns are never felt. No one ever comes to them and asks them anything. Women supervisors are usually better because they understand the problems women have. The only time women supervisors are resented is when they are insensitive to the special needs of women—like getting time off to take care of a sick kid. A woman supervisor who is hard-ass about that is resented. People get more angry at a woman who's insensitive than they would at a man.

They expect more understanding. A woman supervisor who has never married can be a problem. If she's made a career of her job, that's all she lives for.

We don't have too many men in nursing, but those we have freeload more than the women do. They get away with a lot. They say, "I'm going to take a walk," and the women supervisors don't bother them. A woman has to be right there every minute, always running and working. The RNs respect the male LVNs a little more. They don't run up in their faces as often as with other females. And they get very buddy-buddy with them.

It's hard to imagine the way people are treated. I'm knocking myself out, working long hours, and the head nurse is hollering, "Go do this. Go do that." I gulp down my lunch in 15 minutes, and she's still hollering. I'm not a person to get mad. When I do, I shut my mouth so I won't blow up. But I have to let it out, so I go home and scream. My husband used to be proud of my job. If he knew half of what goes on, he'd make me quit.

The head nurse came down the other day and started shaking her finger and screaming at me. I said, "Look, the doctor told me not to get excited, and I'm not going to let you run up my blood pressure." She kept yelling. I walked out and slammed the door. She wanted me to lift a patient but my back hurt and I couldn't do it. They suspended me for three days without pay, but the union got me pay for the days I was off.

What I don't enjoy about the work is the recognition we don't get. Never a "Thank you, you did a good job." Nothing. They like to put you down. One supervisor disliked me and kept writing bad evaluations. But I plugged along and in the end she got fired. So somebody was writing *her* bad evaluations. Some supervisors are poison pen artists, always writing people up, getting them fired. You have to give a person a chance. Conditions at home or on the job can cause people to make mistakes. A supervisor should talk to a person, find out what's disturbing her and try to help her. Before you push a person, walk awhile in her shoes. Then you can understand.

Often you're working with a patient and there's no one at the bedside. Then a doctor will come up, with no apologies, and begin to draw blood. I'll be frank, the doctors are just rude. They ignore you, they don't even see you. You're a flunky to them, a nobody.

People who are a step higher than you don't want to hear what you say. I am very observant of my patients and when I see things are wrong, I tell the doctor about it. He says, "Oh, we know all about that." He walks away and does nothing. Then I get all bent out of shape.

A hospital has to be clean. Germs . . . ugh! So the housekeeper is important because she keeps it clean. Right? But they treat her like dirt, isolate her from other workers, discourage her from working up into other jobs. Even if you're in a menial position, sweeping the floor, you still make up the hospital team. They can't run the hospital without you. But they make you feel like you don't have any brains and, feeling that way, you may do a sloppy job. Supervisors pit one worker against the other one and encourage them to squeal on one another. They play favorites and they're always on top of the older workers because they're trying to get rid of them. We're not here to kiss anyone, but still we should work together and enjoy our day. When your job is pleasant, you face your work with a smile.

Before the union, you'd see the medical director walk out on the floor and fire four people for smoking in the nurses' bathroom. So you worried about job security. They could do anything to you. They'd call you a "dumb son of a bitch" in front of patients. They still try to pull stuff like that.

It was the worst experience I've ever had. The supervisor accused me of having sex with a maintenance man in the locker room. They fired both of us. This other girl and I were watching TV at lunchtime with one of the guys. It's not against the rules. The door was wide open, and this other girl was in there too. Then one day, no warning, no hearing, the supervisor said to me, "I want you to come with me." I had no idea what for. They took me to an office and said, "You're fired." When they explained why, I was speechless. I cried so hard when I called my mother, she couldn't understand what I was saying, but she came and picked me up. The union had just come in, and they got my job back, but it left a bad scar on me.

FAVORITISM

There's so much favoritism. A supervisor may assign vacation time according to whether you give him a fifth of scotch, if it's the right scotch. They discriminate against Blacks, browns, women, old, young. There's no monolithic structure to the discrimination. Each supervisor has his own prejudices, and nobody in administration really gives a shit what they are.

Seniority doesn't count. It's who they like. They're trying to get rid of older people, so they pull them onto the floors for the hard jobs and put the younger ones in their place. I have top seniority, yet they're moving me out of coronary care and onto the floor. I asked the girl that makes assignments, "Doesn't seniority count?" She said, "Only fairness counts." She thinks it's fair to pick on older women.

If your nose isn't as brown as the next person's, they don't need you. They can make it so hard you don't want to stay. A lot of clericals are relatives of higher ups. In one department, almost the whole office staff is related. It's almost like incest. If you see an office job coming up for bid, you wonder whose relative it will go to.

If you're in good with a supervisor, you say, "I want to work in this area. Can you arrange it?" That's how it's done. They put their friends on. If the supervisors want to get rid of a person, they'll pick on her until they find something, then they'll fire her. They might give her a tough schedule. The union tries to stay on top of that and make sure the scheduling is fair. If it's not according to past practice, it looks bad for them. When I became a steward, the first words out of my mouth were: "This favoritism has to stop." One day we'll be able to stop it dead.

COMPETENCE AND CARING

My head nurse doesn't like friction. If you have a problem, she'll say, "I'll take care of it." Then, nothing. She doesn't want any waves. A small problem or a big problem, you can't get anything done. So everybody says, "Why bother? The supervisors don't care."

Supervisors should know more than the people under them. In pediatrics, for instance, the supervisor should know about babies, but she doesn't. How can she direct our work and evaluate us when she doesn't know beans about sick and premature babies?

Supervisors can't even manage the supplies. Nobody's ever stocked. If they want something in emergency, and they want it fast, they don't have it.

Very few supervisors are concerned about patient care. They only worry about things like how many beds they can squeeze into a room so they can get brownie points and the hospital can make more money. We're supposed to have four beds in our wards. We have five. One is squeezed into the middle of the room. You're always bumping into them. They're a hazard. The patient has no phone, no television, and only half a curtain. The inspector is good friends with people on the hospital board, so she sees nothing wrong with cramming these beds in. We got on the health department about it, and they said that only emergency cases could be put in middle beds. So last week there was a big emergency—incision of impacted molars! If there's a big wreck on the turnpike one day, there'll be no beds. They'll be full of teeth extractions from the dentist's office.

DOCTORS

The doctor is your superior, the next thing to God. But after four years at the county hospital, if the doctors learn nothing else, they learn to be human. They can't say, "I'm a doctor. Do this or I'll have your job." They come down to earth fast, and it's "Well, hi there. How are you?" The contract makes them human. We have that protection against harassment. I'm not saying a union is always right, but it's a protection for us. In private hospitals, you genuflect to the doctor when he comes to the nurses' station, and the doctors are always dumping on the nurses. But in a teaching hospital, the interns and residents depend on the nurses and aides to tell them what to do, so they handle them with kid gloves. So we have that protection too.

In medical-surgical at Penn, some of the doctors were mean. They'd throw charts, ignore your questions, yell at you. In obstetrics, the same doctors are entirely different, very nice to you. They trust your judgment. They come when you call them. The same doctors. Why on earth is that? I'll tell you why. Our patients in OB are aware of what's going on, and the surgery patients aren't, so the doctors are better behaved in OB.

There's some beautiful doctors and some nasty ones. I mean real nasty. The housekeepers have to clean the interns' rooms. The interns stick gum on the wall, turn out cigarettes on the floor, use the bed linen to wipe their feet and dry their hands. I can't stand that. I find a lot of wallets, rings, briefcases that they carelessly leave around. I don't touch them. If it's a wallet I take it to the head nurse. If you don't, they come to the housekeeper right away, "Did you see my wallet?" Anything's lost, they think we took it. They take tubes of blood to their rooms, drop them, step all over the blood. They put needles and everything on top of the bed. They sleep on clean sheets with dirty shoes on. I get mad. They couldn't be *my* kids. We're not their personal maids.

You get some interns that are horrendous. A new patient drank a bottle of medicine. We called the pharmacy and they said to pump out the patient's stomach. I told the intern and he just stood there like a zombie. He didn't know what to do with the equipment I had gotten. I told the RN, "Please go over and tell the doctor in your unit to come and pump this lady's stomach for me." I'm the aide and he's the doctor, right? He's supposed to know everything, I'm supposed to know nothing.

BETTER BOSSES

Our boss is really fair. She has no picks. She may like one person better than another but she doesn't show it. She trusts us and gives us a lot of leeway. When we need it, she'll give us a hand, and she can get things done. We call her by her first name because she's easy to communicate with. She treats us as equals, whether or not we are. When we're all guilty of something, she doesn't pick on one, she yells at all of us. You get a lot more out of people by treating them right.

You have to admire my supervisor, but sometimes I'm a little frightened of her. She's totally into her job, and she expects you to be. I couldn't say she's prejudiced because she gets on everyone, regardless of their race or whatever. She's not easy to work for, but she'll back up her employees. She may think the worst of you, but she's not going to let anyone else run you down.

One supervisor was framed by higher ups. She was fantastic in our eyes. She taught us and listened to us. If she didn't know something, she'd read up on it and come back and tell us. They wanted her out, so they set this machine up wrong and she got blamed for it. She got disgusted and left. So that's discrimination, harassment. You name it, we've got it.

UNION COMMENTS

The California promotion system isn't a merit system at all. They can promote damn near anyone they want, and they tend to promote people less competent than themselves. The system's been in place for years and it's gotten worse over time. You take a civil service exam to be promoted to Supervisor I or II. One of the top three on the list has to be offered the job. If that person refuses, they can take anyone on the list. Usually the person is picked ahead of time. The supervisors on the line have a rough time. That's why those jobs are given to women. They take a beating from the doctors and from their own supervisors. They just pass the beatings on down the line.

The Cal medical center employs 70,000 people. That's way too large for a system to run well, but nobody even *tries* to do it. The center is a small city, and its social structure prevents good teamwork at any level. Maybe there are 40 or 50 medical specialties there, which means 40 or 50 very high ego physicians to deal with. Getting them to work together is hard. Getting them to be at all sensitive to people below is even harder. One's making $100,000 a year and the other's making $5,000, so he doesn't perceive the problem.

The upper administration levels are far removed from the clinical setting. They may give lip service, "Oh, you're doing a great job," but it doesn't mean much. Their praise is hollow. That's the cause of the friction down below: the people at the top are out of touch.

There have been stories about women being promoted for sexual favors. The Civil Service Commission won't even listen to this. The Civil Service Commission here would crucify Jesus, in my opinion. They are just not a good third party. They're corrupt and dirty, and just not a legitimate appeal board.

Head nurses aren't trained for their jobs as supervisors. They're trained to be nurses. When they start pushing pencils, they become frustrated. They have no skill in interpersonal relations, and the people they supervise fight them all the way. High level administrators often intimidate and overrule the first line supervisors, who are often women, and that causes a lot of trouble. They take the authority away from the supervisors.

People aren't appointed to supervision based on merit. Usually it's "who you know." I hear complaints constantly about incompetent supervisors. "What did she do to become a supervisor?" They're not talking about sexual favoritism. What you hear is sort of ass-licking stuff. That's why they say, "The fish stinks from the head."

Seventeen

CAREERS, LATERAL MOVES, SCOPE OF PRACTICE

The only way you can promote yourself in here is out of here.

The women's movement has been inspired and sustained by a belief in upward mobility but, while most hospital workers seek to improve their lot, the terms "upward mobility" and "success" or even "careers" do not quite suit either their vocabulary or aspirations. For feminists "careers" may suggest self-fulfillment and acquiring the symbols and trophies of achievement, but for hospital workers the meaning is so much more modest, so much less ego-involved and ego-testing, that the term may not fit their aspirations at all. The term is used here nevertheless because it is so often used in this context and because many hospital workers do seek more opportunity than they have. Perhaps more of them would seek "real" careers if more opportunities were available, but in this case (and others involving workingclass women) values may influence aspirations as much as opportunities do. Upward mobility, in the sense of "making it" or being a "very important person," are simply not very highly valued as life goals.

The hospital is, of course, an ideal setting for developing careers. It is like a city, a service city. It performs most life sustaining services for patients and hence contains most service occupations. The hospital is also very hierarchical; every job fits into another and requires a little more skill to perform. For this reason, the hospital is said to be "the best place in the world to train people." But in most hospitals it does not happen and the result is an excessive turnover of workers and, inevitably, a reduction in the quality of patient care.

In the hospitals studied, not having "many promotional opportunities" was identified by about four in ten women as a *sizeable* or *great* problem—and the same proportion regarded "people are promoted unfairly" as an equally serious problem. Thus, a sizeable proportion of hospital workers deplore the hospital's promotion policies and seek better jobs—though not necessarily "men's jobs" or jobs removed from patient care. Women also questioned the qualifications and training required for certain jobs, and complained about inadequate in-service training for jobs they now perform.

Almost no job training programs were offered in the hospitals surveyed. Even Cal hospital, a giant teaching hospital for a vast range of medical specialties, offered little instruction to its own workers. The hospital closed the LVN school it once operated, and its nursing school recruits almost nobody from inside the hospital or community. At the union's initiative, several training programs, with paid time-off, have been offered to workers, but the initiative is too new to be assessed.

"Career development," the union's response to the hospital workers' desire for upgrading, includes the creation of career ladders, a better division of labor among jobs, apprenticeship training conducted mainly on-the-job, release-paid time for training, credit for experience, and greater relevancy of qualifications to the actual performance of jobs. It also includes expanding the nurses' "scope of practice" and extending the nursing career ladder up into roles now reserved by physicians.

Career ladders do not intensify hierarchies; when they extend into the most highly skilled jobs, they diminish them. In particular, by making the loftiest professions accessible to the lowly, they reduce the caste-like quality of hierarchies. Most highly skilled jobs (especially in the professional and managerial realms) are protected like fortresses by high walls, moats, and sentries. In this case the fortifications are educational requirements and/or being of the right caste (sex, race, social class), or at least looking and acting like the right caste. (In most cases, of course, being of the right caste is prerequisite to getting the educational credentials).

At any rate, most occupational elites protect themselves by caste barriers and impose high educational requirements (the higher the better) that can be met *only* by off-the-job schooling (preferably in a prestigious college or university). Career ladders break down these barriers and penetrate the fortress by (1) reducing excessive education credentialism (lowering the walls), (2) dividing skills into smaller steps to make climbing easier, (3) erecting ladders at the fortress walls so that those below can get inside. What remains of caste then, the selection of supervision, can be corrected through worker participation and approaches that select supervision based on *leadership* ability (as well as other criteria).

Nursing has tried to erect walls around its profession (or semi-profession) but domination by the medical profession has consistently curtailed its ability to do so. Perhaps another strategy might work better: creating career ladders from below into nursing, and joining with those below in extending the ladders into the medical profession.

The cultivation of caste in nursing, perhaps as a reflection of caste in the medical profession, is visible in the early efforts to establish nursing as a "ladies occupation." The movement away from apprenticeship was also to some extent an effort to separate the ladies from the lowly and, in the American example, also the white majority from disadvantaged minorities.

In 1907, one "missionary" nurse wrote, "One cannot have too high-class a nurse for infirmary nursing. There is much a nurse with ideals can do, if she is broad-minded and sympathetic. . . . Oh, there is much in workhouse and infirmary nursing that counts, and I hope girls and women of the right sort will not be deterred from entering."[1] Another woman, asked how she felt about becoming registered when the Register first opened, said that, "it did not really excite her, as her matron had seen to all of that: what she did not like, however, was that the Poor Law nurses got onto the same register as she did."[2]

In developing careers, the union has launched apprenticeship programs following the model of other skilled apprenticeships, and combining the best of hospital and academic training. Over the years, the transfer of nurses' training from hospital to academy has been both applauded and deplored, but perhaps each training approach offers something of value: practical experience in the hospital and "theoretical" knowledge in the academy. In some cases, unions have moved the academy into the union hall, rather than returning it to the "hospital school."

The view that "hospital schools" (and apprenticeships) subjected nurses to paternalism and the male authority of hospital administrators, has considerable validity, as does the view that removing nurses' training from the hospital to college settings altered the male administrator's hold on nursing. As Jo Ann Ashley observes, apprenticeship education "was ideal as a means of keeping a female group in subjection to male dominated groups."[3] And again, "The apprenticeship system of training produced nurses who could not question the status quo. Thus, they fostered defects in existing practices. . . . The education received by nurses in privately controlled service institutions was oppressive and paternalistic, greatly influenced by the institution's own traditions, rituals, and parochial concerns. The power structure in these hospitals was authoritarian, a system that best served an elite few, often functioning to the detriment of staff and patients."[4]

Bonnie Bullough points out, "The major social structure which institutionalized and perpetuated the 19th century subordination of nurses was the hospital training school. . . . . A cornerstone of the hospital nursing school education was a belief that the physician was always right, and even when he was wrong he must be made to appear right."[5]

But to some extent nursing simply jumped out of the frying pan and into the fire when it left the hospital for the academy. Males remained dominant over nursing in hospitals, and while nurses experienced some moments of autonomy in the academy, when they re-entered the hospital, as most of them had to, they were pretty much back to where they had started, except for certain handicaps acquired on the way: lack of practical skill and knowledge, and expectations about autonomy that were shattered by experience. As a "profession," functioning as it has, nursing apparently cannot by itself hurdle the caste barriers constructed by physicians, but as an organized collective, in concert with other hospital workers, it may have a better chance.

Apprenticeship training, which is essentially hospital based and union supervised, may have some positive benefits; it may serve to stabilize the work force, train and retain skilled workers, improve hospital care. It may also strengthen the union by providing needed services to members and thus increasing their identity with the union.

Training and upgrading are women's issues insofar as women (in hospitals and elsewhere) are more likely than men to be stuck in low wage jobs that offer no opportunities for advancement. Employers generally give less training to women, thinking (mistakenly) that women are more likely than men to quit the job and waste training investments. Then too, women have greater home responsibilities than men. They punch time cards at home as well as at work, and they may not be able to take time off for classes. Lengthy training programs also handicap women. Rather few women become MDs, for example: too many years of schooling are required just at the time women start having babies. Women are kept out of other programs by costs, inaccessible locations, the hours classes are held, and age limits.

≈

THE WOMEN—IN THEIR OWN WORDS

QUALIFICATIONS AND REQUIREMENTS

Many times people are already doing a certain job, but they have to take a civil service exam to get the title and the money—and they can't pass the exam. If you can do the job but can't pass the test, the test must be whacky. Right?

Why does an LVN have to go back to school to become an RN? A lot of LVNs already know everything the RN knows. We're taught just about everything the RN's taught, and we give medications just like RNs. Why not test us to see if we can do the job, and if we can, then give us the RN title and the pay.

The union has legislation pending in California to give credit to LVNs and attendants for the work they've been doing. If a woman has worked for five years as an LVN, we'd like that experience applied to getting an RN license. People don't have time to go to school. They need credit for the experience they've already had.

Nurses in California are required to take continuing education credit. It's a full employment program for nurse educators. The people who run nursing try to sell this "professional nurse" viewpoint. They tell nurses they have to go back and take all these goddam courses in order to be recognized. They get hung up on these dinky laws and don't deal with the main issues. It's really harmful.

IN-SERVICE TRAINING

We have a director of in-service training. She shows films on new techniques and equipment. Every six months she shows the same film, the same everything. That's all she does. She takes new employees around for orientation one day and then throws them on the floor to work. She says to me, "*You* work with her." But I'm not getting paid to train people, and I have my own work to do.

I try to gain knowledge on my own. I hear a new term, I write it down and try to read up on it. I'd like something a little better but they keep saying, "You don't qualify for a better job because you don't have the education." We could be taught different things if they'd show us. They're afraid we want their jobs, but we don't. If we try to get an education, we have to quit our job, lose our seniority and our income. We need the money. The hospital should be teaching us.

We had an in-service course in the evening. It was interesting but they taught us about things we have no contact with—alcoholism and drug addicts. We had to pay a fee for this, and I had to pay a baby-sitter and transportation, so I just dropped out. We want an in-service program where we can take off from work, go to a conference or a school and upgrade our skills.

APPRENTICESHIPS

Big changes will be made in hospital training and staffing through apprenticeship programs and career ladders. In the past, unions have set up apprenticeships for plumbers and many skilled and technical workers. Now we need programs to train attendants and LVNs for better jobs, and we need to take these training programs out of the community colleges and bring them into the worksite. That way the union provides something for the workers and creates a work environment that makes the union stronger. The union will organize RNs that way, by taking LVNs (our own members) and training them to be RNs. They'll be our best organizers, and they'll create a more stable work environment. Hospitals have been a secondary labor market basically. The union is trying to make them a primary labor market.

Setting up more apprenticeships and career ladders will be a big help to minorities. If we can take janitors and food service workers and move them up, we'll give minorities a bigger piece of the pie. And they'll do better in apprenticeships than in the schools because schools are basically white middle-class institutions.

MOBILITY

In hospital jobs now, there's very little chance for advancement. If you're licensed, usually the only movement is horizontal, unless you want to go into management. That means you have to go from hospital to hospital, rather than coming up through the system, in order to get a better job.

Jobs should be specialized so that we could have more career ladders, one step leading up to the next one. Hospitals are almost pre-industrial social organizations. Henry Ford had this great idea, the assembly line. It was bad in some ways but good in others. We could adopt the good things in the hospital. Breaking down the tasks of nursing into more specialties would also make scheduling easier. You wouldn't need so many nurses on the floor at one time. Some of our technical classifications could do a lot of the work, and the nursing attendants could be trained in specific skills. The LVNs could supervise most of the work.

Kaiser Permanenty has broken jobs into small segments and trained people to be technically skilled in those areas, and it works. Kaiser has a lot of job mobility programs. For example, the first nurse practitioners came from Kaiser. They've done a lot to promote people, especially from attendant into certain technician jobs. In hospitals like Kaiser, that are highly unionized and that have job mobility programs, you see a dramatic decrease in turnover rates. The turnover rates are about 40 percent in public sector facilities and only about 13 percent in Kaiser.

Career mobility and development, to make hospitals into "primary labor markets," is an idea whose time is coming. We're going to see more flexibility about taking courses on the job in order to go up the nursing career ladder. People will start with no training and get their training on the job up to a certain level. The RNs will be at the top, doing a lot of the ordinary general practitioner care that's usually done by the physician, and probably on an outpatient basis.

People will come up through the system and leave vacancies for new people to come in. The nursing attendants might train for a tech level. If they want to become LVNs, all that training will count, on a competency based level, towards becoming an LVN. And what they've learned as attendants will also count. So you have building blocks, from nursing attendant to tech, to LVN, to RN, to the specialties, and maybe even to physician.

Attendants are very frustrated because they have to go back to school for 18 months to become an LVN or for two years, minimum, to become an RN. To get that training they have to stop work or maybe change shifts and run themselves to death, between school, work, and home.

The training at County shouldn't be just for professionals. Why not train the help that is already there, the people who are familiar with patient care and enjoy their work? Hospital management is short-sighted. They say, "If a housekeeper wants to become a nurses' aide, we have to train her and then get someone to replace her." The union's position is, "Wait a minute. You have a responsibility to provide upgrading and mobility for employees. And if you don't do it, you'll lose them."

We did a career mobility program in Santa Clara county that was really far out. They had about 80 percent minorities in the dietary department but the nursing attendants were mainly whites.

They said, "We can't recruit minorities for those jobs."

We said, "Baloney. They're all in dietary. You can take those workers who have proven work records and move them up."

Attendance records for dietary were horrible, but we said, "So what? Why should people stay there? They don't see they're going anywhere. If they have good records, move them up to nursing attendant."

So we moved them up and management met their affirmative action goals for minorities. The high absenteeism in dietary also stopped because workers were motivated to make a good record. If they missed a lot of work they couldn't qualify for upgrading.

In most hospitals now, a person may be in dietary six years but she doesn't stand any better chance of moving into an attendant's opening than someone walking in off the street.

Training their own workers would give hospitals the nursing staff they need and also help with affirmative action goals. Right now only about two percent of RNs are minorities, even though about 90 percent of hospital workers in most big cities are minorities. Cal Hospital is located in a minority ghetto, but it recruits its RNs from among Asians, whites, and middle-class Blacks, all of whom live far from the hospital. Cal operates a nursing school that graduates about 100 nurses every six months or so, but less than ten percent of the graduates will go to work at Cal. So the hospital doesn't get the nurses it needs, and their own workers don't get a chance to better themselves.

SENIORITY AND TRAINING

To get vertical mobility, you first need seniority to guarantee your job. Very few hospitals have a seniority system—some in the private sector, but certainly not in the public sector. Many hospital workers have been brainwashed into thinking seniority is no good. Private industry uses seniority to guarantee that one worker will train another worker. It's hard to convince a worker to train someone if she thinks the other worker will take her job. But if she has seniority on her job, and seniority for promotions, she doesn't have to worry about the competition. In most hospitals, workers don't train other workers. When people get frustrated with their job and can't train for a better one, they just go on to another hospital. The job market is relatively open, so people don't deal with their jobs or try to improve them, they just move on.

HOSPITAL VS. ACADEMY

Nurses' training has become much more academic in the last decade, and the effects of that are being felt more each year. The training gives nurses a better background in anatomy and other subjects, but it doesn't teach them how to relate the book learning to the patient in the bed.

The colleges stress theory more than practice on the grounds that graduates can get the clinical once they're working. But once they're out there they have to rely on ancillary staff to teach them everything. It's very hard and it's not their job. Sometimes it's comical.

The head nurse says to the LPN, "Take so and so (a new RN) with you and show her how to irrigate a colostomy."

And the LPN says to herself, "Huh, this girl has gone through four years of nursing school and doesn't even know how to do a colostomy. How goddam dumb can she be?" It's like that with everything.

You have to go in to a sick patient and tell him what you're doing.

He knows who the RN is and he knows the LPN is showing the RN how to do things. How does he feel? Pretty nervous. And the RN doesn't like it either. It's one reason you see so much frustration among the RNs now.

The nurse educators tell their students, "You'll pick all that up once you go out to work." They want to keep their jobs too. Many of these graduate nurses go into education and supervision because they don't want to become practicing nurses. But as supervisors, they have no empathy for the people who take care of patients because they've never done it themselves.

A lot of this preference for the academy has to do with the aspirations of nursing instructors (who are the most powerful force in Sacramento lobbying on this issue) and with the idea that it's more professional to be attached to an educational institution.

And then there's the nursing board. People on the board favor academic training, and the more of it the better. These boards are run by administrators and educators. They're the only ones with the time to serve. The RNs certainly can't get time off for it. So the boards serve the interests of educators and administrators rather than nurses.

Nurses used to be trained in the hospitals rather than the academy. Even today about 80 percent of the nurses in California come out of diploma schools—hospital-based programs. They don't have college degrees. And the first LVNs were trained in the hospitals when nurses were scarce during World War II.

The hospital schools were closed primarily because a lot of hospitals used their third year student nurses as staff, without paying them. When they were required to pay students for that third year, to keep students from being exploited, they closed the schools. The graduates of those hospital schools are really prized now. The community colleges and universities can't graduate enough people, which creates the shortage of RNs.

We don't want to revert to those old-fashioned three year hospital schools. We want something better. In those schools you started off scrubbing floors, slinging bedpans, and you curtsied when the doctor came in. They taught you that you were an idiot and needed three different people telling you what to do. After that was beaten through your head for three years, you had a pretty lousy opinion of yourself.

But we shouldn't throw out the baby with the bath. We have to look at the basically good ideas there. Training in hospitals can be a lot better and a lot cheaper than college training. And it can be a lot more satisfying to everyone.

LATERAL MOBILITY

On a day-to-day basis, assignments, transfers, and lateral mobility may matter as much to hospital workers as training and upward mobility. Departments and jobs within them vary greatly, and some are vastly preferred to others. For this reason, workers seek transfers to some jobs and resist transfers to others. "Floating" is a particularly objectionable assignment because when a woman floats she lacks a home base and is required to deal with unfamiliar tools and tasks.

≈

An LVN is like a rubber ball. She's bounced to both the attendants and the RNs when they're short-staffed. We keep a book. Whoever floated last doesn't have to float this time. When you float you don't know where anything is so it's hard to do your work. There's nothing worse than dragging your butt into work, through the ice and snow, "because I can't let the folks on my floor down." You come in and find somebody else didn't show up, so they float you to her job.

People are asked to do things they aren't trained for. A surgical nurse may have to go to intensive care and run a machine that monitors heart beat, but she's had no experience doing it.

Management can transfer and assign pretty much as it wants, simply by alleging that they need people on a job. Unless we can prove discrimination or fraud in the transfers, we don't have much success in overturning them. We have to hang tough, fight it out each year, and get a little more each time. If a job opens, the contract says the top seniority person who bids on it should get it.

≈

JOB ENRICHMENT, ROTATION, INTENSIFICATION

Like lateral mobility, job enrichment and rotation have been proposed as ways of increasing worker satisfaction. Often such enrichment is offered in lieu of wage increases and other costly benefits. In lateral mobility, workers move into better but not higher paying jobs; in job enrichment their present job is improved (made less repetitive) or they are rotated into other jobs in order to reduce boredom. Since hospital workers complain very little about boredom, these approaches may not be very relevant to their work.

Some hospital jobs, of course, are extremely stressful, in which case women may wish to rotate out of them for a time. Usually, however, workers resist rotations into unfamiliar jobs and settings. In some cases, hospital jobs are simple, repetitive and boring—as in dietary departments; enrichment in this case may help to relieve the monotony of the kitchen's assembly line operations.

These approaches—lateral mobility, enrichment, rotation—intensify job satisfaction and create new definitions of "success," rather than relying exclusively on career ladders and upward mobility for satisfaction and a sense of being successful in one's work.

SCOPE OF PRACTICE

"Nursing skills are in a bottle, with a cork at the top, the physician"

"Scope of practice" tries to remove the cork from the nurses' bottle and extend career ladders up into the physician's circles. It has the effect of restructuring jobs and expanding them into male jurisdictions, rather than equalizing male and female wages (comparable worth) or integrating women into male jobs (affirmative action, etc.)

Basic to the hospital worker's problem is that nursing has required more schooling of the RN without achieving any comparable increase in her scope of practice, her occupational territory. The negative consequences of this have included over-trained and hence dissatisfied nurses, excessive medical training and costs, and an ancillary nursing staff that also has a cork in its bottle—the RN. Hospital workers cannot move up very far until the RN does.

Nursing has been ambivalent about how far it should (or can) move into the doctor's private circles. In 1955, for example, the American Nurses Association wrote a model nurse practice act which called for extended schooling but which also included this passage: "The foregoing shall not be deemed to include any acts of diagnosis or prescription of therapeutic or corrective measures." Others in nursing have sought to reduce the historic dichotomy between "caring" (what nurses do) and "curing" (what doctors do), and to push up into both spheres, extending the psychosocial support (the caring) given to patients by nurses, along with progressive increases in diagnosis and treatment (the curing) of their physical ailments. Unfortunately, the success of such ventures has fallen far short of their goal.

A large hole in the physician's circle appeared with the rise of specialization and the consequent shortage of general practitioners, family doctors, primary care physicians. Physician's assistants, recruited mainly from discharged medical corpsmen, moved into that opening but their numbers were limited. During the seventies, most states revised their nurse practice acts to permit nurses to expand into some kinds of diagnosis and treatment of patients. Passing through this legal opening have been thousands of "nurse practitioners"—pediatric, geriatric, adult, maternity, and family nurse practitioners, plus several *thousand certified nurse-midwives—a small but growing fraction of the more than 1.5 million RNs in the country.* *

Scope of practice touches the physician's circle much as self-management touches the administrator's; it extends the circles of hospital workers, provides more opportunity to them, enriches the content of their jobs, and permits more control over their work.

≈

If you want to reduce health care costs, you should use nurses, attendants and LVNs where you're using physicians now. A study at Kaiser Permanenty showed that most people who go to doctors have ailments that a nurse practitioner could treat, and physicians are needed for only 12 percent of all cases.

That's a real battle. Nurses need to take on the doctors but they hate to do that. It's like a private taking on a general. We've been making some inroads through state law though. We got the nurses' practice act adopted in California. Before that, nurses couldn't even take someone's blood pressure without a doctor observing it. That was how the law was written—and it was written by the doctors. Nurses are finally expanding their practice and chipping away at the doctors' practice. The nurse practitioner in an outpatient clinic sees patients on routine problems and does the same things doctors do, and just as well too. But the doctors have powerful political organizations. They want to keep the circle around their territory as big as possible. The nurses also want to make their circle as big as possible. So they push and shove each other.

Often the nurses, instead of pushing the doctors and administration, reverse that and come down hard on the LVN and the nursing attendant. That's related again to being female. The administrators and physicians are usually male, so the RNs are afraid to push them.

Attendants and LVNs are strictly limited by law in what they can do. But the duties intersect at certain points even with the MDs, and organizations representing these groups are constantly trying to expand their own duties.

The California law now allows LVNs to be certified to do IV—intravenous—care. But they can't add solutions or anything else needed to go into the IVs. You need an RN for that. Instead of blocking the LVNs, the RNs should expand their own practice.

Kaiser knows it has to save money to make its hospitals work, so the few RNs it has are supervisors. Most of its staff are LVNs. The

*For descriptions of how two hospital RNs set up a private practice, see: Karon White Gibson, Joy Smith Catterson, Patricia Skalka, *On Our Own*. New York: St. Martin's Press, 1981

LVNs make good money but not as much as the RNs, so the hospital saves, and the LVNs expand their practice.

The RNs and LVNs now have separate nursing boards in California. We want to set up a single board for both. We also want to license some nursing attendants and put them on that board. The RNs will organize against it. They don't like the idea of LVNs being on their board. They're worried that they'll be swallowed up by them. The nurses have a very strong lobby in the state.

We have to decide where the needs are for health care and expand the nurses' practice into those areas. Remember the family doctor who came out to the house? Where is he now? You'd better not wait for him to ring your doorbell. We have this huge gap in family medicine that women could fill.

We need more clinics, and they could be run and staffed by nurses. Most people need to be treated in clinics rather than hospitals. The clinics are also cheaper and more accessible to people. Hospitals are businesses with a vested interest in filling their beds, when patients could be treated just as well on an outpatient basis. That's changing, and the clinics are expanding.

Why always put women into hospitals for childbirth? Birth centers would be more humane and much less costly, and they could be staffed mainly by women. As it is in hospitals, the doctor usually runs in only as the baby's coming out the birth canal. The women have already done most of the work.

We want a law in California to allow women to become midwives and do most of the delivery of babies. That way, you create a real profession, and you make it possible to give better medical care, with lower costs, and have more stability in the nursing profession. Then too, there's very little pre-natal care for women. We should move nursing into that area, where the need is, and where there are probably more satisfying roles for women.

A PEDIATRICS NURSE PRACTITIONER

A nurse practitioner is a nurse in a very extended role. Most states have no legal criteria governing them. The new changes in the California law require that they have at least a bachelor of science degree. Maybe soon they'll be required to have a masters' degree. Nurse practitioners may specialize in several fields, but the overriding difference between her and a regular RN is that the nurse practitioner has a fairly large amount of independent practice. She has her own patients.

One day she will be able to prescribe medicines. Now it's just vitamins and over-the-counter stuff, but we hope it will work up to antibiotics. Nothing terribly profound, but still a giant step forward for nurses.

The "family nurse practitioner" encompasses the entire family, all ages and illnesses. She does physicals and treats the ordinary illnesses, the chronic illnesses, and she consults with the physician when she reaches the limit of her abilities. There are OB-GYN (obstetrics-gynecology) practitioners who insert intra-uterine devices, do pelvics and prenatal stuff. The largest number of nurse practitioners are in pediatrics. In the county of Los Angeles, there are roughly a hundred pediatric nurse practitioners (PNPs). The occupation is growing by leaps and bounds, and some hospitals are actually advertising for them.

In the private sector, most PNPs do physicals and routine counseling. In the county, we also do diagnosis and treat the more common illnesses (strep throats, colds, diarrhea) with a physician's co-sign. The physicians check everything until they get to know you.

The PNP frees the physician for more complicated work. It's ridiculous for a physician with 12 years of post-grad training to take care of colds. Nurse practitioners aren't trying to be junior doctors. We consider ourselves nurses, with additional training, doing a much wider range of work. Nurses and physicians have different orientations. The nurse is taught to evaluate a *patient* and approach the illness from the patient's point of view. Physicians, whether they think so or not, tend to evaluate a *disease.*

Most patients are uncomfortable talking to nurse practitioners at first, but after awhile they develop a lot of confidence in them. Given a choice, many prefer going to the nurse, knowing she will call the physician if needed. We have our own list of patients, and we order the necessary tests on our own.

A lot of nurses want more responsibility and recognition for what they can do. Many doctors owe their license to the fact that a smart nurse pulled their chestnuts out of the fire. Among the young doctors, the rapport with PNPs is good. Many of the older doctors don't accept us and probably never will. They grew up in a medical world where the nurses stood up when the doctor came in the room.

My work is very challenging. You can have ongoing relations with a family and watch the kids grow up. The well-baby care we give is pretty routine. It's all physical exams, and the same counseling, the same shots, year in and year out. But you do have the challenge of different illnesses and different relationships.

There's no end to what you have to learn. It takes a certain personality to get into it, generally someone who enjoys learning. You have to grow a book on the end of your nose in this business.

EIGHTEEN

SELF MANAGEMENT, CONTROL, UNIONISM

Most workingclass people don't have any sense of their own power. Women have it even less than men. When you unionize hospitals, that changes. The women feel: "Do I really *deserve* to be treated with respect and to be paid well?" When they start to unionize, they say, "Yeah—I do deserve it."

The upper administration levels are far removed from the clinical setting. . . . That's the cause of the friction down below—the people at the top are out of touch.

The depth of concern expressed by hospital workers about essentially non-economic issues, particularly with respect to "quality" issues (supervision, patient care, work life) was not altogether anticipated when this research began. Also somewhat unexpected, at least in its intensity, was the profound desire expressed (explicitly or implicitly) by hospital workers for "more say" about a range of problems, including work process and structure, supervision, evaluation, classification, career development, products, assignment of personnel.

The issue of autonomy and control is perhaps most important to those RNs who think of themselves as being among the "free professionals." One study of RNs showed, for example, that the sense of autonomy and control over work were key factors in job satisfaction, while another study showed that giving RNs more opportunity to participate in decision-making helped to reduce their turnover rates.[1]

Hospital workers' comments about the conduct of hospital affairs indicates, moreover, that they have valuable insights and experience to contribute to hospital management, and that listening to what they say may benefit both the public and the employer.

Once the chef's position was vacant, so the staff ran things the way they wanted. They did the supervising. It was a very good deal. After all, they're the ones that know what's going on. When the new chef came in, he wanted to run it his own way, whether it worked or not. They tried to tell him, "If it's working so well this way, why change it?" He wouldn't listen. Sure enough, everything got screwed up and we had nothing but problems. Lots of people have had that experience and lots of them say, "If you want things to run smooth, get rid of the supervisors, and let the people who do the work run the show."

I don't know much about running a place, but I could do better than a lot of our supervisors. Like with scheduling. We're all there on Monday, but during the week, when we need people, we're always short. Then I look at dietary and I say, "These patients are old. They should have different types of food than they're getting." They cook these frozen hamburgers so long all the juices come out, and these poor people can't chew them. They cook the juice and nutrition out of everything.

Then they put a lot of older people in the south wing. After they're in the hospital awhile, and there's nothing more we can do, they should go home with their families or to a nursing home. When patients are kept there any length of time, they get very irritable, and then the staff gets irritable too. We can't help them and it's costing a lot of money.

Some patients I'd like to bring home with me and take care of them there. I could do a better job than they do here because I know how to take care of people. They won't let you do it the right way here. I get a big kick out of doing for people.

Our orderly is not allowed to do patient care, so he floats around and does nothing. I went to meetings and said, "Not that I have anything against that orderly, but I'm sure the girls would appreciate one that works. Couldn't you devise a job for him? Couldn't he do escort service? He'd save the aides thousands of steps by taking patients for x-rays and other tests." They can't fire him because the hospital gets money from some doctor's estate each year he's employed there. But why not give him a job he can do? Supervision can't figure that out, and they won't listen to anything we say.

≈

CONSULTATION

A limited yet meaningful step toward self-management is through consultation, or the participation of workers as advisers to, rather than voting members of, decision-making bodies. The form and substance of consultations can vary, but in any case, workers have a voice and no vote.

A simple form of consultation is the suggestion box, for the deposit of worker ideas about improving jobs. These suggestions may or may not matter to anyone (or even be read by anyone), but they are more likely to matter if they pertain to ways of increasing employer profits and productivity. The suggestion box is the most anonymous and impersonal, and least satisfying and confrontational, form of consultation.

Employers may also conduct opinion polls among workers or set up advisory committees with worker members on them. The substance and form of these consultations may also vary—from the specific to the general, from worker self-discipline to product decisions, from the trivial to the significant, from the worker-defined to the employer-defined. The success of these consultations, from the workers' point of view, depends on how democratic the forms are and how significant the subject matter is—and, of course, on whether management takes the advice given. If it does not, the forms are empty and deceptive.

Of the two hospitals studied, one (Penn) had installed a suggestion box but in such a hidden place that no one knew it existed; while in the other, hospital administrators, in an effort to "change the hospital from an uncaring to a caring institution," had set up several advisory committees, including a Medical Care Evaluation Committee, a Communications Committee, a Nurse Retention Committee and a Nurse Recruitment Committee. The involvement of employees below the RN level was minimal, and union representatives were not involved at all.

Real forms of control evolve when workers are able to *vote* on matters of real substance, but even votes may not count if they are not majority votes. Workers in both hospitals, for example, reported that health and safety committees were a farce since labor members on them were out-numbered by management people. The superior resources (money, staff, time) and technical knowledge of managers usually reinforce the majority votes they may have on such "joint committees."

UNIONS AND CONTROL

Workers do in fact achieve a large measure of control over work through unionism, since virtually every clause in a union contract involves control over some kind of employer practice. Contracts even control supervisory behavior, by imposing the rule of seniority on rewards and the rule of law on punishments given workers, thereby reducing favoritism and arbitrary employer behavior. Unfortunately, not all arbitrary behavior is controlled, nor are other forms of undesirable supervisory behavior—incompetence, uncaring attitudes, resistance to change, etc.

Through the steward system, unions also maintain a continuing presence at the workplace, which allows them to interpret and often enforce the contract on the spot. Since many stewards are unpaid and untrained, the system is far from perfect, but it does give workers some representation and hence control on the job. Other western countries sometimes adopt worker participation schemes only because they lack any comparable system of steward representation.

In other countries, demands for work councils, participation, "quality of worklife programs," worker control, have come from unions, but American unions have been less than enthusiastic about these schemes. They may simply be unfamiliar with them, or they may fear that leadership opposition may develop out of them, but the major resistance is expressed in these union observations:

One, workers often turn to unions because they dislike their bosses. Many worker participation schemes are paternalistic and try to change the workers' perception of the boss from that of adversary to that of "friend" or "father figure."

Two, participation schemes (and other "human relations" approaches) are often used by employers in union-busting drives, to fight unions and defeat them in representation elections. Union experience with such tactics is largely responsible for their negativism on this issue. In any event, forms of participation that presumably promote worker control may have the opposite effect: they may weaken unions and strengthen employer control.

Three, most participation schemes are shallow rather than substantial. They enlist the allegiance of workers not by offering real rewards but by dealing with essentially marginal issues—and in many cases, only with worker productivity. In this way the appearance rather than the substance of more respect and control is given workers. By themselves, "better communications," "listening," and even "better treatment" do not offer what workers in the long run seek.

Four, paternalism undermines the kind of class consciousness needed to advance the interests of working people. Unions, by neutralizing paternalism, tend to strengthen the group loyalties of workers and hence their consciousness of class.

Labor's view of "participation" changes, however, as contexts change and experience grows. In many western societies, the political context is one of greater labor control, and where labor governments have held power (as in Scandinavia, Austria, Germany, England, Israel, France), and where most workers belong to unions, worker self-management schemes have flourished. They function well in most cases because labor has more control over them.

American labor, on the other hand, lacks the political power to legislate such programs, as other countries have done, and in collective bargaining, the issue must stand or fall in competition with other, often more pressing, issues. In the end, even when unions advance the issue, members may not assign it a high enough priority to survive in negotiations. Nevertheless, in industries where unions are strong, they have developed some participation schemes of their own, with generally good results for those involved. Participation is not an alternative to, but an extension of, unionism. Without support from strong and experienced unions, it can become another tool of paternalism, another means of employer manipulation.

Hospital workers want to have a voice and make it heard, hence participation belongs in a total strategy aimed at their needs, and at least one physician (perhaps the only one) would take the strategy to its limit—Vicente Navarro, M.D., writing in *The New England Journal of Medicine:* "A condition for the liberation of the majority of women in the health labor force is the implementation of institutional democracy in the health sector, in which the health institutions are controlled by those who work in it and by those who are served by it."[2] Such *total* control solves the problem of paternalism and manipulation, but it does not solve the problem of how to get from here to there. Total worker control is one of the last achievable steps; most hospital workers have yet to take the first step.

Approaches to participation (short of total control) can often solve daily problems and give workers some sense of self-determination, but they are hardly the panacea some advocates hope they might be. That is, they are unlikely to affect total expenditures within the hospital. In that respect their impact on some major problems (staffing, scheduling, time-off, benefits, and certainly wages, etc.) are limited since all these depend on additional spending. Moreover, it has little influence over decisions that are external to the hospital: the power structure of the health care system, the centralized control of medical occupations and practices, public funding and regulation of health care; yet these issues ultimately control what hospital workers do.

THE STRUCTURE OF POWER IN HEALTH CARE

Control in the health care industry is highly centralized. The industry contains over 20 recognized corporate occupations, including medicine with 20 incorporated specialties. The leading occupations control the others through various organizational arms. In medicine, these include the American Medical Association (AMA), the American Hospital Association (AHA), the Joint Commission on Accreditation of Hospitals (JCAH), the Council on Medical Education (CME), and the American Association of Medical Colleges (AAMC).

"Physicians retain control over industrial production," says Carol A. Brown, "in large part because of their control over other workers."[3] In hospitals, the division of labor is controlled not by local hospitals but by the national JCAH, which is a joint body of the AMA, AHA, and the American College of Surgeons, all of which are composed wholly or partly of doctors. JCAH accredits hospitals and its power to do so is legally approved by the U.S. Public Health Service (which distributes some funds to hospitals) and by local and state health agencies (which license hospitals to operate). To be accredited by JCAH, each medical service a hospital offers must be controlled by a board-certified medical specialist, and specified numbers of professionals must be employed. Accreditation of schools for training allied health workers is controlled by the AMA Council on Medical Education.

Physicians also control other organizations and occupations through the practice of medicine laws (which close down such newcomers as women's self-help clinics). They try (often successfully) to prevent subordinate professions from being licensed, and failing that, they try to control their licensing boards. In fact many lower level occupations have doctors on their boards, frequently as majorities.

"There is an increasing tendency to believe," says Brown, "that physicians are losing control of health services, as hospitals and financial organizations come into dominance. It is my belief that physicians are not the endangered species some think they are. The general practitioner is definitely on his way out, and the ability of the AMA to protect private practice is in decline. But, as the medical profession changes, its organizations of control also change. . . . The chances of any other occupation taking over control of the health industry and becoming the top ranking profession are slim."[4]

As for the participation of women in the power structure, one survey of not-for-profit agencies (environmental, cultural, educational, foundations, hospitals and health care, other health-related, social welfare, legal and public affairs) found that hospitals and educational institutions had the fewest women on their governing boards—only 14 percent in each field, compared with 23 percent in all agencies.[5] Not-for-profit hospitals are among the largest employers of volunteers, and the majority of volunteers are women, as are the majority of employees.

Another analysis found that both women and workingclass people were grossly under-represented on the boards of trustees of reproductive and delivery institutions in the health sector, as shown in the following table.[6]

Estimated Social-class Composition of the U.S. Labor Force and Boards of Trustees

	Corporate class	Upper middle class	Lower middle class	Working class
(figures in parentheses are the percent of women in each class)				
U.S. Labor Force	.5% (.1%)	20% (11%)	30% (70%)	50% (36%)
Health Labor Force	—	17 (6.6)	27 (87)	53 (84)
Members of boards of trustees:				
Reproductive institutions				
Foundations (top ten)	70 (3)	20 (4)	—	—
Private medical teaching institutions	45 (3)	55 (6)	—	—
State medical teaching institutions	20 (5)	70 (8)	10 (1)	—
Delivery institutions				
Voluntary hospitals	5 (.5)	80 (12)	10 (3)	5 (.8)

The pattern shows that both women and workingclass people (and lower middle class) were over-represented as workers in the health system but virtually unrepresented in the power structure.

Expenditures on health care run to over $200 billion a year, so the stakes are high. Conglomerates, multinational corporations, and "multihospital systems" have grown in health care as in other industries. "The entry of large conglomerates into the health field ensures that monopolization will occur much more rapidly than has been the case historically," Gelvin Stevenson forecasts; "They bring with them, indeed are led into health by, management tools and methods well tested in the ways of monopoly profit maximization, i.e. price rises, output restriction, and the manipulation of consumers (or physicians) through advertising and other sales techniques, all geared toward stimulating both the level and composition of demand."[7]

With respect to public policy on health care delivery and spending, the union (like other unions) has advocated national health insurance, efforts to contain wasteful medical costs, new approaches to the delivery of care, more emphasis on preventive medicine, and the expansion of Health Maintenance Organizations (HMOs).

The following comments give some sense of how hospital workers feel about medical costs:

The government allows hospitals to make profits and siphon off all the money to buy new equipment and to pay doctors $100,000 a year. Hospitals pay millions for equipment that's used maybe twice a year, when it could be centralized and used by a lot of medical facilities. So they don't have much left for hospital workers.

There are a number of Kaiser hospitals in southern California. They have *one* hemodialysis unit—very expensive equipment—at the Kaiser Sunset, and it's used all the time. All the other Kaiser hospitals send their patients to Sunset for hemodialysis. They communalize their expensive equipment. That makes total sense. It's like having communal swimming pools. That way each person doesn't have a pool that just sits there and gets used maybe six times a year. Most hospitals don't do that. Each one buys its own expensive equipment, and seldom uses it.

The hospital doesn't treat patients. Doctors treat patients. The doctor admits the patients to the hospital and creates a demand for his own services. In California, the organizations with the most money are the California Medical Association (the physicians), and the California Hospital Association. They are incredibly powerful. We tried to get a cost containment measure through the legislature. It required hospitals to submit their budgets for review if their charges went up more than five percent over the cost-of-living. That would give them about a 20 percent rise in one year. They still wouldn't buy it. They are the most right-wing, reactionary groups in the hospital industry, and they control how health care is given. After all, who's a better lobbyist than a legislator's personal physician? That's how the medical association operates. If they are sponsoring a bill, the legislator's *personal physician* calls him up about it. I mean, really. Health care is run for the physicians, not for patients.

There have been big cost pressures recently. The consumer of health care makes no decision about purchases. The providers make those decisions. The doctor tells you, "This is what's wrong with you. This is what you need. And you don't have to pay for it yourself if you have a third party payer, like insurance." It's like telling someone: "You can have a new car and you don't have to pay for it. Somebody else will." An incredible inflation rate is built into the system. The hospital can go out and buy a cat-scanner, even though there's one next door, and get reimbursed for it. The medical profession wants all the latest gadgets, and they're costly. One machine can cost a million dollars. And, of course, doctors cover their ass with all kinds of tests and procedures that aren't needed. There is nothing to restrain costs.

We've been involved with this for a long time, and there's not much we can do. The hospital says it can't afford to say "no" to buying another cat-scanner, because Dr. Smith will take his business down the street. They have to please the doctor. It's much easier to say, "We'll cut back on the RNs or janitors." That's where it's easy to clamp down. The proportion of hospital costs that go to payroll used to be two-thirds. Now it's only 50 percent. That's because other costs are skyrocketing.

Talk to hospital workers, especially those in patient care, and they'll tell you what's happening, with the machines and the cutbacks. They see this as ridiculous. "When it comes right down to it, I'm the one that takes care of these patients." They all hate the doctors anyway, and they don't trust them.

The nurses complain they can't give quality care. It is a political issue. Without legislation you can't solve the problem of inadequate patient care. Organizing a union at your hospital isn't enough. Legislation is needed to take the profits out of health care. People don't realize that inadequate care is directly related to that. The system isn't built to take care of people. It's built to make money.

Hospital workers are also concerned about quality control, especially of care given to women by male physicians. That the male physician's view of the female body (and mind) have been, at least in some instances, warped and unscientific is illustrated in the comments of Edward H. Clarke, M.D. about sex in education in 1873:

"There have been instances, and I have seen such, of females in whom the special mechanism we are speaking of remained germinal— undeveloped. It seemed to have been aborted. They graduated from school or college excellent scholars, but with undeveloped ovaries. Later they married, and were sterile. The system never does two things well at the same time. The muscles and the brain cannot *functionate* in their best way at the same moment. . . . Force must be allowed to follow thither in an ample stream, and not diverted to the brain by the school, or to the arms by the factory, or to the feet by dancing."[8]

More than a hundred years later, such views have taken new forms. "It is a mystery why physicians are so willing to cut, drug, and bully women. But they do. A hundred years ago, surgery was often performed with the explicit goal of "taming" a high-strung woman. Clitoridectomy and ovariotomy were the methods of preference then. Now, similar results are obtained by telling women that their illnesses are of psychologic origins and then treating them with tranquilizers, psychiatric therapy, shock, or institutionalization. Hysterectomies appear to be another favorite treatment. . . . The surgeons' preference for radical mastectomies, in the presence of clear evidence of their emotional trauma and equally unclear evidence of their curative superiority, is also disturbing."[9]

Hospital workers, being women, are acutely aware of these problems and particularly anxious to have a voice in improving the quality of care for women.

In medicine, women patients get screwed around a lot more than men do. All these goddam hysterectomies, and the way child birth has been handled by male doctors. It's important that some governing body say, "Listen sucker. You don't have to do an epesiatomy 95 percent of the time, as you're doing. And you'd better show us you're not doing it too much, or you're not going to get paid." You don't have to do Caesarian sections 40 percent of the time (which is what it's getting to be over in the women's hospital). You better not, because you're not going to get paid for anything over five percent. So think about it. Don't strap all that monitoring equipment on a mother's belly so she can't move. Don't put probes up on the baby's scalp and make him bleed before he's even born, just to get results you don't even know how to interpret yet."

If anybody asked us, the nurses could tell them how to keep women healthy, pre-natal to the grave. And if they took the lid off us, we could tell the politicians how to keep the doctors from messing up women patients. Cut off their money, that'll do it. National health would do it, and letting the nurse midwives take over would do it. Listen to the nurses. We can tell you anything you want to know, if you want to listen.

THE IMPACT OF UNIONS ON HOSPITALS

If workers and unions seek more control over hospital decision-making, their impact on the hospital and the quality of care is a relevant matter. Though this study does not deal with that impact, a strong hypothesis has nevertheless surfaced: "Organizing workers has a positive effect on the quality of patient care in hospitals"—and a second hypothesis, "The quality of patient care rises as the participation of workers in decision-making rises and as stability of the work force increases." These hypotheses are suggested, not tested, by the present study. What is apparent in the study, however, is that unions reduce worker turnover and increase the stability and experience of hospital workers, and thereby undoubtedly improve the quality of care.

Some evidence on "impact" comes from a national study of the perception of hospital managers about unionization.[10]

Hospital Managers Perception of Unionization

	Percent of Managers Responding	
	Union has	Union has
Area of Impact	positive effect	negative effect
	%	%
Employee interest in long-term employment	57%	15%
Hospital's ability to retain employees	55	20
Employee interest in promotion	47	22
Overall quality of management	61	12
Centralized policy making	77	11
Employee morale	45	35
Employee wages	64	20
Overall quality of care	25	33

In all but one of these instances, more managers saw a positive than a negative impact of unionism on hospitals, with the greatest proportion of doctors seeing a positive impact on "centralized policy making," "employee wages," and "overall quality of management."[11]

"Decision and policy making had become more centralized, with senior administrators and personnel/industrial relations specialists assuming an expanded role. Employee relations policies were seen to have become more formal, more similar across organization sub units, and applied with greater consistency."[12] In other words, unionization results in the adoption of the rule of law, a formalized system with written rules governing employee rights (a bill of rights) which can be applied impartially. Establishing and enforcing these rules are the positive aspects of "bureaucratization," in the sense that they reduce favoritism, inequities in the application of rules, and arbitrary employer behavior.

As for impact, even among these managers (the official antagonists and most outspoken adversaries of unions), 25 percent said that unionization of their hospitals had a positive effect on the "overall quality of care," only 33 percent said it had a negative effect, while the others saw "no effect." Thus, even among its severest critics, the view that the impact of unionism was positive was almost as prevalent as the view that it was negative.

On the issue of productivity, another study of union impact (but not specifically on hospitals) conducted by Charles Brown and James Medoff found that unionized establishments were about 22 percent more productive than non-union establishments, and that this advantage could be as high as 30 percent.[13]

UNIONS AND WOMEN'S ISSUES

Unionism is perhaps the major strategy available to workingclass women who seek a better work life.[14] The progress they can make through unionism, however, tends to be incremental rather than instant and total, and in anti-union environments it is sometimes agonizingly slow though nevertheless substantial over time.

Unions give workers a voice and some collective influence in at least three arenas: within the union through the extension of opportunities for leadership; with their employers through collective bargaining; and in the political arena through legislative activity. Unions play a central role in shaping legislation on the structure and financing of health care, the regulation of the medical professions and hospital operations, and the designation of duties, training, and licensing of health care workers.

Union women have been responsible for raising the issue of comparable worth to a position of prominence, and unions have systematically addressed most other issues of importance to women. One issue on which progress has been especially slow for hospital workers is "staffing," despite various union efforts to improve conditions, including: direct action, collective bargaining, efforts to enact legislation regulating worker-patient ratios in hospitals, and demands for adequate funding of hospital labor costs. The sense of how many hospital workers feel about unionism is apparent in the following comments:

The great thing about unions is that with them you can take on the power structure, and within a framework that recognizes you and gives you protection. If you don't like your boss and you don't have a union, you don't stay. That's the reality. The RNs have been afraid of the power structure. They have been so socialized to subserviance by professional associations that the union has to overcome a lot of the brainwashing given them.

But many features of the work environment can't or aren't being dealt with through the contract. The union contract can go just so far. Unless the employees get a bigger political outlook they'll never move beyond certain bread and butter issues. But their concerns, their ability to struggle, their knowledge and their confidence in themselves is much greater today because they're organized. It's a tremendous boost for their morale. It's so much better for them with a union. They can fight. They know that if they stick together they can win. That in itself is a tremendous boost for them. And they have something they are respected for. Just getting organized is the overwhelming issue. Unorganized workers have nothing, but organized workers have some power. Then it's a question of how well they use that power.

Notes

Chapter 1

1. Meredith Tax, *The Rising of the Women,* Feminist Solidarity and Class Conflict, 1880–1917. New York: Monthly Review Press, 1981.
2. Robin Morgan, *Going Too Far,* The Personal Chronicle of Feminism. New York: Vintage, 1978, p. 92.
3. Ibid, p. 132.
4. Ibid, p. 151.
5. Helen I. Marieskind and Barbara Ehrenreich, "Towards Socialist Medicine: The Women's Health Movement," *Social Policy,* V. 6 no. 2, 1975, p. 34.
6. Kate Millett, *Sexual Politics,* New York: Avon, 1969.
   Shulamith Firestone, *The Dialectic of Sex:* The Case for Feminist Revolution. New York: Bantam, 1970.
7. Firestone, Ibid, p. 11–12.
8. Barbara Easton, "Feminism and the Contemporary Family," *Socialist Review* no. 39, 1978, p. 34.
9. John and Barbara Ehrenreich, "Hospital Workers: A Case Study in the 'New Working Class," *Monthly Review,* Jan. 1973, p. 19.
10. Carol Hatch, "Socialist-Feminism and the Workplace," *Socialist Review,* No. 47, 1979, p. 119.
11. Ibid, p. 120 and 127.
12. Ibid, p. 127–128.
13. Ibid, p. 128 and 130.
14. *Health Care Week,* May 29, 1978. In hospitals, psychiatric nurses (27 percent of the total) were the most dissatisfied, followed by obstetrical-gynecological nurses (25 percent), medical-surgical nurses (25 percent) and geriatric nurses (22 percent). The least dissatisfied were nurses in emergency rooms (12 percent), nurses in administration (13 percent), education (14 percent) and pediatrics (20 percent).
15. Florence Nightingale, *Cassandra.* Old Westbury, N.Y.: Feminist Press, 1979; and Elaine Showalter, "Florence Nightingale's Feminist Complaint: Women, Religion, and Suggestions for Thought," *Signs:* Journal of Women in Culture and Society, v. 6, no. 3, 1981, pp. 395–411.

Chapter 4

1. E. G. Hughes, H. M. Hughes, and I. Deutscher, *Twenty Thousand Nurses Tell Their Story.* Philadelphia: Lippincott, 1958, p. 68.

Chapter 11

1. See Pamela Roby, *Women in the Workplace,* Proposals for research and policy concerning the conditions of women in industrial and service jobs, Cambridge, Mass.: Schenkman Publishing Company, Inc., 1981.

Chapter 14

1. Edward A. Brann, and Miriam Ostow, Conservation of Human Resources, Columbia University, *New York Times,* September 5, 1981, p. 18.

Chapter 15

1. See: U.S. Dept. of HEW, NIOSH, Health and Safety Guide for Hospitals, Washington, D.C. U.S. Government Printing Office, 1978; and Hospital Occupational Health and Safety, NIOSH, 1977.
2. Jean D. Watkeys, M.D., "Women in the Work Environment," *Journal of Occupational Medicine,* May 1975.
3. Pamela K.S. Patrick, "Burnout: job hazard for health workers," *Hospitals,* Nov. 16, 1979, p. 87.
4. Donald L. Tasto et al., "Health Consequences of Shift Work," U.S. Dept. of HEW, NIOSH, March, 1978.
5. Howard Rowland, ed., *The Nurse's Almanac,* The Aspen Systems Corp., Germantown, Md., 1978, p. 89.
6. David Margolick, "The Lonely World of Night Work," *Fortune,* Dec. 15, 1980, p. 113.

Chapter 17

1. Christopher J. Maggs, "Towards a Social History of Nursing," *Nursing Times,* May 18, 1978, p. 56.
2. Ibid, p. 55.
3. Jo Ann Ashley, *Hospitals, Paternalism, and the Role of the Nurse.* New York: Teachers College Press, 1977, p. 75.
4. Ibid, p. 128.
5. Bonnie Bullough, "Barriers to the Nurse Practitioner Movement: Problems of Women in a Woman's Field," *International Journal of Health Services,* Vol. 5, No. 2, 1975, pp. 228–9.

Chapter 18

1. As reported in Paula Span, "Where Have All the Nurses Gone?," *New York Times,* Feb. 22, 1981, pp. 70–100.
2. Vincente Navarro, M.D. "Women in Health Care," *The New England Journal of Medicine,* Feb. 20, 1975, p. 402.
3. Carol A. Brown, "The Division of Laborers: Allied Health Professions," *International Journal of Health Services,* Vol. 3, No. 3, 1973, p. 440.
4. Ibid, p. 443.
5. *Trustee,* Feb. 1978, p. 24.
6. Navarro, Op. Cit., p. 401.
7. Gelvin Stevenson, "Profits in Medicine: A Context and an Accounting," *International Journal of Health Services,* Vol. 8, No. 1, 1978, p. 53.

Also see: Donald E. L. Johnson, "Multi-hospital System Survey," *Modern Healthcare,* April 1980, pp. 57–96.

8. Edward H. Clarke, M.D., *Sex in Education; or, A Fair Chance for the Girls.* Boston: James R. Osgood and Co., 1873.

9. Jerry L. Weaver and Sharon D. Garrett, "Sexism and racism in the American health care industry: a comparative analysis," *International Journal of Health Services,* Vol. 8, No. 4, 1978.

10. Charles Maxey, "Hospital Managers' Perceptions of the Impact of Unionization," *Monthly Labor Review,* June 1980, pp. 36–38.

11. In 1977 unionized service workers had usual weekly earnings that were 58 percent higher than those of non-union service workers. The fringe benefits of union workers overall were 143 percent higher than non-union workers. Bureau of Labor Statistics, "Earnings and other characteristics of organized workers," based on a May 1977 survey.

12. Maxey, op. cit., p. 38.

13. Charles Brown and James Medoff, "Trade Unions in the Production Process," *Journal of Political Economy,* Vol. 86, No. 31, 1978.

14. See: The Women's Labor Project, National Lawyers Guild, *Bargaining for Equality,* A guide to legal and collective bargaining solutions for workplace problems that particularly affect women, 1980; and

The Coalition of Labor Union Women, *Effective Contract Language for Union Women,* 1979.

APPENDIX A

1. Please check your job classification:

____ dietary
____ housekeeping
____ maintenance
____ clerical
____ lab, x-ray, or other technician
or lab assistant

____ RN
____ LPN or GPN
____ nursing assistant
____ ward clerk
____ other (specify)

_____

_____

2. How old are you?

____ 16 to 24
____ 25 to 34
____ 35 to 44

____ 45 to 54
____ 55 to 64
____ 65 and over

3. What is your race or ethnic group?

____ White
____ Black
____ Asian-American

____ Hispanic
____ Other

4. What is your religion?

____ Protestant
____ Catholic
____ Jewish

____ Other
____ None

5. Your education

____ Did not finish high school
____ High school graduate
____ One or two years of technical
       training
____ Some college
____ College graduate

6. Marital status

____ Single, never been married   ____ Separated
____ Married   ____ Widowed
____ Divorced

7. Husband's occupation

____ Blue collar, manual or factory
____ Blue collar, skilled trade
____ White collar, non-professional
____ White collar, professional or
       managerial

8. Your current hourly rate of pay

____ $3.00-3.99 per hour   ____ $6.00-6.99 per hour
____ $4.00-4.99 per hour   ____ $7.00-7.99 per hour
____ $5.00-5.99 per hour   ____ $8.00 or over per hour

9. Total family income

____ $6000-$999   ____ $18,000-21,999
____ $10,000-13,999   ____ $22,000 and over
____ $14,000-17,999

10. Number of children

____ none   ____ 3
____ 1   ____ 4
____ 2   ____ more than 4

11. Check the age groups in which you have children

____ Under 2½ years   ____ 12 to 6 years
____ 2½ to 5 years   ____ over 16 years
____ 6 to 11 years

12. Where are your children taken care of while you're working?

_____ in your home   _____ not in your home

13. Who takes care of your children while you're working?

_____ husband   _____ non-relative
_____ older children   _____ child-care center
_____ other relative   _____ they take care of themselves

14. How long have you worked here at the hospital?

_____ under 1 year   _____ 4 to 10 years
_____ 1 to 3 years   _____ over 10 years

15. How long do you intend to work here at the hospital?

_____ under 1 year   _____ over 5 years or till retirement
_____ 1 to 5 years   _____ don't know

16. Which of the following schedules best describes your own?

_____ the exact same hours all the time
_____ the same shift all the time, but different hours within that shift
_____ shift changes every month
_____ shift changes more often than once a month
_____ none of the above

17. How often do you attend union meetings or other union activities?
(Check one line only)

_____ more than once a month
_____ once a month
_____ 3 or more times a year
_____ 1 or 2 times a year
_____ not at all

18. From the following items, pick the three that you *most dislike* about your
    job, or have the most problems with. Put a number 1 next to the biggest
    problem you have; put a number 2 next to the second biggest problem
    you have; put a number 3 next to the third biggest problem you have.
    Only mark 3 items.

_____ my schedule   _____ health and safety problems on
_____ physically tiring work   the job
_____ not enough sick days   _____ the way I'm treated—lack of
_____ boring or uninteresting work   appreciation, respect, dignity
_____ dealing with patients   _____ the people I work with
_____ wages   _____ opportunities for promotion

_____ not enough vacation, personal days and holidays

_____ trying to work and raise a family

_____ supervision

_____ fringe benefits—health insurance, pension, etc.

_____ not enough staff

_____ other (please specify)

19. From the following items, pick the three that you *most like* about your job. Put a number 1 next to the item you like best about your job; put a numer 2 next to the item you like second best; put a number 3 next to the item you like third best. *Only mark 3 items.*

_____ the people I work with

_____ interesting work

_____ wages

_____ the work is not too hard

_____ opportunities for promotion

_____ pleasant place to work

_____ job is near my home

_____ useful work; helping sick people

_____ good supervision

_____ chance to meet people

_____ the way I'm treated— appreciation, respect, dignity

_____ steady work

_____ my schedule

_____ good fringe benefits

_____ other (please specify)

20. In your current job, do you have a problem with any of the following? (Check one box, for each item. If question does not apply, check "No Problem at all").

	1 No Prob- lem at all	2 A Slight Problem	3 A Sizeable Problem	4 A Great Problem
Having to work more than 5 days in a row.				
Patients expect too much of me.				
Supervisor watches my work too closely.				
Wages not high enough considering the work I do.				
My job does not let me use my abilities fully.				
Too much standing.				
Not having enough time to spend with my family.				
Having my schedule posted only two weeks in advance.				
Having to work too fast.				
Supervisor doesn't try to solve				

	1 No Prob- lem at all	2 A Slight Problem	3 A Sizeable Problem	4 A Great Problem

problems brought to her/him. _____

Harassment for using sick
   days. _____

Discrimination because of my
   age. _____

Cuts, bruises or burns. _____

My job is not considered very
   important in the hospital. _____

Wages not fair compared to
   what other employees in the
   hospital make. _____

Going home tired at the end of
   the day. _____

Pension won't be adequate
   when I retire. _____

Work is boring. _____

Getting to and from work. _____

People are promoted unfairly. _____

Supervisor is too busy. _____

Some people won't help out
   when needed because they
   think my work is beneath
   them. _____

Lifting and bending. _____

Working weekends or
   holidays. _____

Not being able to take my
   breaks. _____

Health insurance doesn't cover
   long illnesses. _____

Getting along with the people I
   work with. _____

Finding good child care or
   babysitters for my children
   while I work. _____

Lack of materials and
   equipment to do a good job. _____

Supervisor doesn't ask for my
   opinion about things. _____

Catching disease because I
   work in a hospital. _____

My department is not
   considered very important in
   the hospital. _____

	1 No Prob- lem at all	2 A Slight Problem	3 A Sizeable Problem	4 A Great Problem
Wages not high enough to support my family.				
Supervisor doesn't work hard enough.				
Patients don't appreciate the work I do for them.				
Falling down.				
Work schedule interferes with my family life.				
Having to do work I'm not adequately trained to do.				
Discrimination because I am a woman.				
Not many opportunities for promotion.				
My husband does not help out enough at home.				
No convenient or pleasant lounge area or other place to take a break.				
Supervisor doesn't treat people fairly.				
No able to schedule my vacation when I want it.				
Dangerous chemicals, gases, or radiation.				
Not having a steady, permanent shift.				
Not enough staff.				
Not able to go back to school and train for a better job.				
Discrimination because of my race or ethnic background.				
Supervisor doesn't know enough to be able to answer my questions.				
Emotional stress from my work.				
Hard to work all day, then go home and do housework.				
Wages not as high as I could earn elsewhere.				
Working evening or night shift.				

	1 No Prob- lem at all	2 A Slight Problem	3 A Sizeable Problem	4 A Great Problem
Doing the work of two people when someone doesn't show or calls off.				
Dangerous tools, machinery, equipment.				
Supervisor tries but isn't able to solve problems brought to her/him.				
Not enough training to do my job.				
Too hard to get things changed that need changing.				
No time for leisure.				

21. From the following list of fringe benefits, pick the three you would most like to receive or have improved. Put a number 1 next to the most important; put a number 2 next to the second most important; put a number 3 next to the third most important item. *Only mark 3 items.*

_____ Health insurance
_____ Dental coverage
_____ Optical and eyeglass coverage
_____ Prescriptions
_____ Pension and retirement system
_____ Holidays

_____ Vacation
_____ Personal days
_____ Sick days
_____ Education, assistance programs
_____ Good, inexpensive child care centers
_____ Free legal assistance when needed

22. Which would you rather have—a 15% wage increase or: (Check one box for each item)

	This item	The 15% wage increase
More control over your schedule		
More staff to help with the work		
Better supervision		
Improved fringe benefits— health insurance, pension, etc.		
Less tiring work		
More opportunities for promotion		

This item The 15% wage increase

Better treatment—more respect
  and appreciation _____
More interesting work _____
More vacation, personal days,
  holidays _____
Safer and more healthy work
  place _____

23. How much do you agree or disagree with the following statements?
    (Check one box for each item)

	1 Strongly Agree	2 Agree	3 Disagree	4 Strongly Disagree
The union has done a good job for me here at the hospital.				
The union cares about what its members think.				
Women in the union have an equal chance with men of becoming officers and staff for the union.				
I would be happier if I didn't have to work at all.				
Women workers have different problems and concerns than men workers.				
The women's rights movement has caused men to treat women less courteously or less respectfully.				
Women are getting jobs for which they are not qualified, just because they are women.				
The women's rights movement has helped women get better jobs and better pay.				
More and more, women are expected to do work that should be done by men.				
The women's rights movement has encouraged me to stand up more for my rights.				

	1 Strongly Agree	2 Agree	3 Disagree	4 Strongly Disagree
There is a need for an organization which brings women together from many different unions to work on common concerns.				
There should be more women in the higher positions here at the hospital—such as doctors and administrators.				
The hospital cares more about money than it does about giving the patients good care.				
Sex discrimination in this country is a serious problem.				
The hospital could give people more regular schedules and still cover the needs of the hospital.				
The Equal Rights Amendment (ERA) will have a positive effect on the lives of women.				

APPENDIX B

A CONTRACT SETTLEMENT AT PENN HOSPITAL*

SECURITY

The new contract provided a grievance procedure as a means of enforcing the contract. No means existed before the strike to allow workers an appeal from any management decision.

The contract stipulated that workers be disciplined and discharged for "just cause" only. Before, discipline and discharge were at the discretion of the hospital.

Seniority provisions on job bidding were introduced for the first time. These require that employees with the greatest hospital seniority, who have qualifications and ability, *shall* be awarded the job. Before no means existed to formally challenge sex, age, or race discrimination or favoritism in job bidding.

Seniority provisions also required layoffs in inverse order of classification seniority, and permitted seniority employees the right to bump junior employees in other classifications. Recalls from layoffs would proceed according to seniority. Before, no means existed to challenge discrimination or favoritism in layoffs or recall.

HOURS AND TIME-OFF WITH PAY

Before, employees had to work 10 years to get more than ten days vacation, and 20 years to get more than 15 days. After 15 years, the maximum time was 20 days.

The new contract introduced yearly increments of vacation days, so that a woman with 9 years seniority, for example, would get 15 days and a woman with 19 years would get 25 days of paid vacation.

*Calculations cover the technical unit and the service and maintenance unit and are based on an analysis of the contract and a review of conditions before the contract.

213

For part-time employees, the contract offered a pro-rated share of vacation days based on the ratio of time worked to full employment in the previous year. Before, part-timers were entitled to a maximum of only three days vacation after one year of service.

The contract added one paid holiday, for a total of 8, plus two guaranteed days of personal leave. Before, only one personal day was allowed, awarded at the discretion of supervisors. Part-timers were given five paid holidays. Before the contract, they had none. Hours worked on a holiday were paid at straight time before the contract. After, they were paid at time and a half.

Before, part-timers got no "bereavement leave" with pay. After, they were entitled to the same leave as fulltimers (3 days for close relatives, one day for more distant ones).

Before, workers accrued no seniority during leaves of absence. After, they accumulated seniority throughout their absence.

WORK SCHEDULES

Before the contract, work schedules were made up solely at the discretion of the supervisors. After, it was required that schedules be posted at least two weeks in advance and that they be changed only in an emergency or with worker consent. It also required that people reporting to work be guaranteed work for the scheduled number of hours, or pay in lieu of work, unless notified 24 hours in advance. Split shifts were abolished. Twelve hour intervals between shifts were required, and no one was any longer required to work more than two consecutive weekends.

PAY AND REIMBURSEMENTS

The new contract provided a 25 cent per hour premium pay for the second shift, and a 20 cent an hour premium for the third shift. Before, workers on these two shifts were paid only 75 cents *per day* premium.

The contract provided time and a half pay after an 8 hour day. Before, workers got time and a half only after 80 hours of work in a pay period. Paid time off (vacation, holidays, etc.) were included for the first time in the computation of overtime.

The contract allowed $300.00 per school year as tuition reimbursement of hospital-related credits.

The contract stipulated pay increases in most cases averaging about 40 percent during the first three years of the contract. It also substituted seniority for the arbitrary assignment of hourly rates within classifications.

HEALTH AND WELFARE

Before, the *employee* paid 100 percent of the premium for dependent coverage on Blue Cross-Blue Shield. After, the *hospital* paid 85 percent of such coverage.

SELECTED BIBLIOGRAPHY

American Public Health Association. *Women in Health Careers: Chart Book for International Conference on Women in Health.* Washington, D.C.: American Public Health Association, 1976.

Appelbaum, Alan L. "Women in Health Care Administration," *Hospitals, Journal of the American Health Association,* 49 (Aug.), 1975.

Ashley, Jo Ann. "Nurses in American History—Nursing and Early Feminism," *American Journal of Nursing* 75(9): 1465–1467, 1975.

———. *Hospitals, Paternalism, and the Role of the Nurse.* New York: Teachers College Press, 1977.

Bayrs, Marjorie and Newton, Peter. "Women in Authority: A Sociopsychological Analysis," *Journal of Applied Behavioral Science* 14 (1): 7–20, 1978.

Beates, Henry. *The Status of Nurses: A Sociologic Problem.* Philadelphia: Physicians' National Board of Regents, 1909.

Bernstein, Arthur H. "Equal Employment Opportunities in Hospitals," *Hospitals, Journal of the American Health Association,* 1978.

Bettman, Otto L. *The Good Old Days—They Were Terrible!* New York: Random House, 1974.

Bloom, Barbara and Plant, Janet. *Health Manpower: An Annotated Bibliography.* Chicago, Illinois: American Hospital Association, 1976.

Boyarski, Robert Philip. "Nursing Workweek Equalizes Shifts, Time Off," *Hospital Progress,* July, 1976.

Brown, Carol A. "Women Workers in the Health Service Industry," *International Journal of Health Services* 5(2): 173–184, 1975.

———. "The Division of Laborers: Allied Health Professions," *International Journal of Health Services* 3(3): 435–444, 1973.

Bucher, R. "Autonomy and Monitoring on Hospital Wards," *Sociological Quarterly* 13: 431–446, 1972.

Bucher, R. and Stelling, Joan G. *Becoming Professional.* Beverly Hills, California: Sage, Inc., 1977.

Bullough, Bonnie. "Barriers to the Nurse Practitioner Movement: Problems of Women in a Woman's Field," *International Journal of Health Services* 5 (2): 225–232, 1975.

———. *The Law and the Expanding Nursing Role.* New York: Appleton-Century-Crofts, 1975.

Bullough, Bonnie and Bullough, Vern. "Sex Discrimination in Health Care," *Nursing Outlook* 231 (1): 40–45, 1975.

Campbell, Margaret A. *Why Would a Girl Go Into Medicine? Medical Education in the United States: A Guide for Women.* Old Westbury, New York: The Feminist Press, 1973.

Campbell, Roy. *Minorities in Nursing.* San Francisco, Calif.: California Nurses' Association, Minority Group Task Force, 1973.

Cannings, Kathleen and Lazonick, William. "The Development of the Nursing Labor Force in the United States: A Basic Analysis," *International Journal of Health Services* 5 (2): 185–191, 1975.

Caress, Barbara. "Health Manpower," *Health/PAC Bulletin* 62 (Jan./Feb.), 1975.

Carpenter, Eugenia S. "Women in Male-Dominated Health Professions," *International Journal of Health Services* 7 (2): 191–207, 1977.

Claus, Karen E. and Bailey, June T. *Power and Influence in Health Care: A New Approach to Leadership.* St. Louis, Mo.: C.V. Mosby Co., 1977.

Cleland, Virginia. "Sex Discrimination: Nursing's Most Pervasive Problem," *American Journal of Nursing* 71 (8): 1542–1547, 1971.

Cook, Sir Edward. *The Life of Florence Nightingale.* New York: The Macmillan Co., 1972.

Cray, Edward. *In Failing Health: The Medical Crisis and the A.M.A.* New York: Bobbs-Merrill Co. Inc., 1970.

Cunningham, Letitia. "Nursing Shortage? Yes," *American Journal of Nursing,* March, 1979.

Davis, Fred (ed.). *The Nursing Profession: Five Sociological Essays.* New York: John Wiley and Sons, 1966.

Donovan, Lynn. "Is Nursing Ripe for a Union Explosion?" *RN,* May, 1978.

Duff, Raymond S. and Hollingshead, August B. *Sickness and Society.* New York: Harper and Row, 1968.

Edelstein, Ruth Greenberg. "Equal Rights for Women: Perspectives," *American Journal of Nursing* 71 (2): 294–298, 1971.

Ehrenreich, Barbara. "Health Care Industry: A Theory of Industrial Medicine," *Social Policy* 6 (3): 4–11, 1975.

———. "The Status of Women as Health Care Providers in the U.S.," paper presented at the International Conference on Women in Health, Washington, D.C., June 16–18, 1975.

Ehrenreich, Barbara and Ehrenreich, John. *The American Health Empire: Power, Profits, and Politics.* New York: Vintage Books, 1971.

Ehrenreich, Barbara and English, Deidre. *Complaints and Disorders: The Sexual Politics of Sickness.* Old Westbury, N.Y.: The Feminist Press, 1973.

———. *For Her Own Good: 150 Years of Experts' Advice to Women.* Garden City, N.Y.: Anchor Press, 1978.

Ehrenreich, John. "Toward a Healing Society," *Social Policy* 8 (5): 16–21, 1978.

Ehrenreich John and Ehrenreich, Barbara. "Hospital Workers: A Case Suty in the 'New Working Class,'" *Monthly Review,* Jan., 1973.

Freidson, Eliot. *The Hospital in Modern Society.* New York: The Free Press of Glencoe, 1963.

Grissum, Marlene and Spengler, Carole. *Womanpower and Health Care.* Boston, Mass.: Little, Brown & Co., 1976.

Haase, J.; Wyshak, G.; Kole, J.; Whittenglon, A.; and Lesowitz, A. *A Study of the Participation of Women in the Health Care Industry: Labor Force Executive Summary.* Cambridge, Mass.: Radcliffe Programs in Health Care.

Health/PAC. *Health/PAC Bulletin* no. 64. New York: Health/PAC, 1975.

Health Care Financing Administration. *Health Care Financing Trends.* Washington, D.C.: Health Care Financing Administration.

Heide, Wilma Scott. "Nursing and Women's Liberation, a Parallel," *American Journal of Nursing* 73 (5): 824–827, 1973.

International Conference on Women in Health. Proceedings of the International Conference on Women in Health. McLean, Va.: MITRE Corporation, 1975.

Kotschever, Lendal H. "Labor Shortage Intensified by High Turnover, Low Productivity," *Hospitals, Journal of the American Hospital Association,* 46 (9), May, 1972

Kritek, Phyllis and Glass, Laurie. "Nursing: A Feminist Perspective," *Nursing Outlook,* March, 1978.

Loeser, Herta and Falon, Janet. "Women: the Second Sex in the Boardroom, Too," *Trustee,* Feb., 1978.

Maggs, Christopher J. "Towards a Social History of Nursing, Parts I and II," *Nursing Times,* May, 1978.

Marieskind, Helen and Ehrenreich, Barbara. "Toward Socialist Medicine: The Women's Health Movement," *Social Policy* 6(2): 34–42, 1975.

Meyer, Genevieve Rogge. *Tenderness and Technique: Nursing Values in Transition.* Los Angeles: University of California Institute of Industrial Relations, 1960.

Navarro, Vincente. "Women in Health Care," *New England Journal of Medicine* 292 (8): 398–402, 1975.

Patrick, Pamela K.S. "Burnout: Job Hazard for Health Workers," *Hospitals, Journal of the American Hospital Association,* Nov., 1978.

Price, Elmina N. "A Study of Innovation Staffing," *Hospital Progress,* 1972.

Reverby, Susan. "Health: Women's Work," *Health/PAC Bulletin* 40 15–20, 1972.

Russell, Louise B. and Burke, Carol S. "The Political Economy of Federal Health Programs in the United States, An Historical Review," *International Journal of Health Services* 8 (1): 55–57, 1978.

Ruzek, S. and Bourne, P. (eds.) *Women's Leadership and Authority in the Health Professions.* San Francisco, Calif.: University of California Program for Women in Health Sciences, 1977.

Service Employees International Union. *Health Care Corporations.* Washington, D.C.: SEIU Report no. 21, 1980.

Stevenson, Gelvin. "Profits in Medicine: A Context and Accounting," *International Journal of Health Services* 8 (1): 41–54, 1978.

Tasto, Donald L. et al. *Health Consequences of Shift Work.* Washington, D.C.: National Institute for Occupational Safety and Health, Technical Report, 1978.

Urban Planning Aid: Occupational Health and Safety Group. *Hospital Hazards.* Cambridge, Mass.: Urban Planning Aid, Occupational Health and Safety Group, 1977.

U.S. Department of Health, Education, and Welfare. *Health Womenpower: Attaining Greater Influence of Women in the Health Care System.* Washington, D.C.: U.S. Supt. of Documents, 1977.

———. *Barriers to the Achievement of Increased Representation of Non-Whites and Women in the Health Professions.* Washington, D.C.: U.S. Supt. of Documents, 1973.

———. *Women and Their Health: Research Implications for a New Era; Proceedings of a*

Conference Held at the University of California, August 1–2, 1975. Washington, D.C.: U.S. Supt. of Documents, 1977.

———. *Hospital Occupational Health and Safety.* Center for Disease Control. Washington, D.C.: U.S. Supt. of Documents, 1977.

———. *Health and Safety Guide for Hospitals.* Center for Disease Control. Washington, D.C.: U.S. Supt. of Documents, 1978.

———. *Minorities and Women in the Health Fields: Applicants, Students, and Workers,* Bureau of Health Manpower. Washington, D.C.: U.S. Supt. of Documents, 1978.

———.*Women and the Health System: Selected Annotated References.* Public Health Service. Washington, D.C.: U.S. Supt. of Documents, 1978.

Watkeys, Jean D. "Women in the Work Environment," *Journal of Occupational Medicine* 17 (5): 308–312, 1975.

Ward, Joan S. "Sex Discrimination is Essential in Industry," *Journal of Occupational Medicine* 20 (9): 594–596, 1978.

Wash, Patrick. "Occupational Mobility of Health Workers in the United States," *International Journal of Health Services* 8(4): 665–676, 1978.

Weaver, Jerry L. and Garrett, Sharon. "Sexism and Racism in the American Health Care Industry: A Comparative Analysis," *International Journal of Health Services* 8 (4): 677–703, 1978.

Wilson, Victoria. "Analysis of Feminity in Nursing," *American Behavioral Scientist* (Nov.): 213–220, 1971.

Women's Work Project of URPE. "Women Health Workers," *Women and Health* 1 (3): 14–23, 1976.

Yerxa, Elizabeth J. "On Being a Member of a 'Feminine Profession'" *The American Journal of Occupational Therapy* (Nov./Dec.), 1975.